50 YEARS

OF CAMRA

LAURA
HADLAND

CAMRA
BOOKS

T0323114

For Pixie

For Willow – thanks for teaching me to type with one hand

Published by the Campaign for Real Ale Ltd.
230 Hatfield Road, St Albans, Hertfordshire AL1 4LW
United Kingdom

www.camra.org.uk/books

Paperback ISBN 978-1-85249-369-1
Hardback ISBN 978-1-85249-375-2

A CIP catalogue record for this book is available from the British Library

Printed and bound in the United Kingdom by CPI Antony Rowe

Commissioning Editor: Katie Button, Alan Murphy
Copy Editor: Alan Murphy
Design/Typography: Dale Tomlinson
Cover Design: Jack Pemberton
Sales & Marketing: Toby Langdon

Contents

Introduction

WHEN I began researching this book, I chewed thoughtfully on a well-gnawed pencil and pondered what the next fifty years had in store for the Campaign for Real Ale (CAMRA). I wrote BREXIT carefully in capital letters, underlining it twice. This was the easy part of planning my narrative – Brexit was obviously going to be *the* big issue as CAMRA moved forward.

But the future had other plans. The Covid-19 pandemic has unfolded while this book was being researched and written. Rather than a single event that punctuates our lives and sends us off on a new trajectory, Covid-19 has been an unprecedented interruption of regular life for almost a year (at the time of going to press). It has had an unprecedented effect on CAMRA's sphere of influence.

I had carefully organised a tight schedule of interviews with nearly forty people for the CAMRA Members' Weekend in York at the beginning of April 2020. Two weeks before my trip, the prime minister announced that pregnant women were considered high risk and should stay at home with immediate effect.

We had seen lockdowns taking place in China, but most people hadn't really even imagined that it would happen in the UK too. I was thirty weeks pregnant, and except for hospital appointments (including the birth of my daughter) I would barely leave the house for the next five months. Plans to meet CAMRA members old and new were rescheduled and then cancelled as the national lockdown took hold. Archives that I was looking forward to visiting to corroborate the oral testimonies were closed to physical visitors, and many have still not reopened.

This is a very different book to the one I had planned and might have written under 'normal' circumstances.

However, I have still had the privilege of interviewing more than a hundred wonderful people, mainly over the phone, to research this book. They include active participants in the Campaign, brewers, publicans, journalists, politicians and many others who are involved with beer and pubs. Their lives have all been touched by the remarkable story of the UK's biggest single-issue consumer organisation. This book provides an account of the development of the Campaign for Real Ale by weaving together these living histories.

It is not a fully comprehensive account because CAMRA has embarked upon tens of thousands of campaigning activities over their fifty years. On a national, regional and local level there have been marches, printed beer mats and poster campaigns, brewery closure protests, petitions, not to mention beer competitions, pub guides, t-shirt slogans, beer festivals and much more besides. There has even been the occasional pair of CAMRA cufflinks.

In order to select the most interesting and impactful of these campaigning activities, I have relied on events that have made the biggest footprint on the popular memory, and I have been guided by the stories that the members remember most vividly or fondly.

Some key events that I had expected to cover in great detail when I embarked on this project have hardly warranted a mention in the final analysis. Some changes took place independently of CAMRA's activities, like the evolution of drink driving laws. Other events made the front page of *What's Brewing* at the time, but lack any gripping narrative, such as the various changes to licensing laws that have taken place over the course of CAMRA's lifetime. It is a similar story with Mild Month. Despite being one of the longest continuously running campaigns, 'Mild in May' was barely mentioned by the people interviewed for this book, so it barely gets a mention here.

I give my heartfelt thanks to the scores of people who shared their stories and memories so generously with me, and especially to those who took the time to reply to my follow-up questions and even check over the veracity of my text. I hope that this book has done you proud. In particular I would like to mention Jessica Boak, Michael Hardman, Gillian Hough and Roger Protz for their endless patience with me.

In some cases my research has allowed me to tweak a detail of the stories I was told. I will never forget the surprise in CAMRA founder Bill Mellor's voice when I told him that he didn't read about weak British beer in a newspaper on the way to Ireland, because the story in question wasn't published until they were on their way home! All of our memories are fallible, especially when lubricated by a pint or two of real ale. I have tried to recalibrate the narrative sensitively when required by the cold hard facts. Some quotes have been adapted slightly from their transcription for readability.

*   *   *

CAMRA has created life-changing experiences for its members and advocated for beer drinkers for half a century. Its achievements are all the more remarkable when you consider that it is truly a grassroots organisation. Despite having no commercial backing or private financial support CAMRA has brought huge change to a multi-million pound industry for the benefit of the consumer. We will explore how and why the Campaign for Real Ale began, and how it works. Next we examine their campaigning activities, from the early protest marches to sophisticated parliamentary lobbying. The Campaign's main activities can broadly be divided into three areas, beer, breweries and pubs, so we look at each of these areas in turn before reflecting on what the future of the organisation might be.

Early History: Why Cask Ale Needed Saving

I don't remember much about local brands in the pubs where I was brought up – just national keg brands. I remember my parents drinking Party Sevens and Party Fives at home – big cans of keg beer.

MARK TETLOW, a qualified brewer of over thirty years' experience

BRITAIN's history is the history of a great brewing nation. Notable beer writer and key CAMRA pioneer Roger Protz is rightly proud that 'we brew something really rather different in this country.' It's a simple product of water, yeast, malt and hops, but various styles of hopped beers and unhopped ales have been developed over the centuries to suit different purposes. For example, India Pale Ales were strong and well hopped so that they could survive the long sea journey to India. Porters were dark in appearance due to the use of brown malts on the grain bill, and gained their name from their popularity with the local London street and river porters who drank them.

British brewing first became ubiquitous in the hands of women, or brewsters as they were known. During the medieval period this cottage industry was gradually overtaken by commercial in-house brewing at ale houses, thus setting the tone for the story of brewing, which has always been intrinsically linked with where the beer was consumed and how it was taxed.

After it is brewed, cask beer is racked into containers, 'casks', of various sizes. These casks are mostly aluminium these days, but historically they were made from wood. A living product, the beer is unfined and still contains its yeast sediment, which means that a small secondary fermentation takes place in the barrel. This conditioning process adds extra flavour and a light, natural carbonation to the product. The beer must be carefully stored to allow the sediment to settle at the base of the container so that the beer is clear when it is poured. Being able to store, condition and serve cask ale properly is no simple task, so the art of cellarmanship is a respected craft that takes time and skill.

In the late eighteenth century an English inventor, Joseph Bramah, finessed a system of pumping beer up from the casks stored in an ale house's cellar. The mechanics had first been developed nearly 100 years before by a Dutchman living in London, John Lofting. Bramah perfected Lofting's invention and patented the beer engine in 1785. It allowed beer to be manually siphoned from the cask thanks to an airtight piston chamber and two one-way valves. The bartender operates the system using a vertical handle, and three or four smooth pulls creates a perfect pint. The mechanical hand pull or hand pump has become the iconic symbol of traditional British cask ale.

The World Wars had a notable impact on pub use in the UK. During the First World War, War Minister David Lloyd George saw alcohol as a significant threat to productivity, leading to the passing of much stricter licensing laws. The hours that pubs could open were drastically reduced and beer duty was trebled. The 'Carlisle Experiment' saw a number of pubs being nationalised to allow greater state control of the drinks trade. It began in Carlisle in 1916 with more than 300 pubs and breweries being taken over by the government. The aim was to keep munitions workers safe by keeping them sober. Alcohol content was reduced and prices were increased to decrease the value for money that punters were getting. External advertising for alcohol was removed from pub buildings and serving food was heavily promoted. The scheme was so successful that it was not abolished in law until 1971 and the Carlisle State Brewery was sold to Theakstons in 1974.

During the Second World War, conversely, the pub trade was seen as an important morale booster, so there were no restrictions to licensed hours. Pubs were even allowed to stay open when air raids took place. Bumper barley harvests meant that brewing was unaffected by rationing, but prices continued to go up thanks to tax hikes.

By the 1950s and 1960s the way the beer industry operated was changing. Some larger breweries had grown, controlling pubs around the country rather than just serving their immediate communities. These pubs existed solely as outlets for the breweries' beer – at least in the eyes of the company accountants. National beer brands had been created for the first time, although in a static population any one consumer would have been unlikely to notice the creeping homogenisation of beer. This phenomenon was the origin of the tied system which links breweries and pubs, for better or for worse, to this day.

Many of the varied historic beer styles became rarities under this system. Limiting choice and creating bland beer that would not offend anyone's palate was a conscious decision to increase profit. The breweries had their own pubs to serve their own bitter, their own mild (and possibly Guinness as the dark beer choice) and that would be the sum total of cask products available. Free houses, which had a free choice of which breweries to serve beer from, became rarer as more pubs became tied. Smaller breweries struggled to survive and were often bought out by their bigger, more aggressive rivals.

*   *   *

Beer had been the preferred drink of the masses for centuries in the UK. Several pints of beer after a long day of manual graft was considered standard for working men, and with good reason. After a day in the steelworks, factory or pit a substantial volume was needed to slake the thirst. An easy to drink 3% ABV mild was also easy on the pocket because drinks were taxed by alcoholic strength. It was common for a pub next to the factory gates to have 200 pints poured and ready to serve at knocking-off time.

The main problem with traditional cask ales was consistency. Draught ale was signing its own death warrant because publicans didn't know how to keep or serve it correctly. Not every publican had taken the time to learn proper cellarmanship and it showed. Lifetime CAMRA member Geoff Paddle remarks that beers from the hand pump could occasionally 'bear a passing resemblance to brown Windsor soup.' Another early member, Richard J Abrahams, remembers popping out for a pint in the 1960s: 'Often the ale was somewhat less than see through and had bits floating within! This was obviously yeast but we always called them "fishes" and were told to "get it drunk up boy, it won't harm you!"'

A new product hit the market where every pint was as clear as a bell – kegged beer. These beers were filtered, racked, infused with carbon dioxide and served under pressure. This slashed the amount of time needed to condition the beer and no particular skill was required to serve a consistent, clear pint. The very first of these new products was Watneys Red Barrel, released in the 1930s, but the first to be promoted specifically as 'keg beer' was Flowers Keg Bitter in 1957. It was more expensive than cask beer and heavily marketed as a premium product.

A white plastic barrel with a light inside sat on the bar top. Every pint of its product came out the same and see through, we were in heaven! Of course it took years before original gravity was required to be displayed and so we didn't know it was weak as, and not far removed from, water. We did always refer to it as "boys bitter" or, after passing our tests, "driving beer".

Richard J Abrahams

These beers were served colder and fizzier than their draught counterparts. Without the extra conditioning, and because of their low temperature, they tasted of comparatively little. The forced carbonation was notorious for leaving the drinker bloated, but every pint was clear and consistent without the cellar manager needing to expend any effort at all. Soon big brand keg beers with big advertising budgets were popping up in pubs up and down the country.

Some drinkers thought they had never had it so good, but traditional cask beer suddenly found itself on the endangered list. Even iconic London brewery Fuller's were considering giving up on their cask production and switching solely to keg. CAMRA's existence would provide them with the encouragement they needed to keep going, by demonstrating that there was still a market for cask ale.

What is real ale?

Real ale is a "living" product, which is typically produced and stored in a cask container. In comparison to other types of beer that kill off the yeast and artificially inject the beer with CO_2 prior to serving, real ale contains live yeast which continues to condition and ferments the beer until it is served.

Like any artisan product, real ale requires special handling and storing to ensure the quality of taste. Well-kept real ale served at the right temperature should be lively, naturally carbonated and flavourful – representing the pinnacle of brewing art.

CAMRA's official definition

The founders of CAMRA liked cask ale because they were volume drinkers. They enjoyed nothing more than spending a few hours in the pub with friends, sinking a few pints. Keg beers were too carbonated for them to be able to comfortably do this. An intense dislike of all carbonated drinks is a common trait amongst early CAMRA members, applicable to beer and soft drinks.

Real ale is a vital part of the British pub culture.
It is our contribution to the world of beer really,
the thing that we do better than anyone else.

PETE BROWN, Chair of the British Guild of Beer Writers

CAMRA coined the term 'real ale' to distinguish cask conditioned traditional ales from the processed and highly carbonated beers produced by the large national brewery brands. The first scientific definition was settled at the AGM in Cardiff 1978, where National Chairman Chris Bruton's knowledge of yeast and fermentation was invaluable in clarifying a more technical interpretation for the first time. A Code of Policy was developed by the National Executive in 1973 to codify their position and gives one of CAMRA's earliest written descriptions of draught beer: a 'living beer kept in natural condition and not pasteurised; it should be dispatched and kept without the addition of extraneous carbon dioxide, it should be drawn from casks or barrels by methods other than those requiring carbon dioxide pressure; and it should taste pleasant and wholesome.'

As the landscape has changed over the decades, CAMRA has needed to rethink its ideas around real ale. The Technical Advisory Group was recently tasked with improving the definition and making it technically accurate, applicable to all beer formats but also continuing to uphold the Campaign's focus on the primacy of cask ale. This exercise has led to two new definitions for 2021, 'live beer' and 'cask-conditioned beer', because the invented term of 'real ale' was held to no longer be relevant.

CAMRA defines a live beer as any that when first put into its final container contains at least 0.1 million cells of live yeast per millilitre, plus enough fermentable sugar to produce a measurable reduction in its gravity while in that container, whatever it may be.

CAMRA defines a cask-conditioned beer as a live beer that continues to mature and condition in its cask, any excess of carbon dioxide being vented such that it is served at atmospheric pressure.

CAMRA's official definition

*   *   *

The Campaign for Real Ale's first campaigning targets were known as the 'Big Six': Allied Breweries (composed of Ansells, Ind Coope and Tetley), Bass Charrington, Courage, Scottish & Newcastle, Watney Mann & Truman, and Whitbread. They were the breweries that dominated the market through aggressive expansion, and they had also introduced keg beer. Despite being one of seven businesses that made up over 80% of beer sales, Guinness was never included in this unholy Hall of Infamy as they did not own any pubs and did not make any reduction in the strength or flavour of their product during the early seventies. This fact was first noted by Chris Hutt in his seminal 1973 work, *The Death of the English Pub*, a work that would inform and inspire the nascent Campaign for Real Ale:

> Pressurisation is alien to a well-brewed and well-kept pint of draught beer, and yet it is now the rule rather than the exception in most parts of the country. It is an innovation that is designed to cover up the weaknesses of an inferior product, served by a landlord who cannot be bothered to keep his pipes clean.
>
> *CHRIS HUTT*, The Death of the English Pub

The Big Six were large regional firms that had expanded rapidly and aggressively in the 1960s. They gobbled up rival breweries and took over pubs the length and breadth of Britain to make themselves into national brands. These actions were made possible by improvements to the motorway network and other technological developments which assisted the businesses with moving large quantities of beer around the country. Between 1966 and 1976 the number of British beer brands halved to less than 1,500 thanks to these predatory brewers.

It was Watneys that first introduced keg beer to the UK, but this wasn't the only threat to cask ale. In 1969 Whitbread signed a deal to produce a version of Heineken in Luton on behalf of the Dutch parent company. This was the beginning of a rise in popularity of draught European-style lagers which is still with us today. Lager has consistently held on to the lion's share of beer consumption in the UK since the 1980s. The new European-style lagers introduced in the seventies found favour as they were served at a more refreshing chilled temperature. Previously, only unappetisingly ambient bottles of lager lurked under the counters of backstreet boozers. As package holidays increased in popularity more Brits acquired a taste for the lagers they had tried abroad, contributing to a perfect storm for traditional ales.

*   *   *

Meanwhile, future CAMRA members were having their first encounters with beer – some much more positive than others. Traditional beer had not vanished everywhere … yet. It was a lottery as to whether young drinkers were exposed to an isolated pocket of locally produced ale or stuck with keg beers. The current vice-chair of CAMRA's Birmingham branch, Mark Parkes, saw both highs and lows as he grew up:

> When I first started drinking, Birmingham was basically a duopoly of Bass Charrington and Ansells. Where I lived in the Black Country we had three or four breweries. But we were seeing the takeover of a lot of small breweries at that time leading to closures, mergers, the growth of the big boys and the annihilation of the small ones.
>
> *MARK PARKES, CAMRA member*

In total contrast, former CAMRA National Chairman Tony Millns enjoyed a wonderful selection of beer in the back streets of Doncaster where he grew up: local breweries like Sam Smiths and John Smiths, Sheffield brewers Wards and Stone, Shipstones from Nottingham and more. South Yorkshire workers would regularly sink five or six pints on the way home from work, not just to replace fluids but also to 'lay the dust'. Tony remembers his mother wiping round the window sills of the family home each day and the cloth would be black with industrial soot and dust by the time she had finished.

After his positive introduction to beer, Tony went up to Merton College, Oxford. Unfortunately, the charming college bar with beer on stillage from the barrel that he had encountered during his interview had been ripped out and replaced by a 'huge new student vomitorium', replete with modern formica tables and all keg beer. Tony first tasted beers like Whitbread Tankard here in 1969. He came away at first with the opinion that northern beer was good and southern beer could not compare.

It was a triumph of marketing over common sense and taste.

BILL MELLOR, CAMRA founder

One of CAMRA's four founders, Michael Hardman, grew up in Warrington. Two thirds of the local pubs there were operated by Greenalls and the rest Walkers, with one solitary Burtonwood pub and one Tetley's pub in the whole town. There was no choice. Beer didn't travel the same distances that it does do now. Michael remarked how one of his current locals in Putney serves the entire range of Timothy Taylor's from Yorkshire. This would have been unthinkable fifty years ago. Those beers wouldn't have got as far as Sheffield, never mind all the way to London.

These nascent beer lovers were irked that traditional draught beer was being replaced by keg. Arguably, if publicans had chosen to put keg beer on their bars *alongside* traditional draught beers, then CAMRA would never have existed. Choice was the most important thing to our young pub goers. According to Great British Beer Festival volunteering veteran, Denny Cornell-Howarth, without CAMRA the UK would have eventually become a 'keg beer desert'.

We'd go to the pub and there would be 6 types of rum, 7 types of whisky, 4 types of gin, all sorts of soft drinks, but only 2 types of beer – mild and bitter – and they were being shown the door by then and were being taken out of pubs. We thought it was an absolute cheek.

MICHAEL HARDMAN, CAMRA founder

Let battle commence!

I think for my generation all the big topics like love and peace and stuff like that had all been taken by the hippy generation. I was a child of the 70s and we weren't left with much, so beer was quite a good [protest].

TIM WEBB, CAMRA member since 1974,
co-author of The World Atlas of Beer

A number of people around the UK were independently waking up to the threat that traditional beer was facing. Some of them were motivated enough to take action. The Society for the Preservation of Beers from the Wood (SPBW) began in 1963. It was founded more as a drinking society than a campaigning organisation and still exists in modest numbers today. Their romantic ideal of serving beer 'from the wood' – direct from wooden barrels – championed nostalgic ideals of quality and flavour, in opposition to keg beers that were served from 'sealed dustbins'.

Metal casks became the norm in the 1970s but the group retained their name for the sake of tradition. While wooden vessels are still occasionally used to mature beer, their permeable surfaces are inherently difficult to keep spotlessly clean. They are also extremely heavy and difficult to move safely. Many wooden barrels are supplied with a polymer lining to prevent any infection, so any perceived benefits to flavour from the wood are probably a red herring.

By the time CAMRA came on the scene, the SPBW had a membership numbering in the thousands, and garnering some publicity from low-level protesting. The SPBW approach included holding mock funerals at pubs that were 'blighted by dustbin beer'. This concept was later borrowed by CAMRA activists who couldn't resist a high-profile wake for a brewery or beer under threat.

You felt you were doing something really worthwhile, that somehow drinking was a cause and you were championing those traditions. *DAVE GAMSTON, pub campaigner*

The SPBW merrily continued to do their own thing, but they weren't intending to take the world by storm. There was a gap in the market for a new kind of organisation to pick a fight with the beer establishment on behalf of the consumer.

Enter four men enjoying a few quiet pints in Kruger Kavanagh's near Slea Head, Ireland, the most westerly pub in Europe.

*   *   *

The year is 1971. The four men are Michael Hardman, Graham Lees, Bill Mellor and Jim Makin: three journalists and a member of a brewery's office staff. Jim and Graham were school friends from Salford. Graham and Bill were journalists who worked together on local newspapers in Cheshire. They had happened to meet Warrington-born Michael socially. The four had all independently come to the conclusion that good beer was getting very hard to find. This mutual interest in beer cemented their friendship.

The Campaign came about by accident, as a bit of a joke. The four young men had gone on a package holiday to Ireland to drink beer. They had been out on the town in Chester the night before leaving for the trip and remember being appalled by the poor quality beer and lack of choice available. They found beer was becoming more expensive and fairly tasteless. When they talked to the older people they came across in pubs they heard similar grumbles and wondered what the reason for it was.

Their holiday was 'basically a pub crawl around Ireland' so conversation naturally kept returning to beer and related matters, particularly as there were so few non-keg alternatives to drinking the ubiquitous (albeit tasty) Guinness. They visited the Guinness brewery on their first full day and stayed in Killarney that night. The next day they visited the Dingle Peninsula. It was 16 March 1971 and their ideas about beer had been crystallising into something tangible. Michael Hardman remembers the date very well because it was the day before St Patrick's Day, when they visited Cork. They resolved to start their own society to push for better beer quality and choice. Graham Lees suggested they held the first meeting in Kruger's: 'It was a boozy, jokey, jolly, frolicking week. At the outset no one had any idea of creating something like CAMRA.'

The first order of business was to give themselves a name. Michael had dreamed up the acronym CAMRA during their visit to the Guinness factory. He thought it slipped pleasingly off the tongue. It put together the 'cam' of *cam*paign with 'ale', which Graham insisted on as sounding less pretentious and more pleasingly northern than 'beer'.

The Campaign for 'Something-Beginning-With-R' Ale.

It isn't remembered which of them suggested 'Revitalisation' to finish the name off, but they went with it, and so The Campaign for the Revitalisation of Ale was born. They weren't particularly serious about it. They certainly didn't realise they would ever get more than the four members sat round the table, so the name didn't seem particularly important. 'Why we stuck with it when we did go public, I don't know,' muses Michael.

Apart from working on the name, the only other achievement of that first meeting in Kruger's was the election, such as it was, of a rudimentary committee. Michael Hardman was made chairman as he spoke first. By dint of holding a crumpled piece of paper and pen, Graham Lees was named secretary. Jim Makin was the only office worker and apparently that made him the obvious choice for treasurer. 'We couldn't think what to do with Mellor so we called him the events organiser,' says Michael. 'He never did arrange an event for us, but he's a fine chap.' Bill concedes the point, 'I was probably the most incompetent events organiser they could possibly have considered.'

The rest of the trip was occupied with celebrating St Patrick's Day, followed by travelling around Limerick, Galway and Dublin. They flew back to Liverpool on Sunday, 21 March, where the campaigning fire was fuelled further by an article in the *Sunday Mirror*[1] decrying how weak British beer was. One brand

---

1. 21 March 1971 'The sobering truth about the British pint'

of Watneys beer was described as so low in alcohol that it could legally have been sold during Prohibition in the United States, or sold to children as shandy. This article and subsequent follow-ups that analysed the strength of various big-name brands caused a good deal of outrage. This undoubtedly helped to awaken the public to the potential need for beer campaigning.

*   *   *

The founders went back to their respective lives without another thought for their new society. The idea was only rekindled at Christmas 1971 when Graham was working in Chester. Another journalist in the newsroom had his own version of a John Bull printing kit, so Graham asked him to print a custom Christmas card.

A run of about fifty CAMRA Christmas cards were made up and sent to various friends as a bit of a laugh. They offered 'Christmas & New Year Greetings from CAMRA' on the front and contained Graham's self-penned daft ditty:

> Whether in city bar you sup
> Or in village vault you get tanked up
> Be on your guard against bad ale
> Or you'll never live to tell the tale...
>   of CAMRA.
>   *Merry Slutching*

Slutching was their colloquialism for drinking. The spark to this light-hearted tinder was the fact that most of Graham's friends were journalists. The people who received this slightly cryptic festive greeting were young professionals in their twenties working for newspapers. Unexpectedly, Graham's message resonated with them and he received lots of calls asking who CAMRA were and what they were doing about the state of beer.

The truth was that they weren't doing anything. But this wave of reaction spurred the four founders into developing a more serious organisation in early 1972. People were complaining about being served poor quality beer, so they wanted to address the problem practically. As more of their journalist friends got interested in the idea, there was more publicity for the Campaign in local and regional newspapers. These early members were writing about CAMRA as an established organisation, even though in reality it had barely got off the ground.

Graham had put his mother's address, at 207 Keats Court on the Kersal Estate in his hometown of Salford, on his handmade Christmas cards as CAMRA's correspondence address. This became the de facto Campaign office until at least the end of 1973. Much to everyone's surprise, and especially to the surprise of Mrs May Lees, big mail bags of letters from all over the country started to arrive. She would forward it all on to her son. 'What is it all about, Graham?' she'd say, 'I keep going to the post office and they ask me what's all this post for and all I could say to them is I think it's something to do with beer!' She wasn't a beer drinker and it was always a bit of a mystery to her.

Newspaper pieces about the state of British beer inspired members of the public to write to the Campaign in their droves, voicing their own complaints. They asked what CAMRA was going to do and how could they get involved. They sent in details of local issues where breweries were closing or being taken over. Graham remembers:

> We were ignorant to start with, completely ignorant. We just had a view, an idea. But the more information that came in, the more it became apparent that the industry was changing. We began to realise that the industry was being coalesced into six major brewing groups. Their objective was to monopolize output and the way they were doing it was to buy up breweries in order to acquire their tied estate so that they could have more pubs. But they didn't want the beer that those little brewery

companies were producing, so they were quickly closing down breweries and then pushing in their national brands.

They were selling it on the lines that it was consistent.

It was certainly consistent, but it was consistently bad.

GRAHAM LEES, CAMRA founder

So the stage was set for the newly formed CAMRA to grow into what was soon described as 'the most successful consumer organisation in Europe' by Lord Young of Darlington, the founder of the Consumers' Association and the National Consumer Council. The early members of the nascent organisation were delighted by this description; the Big Six brewers were not.

Revitalisation to real ale

For me, as for so many others, it was what I'd unwittingly been waiting for, having always had a passion for good pubs, the complete cross-section of society in them and good beer. We now had a banner to march behind. Wow! Something to believe in. Anything and everything was now possible. There was a drive, an energy – largely youthful – a purpose, a dynamism, a determination to succeed, a flat refusal to accept no for an answer or to fail.

Early National Executive member JAMES LYNCH

CAMRA held its first annual general meeting at the Rose Inn, Nuneaton, in May 1972. The event is commemorated with a brass plaque at the pub, which was named an Asset of Community Value in 2017. This venue was selected by the organiser Bill Mellor because he rented a room there at the time. The twenty or so members who came along were mainly friends of the founders.

The only secretarial experience Graham Lees had was as secretary of a branch of the National Union of Journalists (NUJ). When CAMRA began to coalesce into a more serious organisation run by volunteers, he proposed they modelled themselves on the administrative structure of the NUJ. This is why CAMRA has a National Executive along with branches, regions and local organisers at the heart of its system. A make-do constitution that enshrined this structure was tabled and approved.

Michael Hardman's legendary fierceness and tenacity – one of the key factors that drove CAMRA forward at the beginning – was in evidence during this meeting. The group was being so loud and argumentative that some of the locals complained and the landlord of the Rose asked Bill to get them to tone it down. Apparently they caused such an affront to the delicate sensitivities of the locals that parochial journalist Roy Derry got hold of the story.

He printed a piece in the *Nuneaton Observer* implying that the group were a bunch of con artists, questioning who this 'fake organisation' was and naming Bill in the piece, saying he 'couldn't be reached for comment', even though they worked on rival newspapers in a small town. Somewhat outraged, Michael Hardman decided to have a 'quiet word' with Derry in his inimitable way. This apparently resulted in a grovelling apology being printed a week or two later, along with a full explanation of who they were and what they were doing. According to Bill, Michael 'was a pretty formidable guy in those days,' but has 'mellowed quite a lot' now.

This was the first piece of controversy the Campaign courted and it served to make the new group better known and more attractive to the public: CAMRA the protest group. They were predominantly young people who had a passion for their cause, and could comfortably be pigeonholed beside the other campaigning groups of the period like the Campaign for Nuclear Disarmament as unapologetically militant forces within their own spheres. The Campaign was exciting, obdurate and a little bit wild.

*   *   *

Unfortunately, so the legend goes, the first National Executive was so useless that the fledgling group had to have an Extraordinary Meeting just a few months later to elect some new office holders. According to Michael Hardman, the original constitution wasn't very good either: 'we [him and Graham Lees] altered it behind everyone else's back later, because there were some stupid phrases in it.' But these minor trips caused no setbacks in the growth of the organisation. Word was spreading and the ranks were beginning to swell, much to the surprise of the four founders of the enterprise.

Graham Lees remembers a wide range of people coming together. They weren't all young professional men, although the organisation's average age was a spritely twenty-five. Letters were flooding in from people of all demographics: housewives, vicars, postmen, bus drivers, lecturers, any profession you can name. The new National Executive quickly realised their Campaign wasn't restricted to any age or class: 'it was an across the board kind of social revolution which was happening' Graham remembers. Crucially, people who already had significant knowledge and experience of beer were getting involved, like beer writing pioneers Frank Baillie and Christopher Hutt. The injection of their expertise was another huge step in CAMRA's development.

Roger Protz, who came to work for the Campaign from 1976, liked how they 'covered a broad spectrum of people's views … we had one central aim in mind, which was to protect and to preserve and revive the fortunes of real ale.' Others, like early member Andrew Cunningham, think that it was exactly the involvement of people like Roger, with his background as editor of the *Socialist Worker*, that gave the media and other external parties the impression that CAMRA had a left-leaning nature in the early days.

This impression was apparently widely held. Tim Amsden represented CAMRA in 1978 at a meeting held to approve the merger of Allied Breweries with Lyons Cakes. Tim suggested the move was inappropriate and reports that the 'crimson-faced bully', Chairman Keith Showering, rounded on him, saying that 'CAMRA was a bunch of left-wing activists determined to bring down capitalism.' A CAMRA delegation was later to meet with Mr Showering. That meeting was chaired by John Camp, who was not only a member of the Campaign's National Executive, but also chairman of both his local Conservative branch and of the Tory Barristers, so even Mr Showering must have had to concede that not quite all CAMRA members were trendy lefties.

*   *   *

Graham Lees recalls that the 'revitalisation' name served their initial purposes because they felt that a lot of traditional beer being served in pubs was becoming a little bit indifferent. 'Some of the traditional ale being pulled out by hand pump was a bit insipid, so "revitalisation" was to revitalise the idea of good beer, for good beer to be widely available. We weren't actually opposed to keg beer, right from the start our view was people should have choice.' However, the fledgling organisation had great momentum, and the only thing holding them back now was that name.

At the second CAMRA AGM, held in London in 1973, it was agreed that 'revitalisation' was confusing as well as inconvenient to say after a few pints. The decision was made to change the word but keep the acronym. After some grasping for another word beginning with 'R', the Campaign for Real Ale was hit upon as CAMRA had, since its inception, been talking about real ale, real beer and real brews in their communications to members. The term reflected the idea of this type of product being something traditionally British, something right and proper, which helped to broaden yet further the base of appeal. An early editor of the *Good Beer Guide*, John Hanscomb, claims that he first coined the term 'real ale' at an early branch meeting: 'I mentioned the fact that it's proper beer, so it should be called real ale and we adopted that name.'

Whoever the original architect was, Michael Hardman muses that if they had a pound for every time the term real ale was used they'd be millionaires. The phrase, and the organisation's new name, was easier to say and it required less explanation. People grasped what CAMRA was about. Though it may be simple coincidence, they flourished from that point on.

Why did the Campaign for Real Ale take off?

> Everyone who frequents a pub and averages a pint or so a day
> considers himself the country's leading authority on the
> decline of British beer, pubs and the moral fibre of the nation.
>
> *RICHARD BOSTON in his first beer column for* The Guardian[2]

There was a groundswell of popular support in the UK for traditional products whose very survival was coming under threat in the 1960s. As new technologies and time-saving products were being introduced so there was an equal and opposite reaction. People became nostalgic about the good old days, where everything was remembered to be homemade and high quality, regardless of the reality. This was a reaction against the disposable, cheap, replaceable 'space age' culture that was being introduced. Along with this, for some people, came the desire to protect cask-conditioned beer, a uniquely British product. The pint of draught mild or draught bitter was seen as the ubiquitous drink of the working class. The time was right for an organisation like CAMRA to flourish.

> [CAMRA] was basically a PR factory, or a PR consultancy
> that didn't charge for its services. The group of people were
> very successful at placing stories and then people responded
> to those stories.
>
> *CHRIS HUTT*

It has already been emphasised that the journalists and marketeers who were the first members of the Campaign for Real Ale were pivotal for gaining notoriety. They were loud-mouthed and opinionated. Being part of the generation that grew up during the 'Summer of Revolution' it was pretty much expected that they would rebel. A further boost was given via the election of television and radio presenter Jeremy Beadle to the National Executive, although, according to veteran campaigner Andrew Cunningham, trying to call Jeremy was problematic as

---

2. The *Guardian* 11 August 1973

he was never in so you had to leave a message with his mother. In Jeremy's nine-month or so tenure he went on to secure the Campaign's first radio coverage – on the BBC Radio London programme that he hosted.

> Michael Hardman said that within about eighteen months of the start of the Campaign, there was a CAMRA member in every newsroom in the country.
>
> *CHRIS HOLMES, Former National Chairman*

Originally, the aspiration had been to get enough members to 'fill a shoebox', when members' details were kept on slips of paper in a shoebox at Graham Lees' house. He was amazed that CAMRA grew so big, so quickly. He said that 'in the early days I thought if we got a thousand members we'd be really going places,' so reaching for 200,000 now is truly 'mind boggling'.

One of the most iconic beer commentators of the time was Richard Boston. His regular *Guardian* column, Boston on Beer, began in August 1973 and is rightly regarded as a watershed moment in UK beer writing. His occasional references to CAMRA, and indeed printing their correspondence information and membership fees, helped them to reach a new audience that were inspired to action by the Campaign's message. Tim Amsden, later a National Chairman, remembers giving up his time to support the secretary, John Green, in processing the enquiries that flooded in as a result of Richard's column. They were truly overwhelmed and it took many months to sort out.

Less than a year later, celebrated writer and architectural correspondent Ian Nairn wrote a piece about CAMRA for the *Sunday Times*, which was published on 30 June 1974. The several-thousand-word article headed up the front page of the arts section. Nairn interviewed National Chairman Chris Hutt for the piece and included the address of CAMRA HQ in the finished article. Chris says that this was his 'price' for collaborating with the journalist. Nairn's loyal readership was so large that the numbers of prospective members who got in touch subsequent to publication again overwhelmed them. Membership levels shot into the thousands for the first time.

Chris tended to make the most of any opportunities for publicity while he was chairman. He wrote a letter to the *Financial Times* about CAMRA, including their address, which garnered more new members. To his surprise, the following week the PR manager for Watney Mann wrote a response saying how inaccurate Chris's letter had been. This contentious letter opened the floodgates, enabling Chris to extend the printed exchange over several weeks and compound the beneficial effect for the Campaign. Chris thought the Watney Mann PR man 'would have been better off if he had just kept his mouth shut.'

Unsurprisingly, the Campaign for Real Ale was not well received in all quarters. While it appears to have tapped into a general sense of disillusionment amongst the general public, the CAMRA newsletter *What's Brewing* of 1974 is filled with stories about the various organisations they had been rubbing up the wrong way. It seems that Watneys were prepared to fight dirty and it was reported that the brewer had tried to enlist the services of an unnamed freelance journalist to write anti-CAMRA stories for the national press. The journalist himself is quoted as saying Watneys left him 'with a feeling partly of being insulted from a professional and ethical point of view and partly of being amused that Watneys would try to do such a stupid thing as to buy their way into the newspapers through the back door.'

The PR men at Allied Breweries, Bass Charrington, Whitbread and Courage all accused CAMRA of being 'a very small bunch of people who do rather a lot of shouting and get headlines' at various times in 1974, while the June edition of *What's Brewing* reported that the Campaign's cheque for £5 for an annual subscription to the *Brewer's Guardian* had been returned by a 'man with a condescending tone' who phoned to say they didn't want CAMRA to receive the publication as the director had been upset by a previous mention in *What's Brewing*.

However, generally speaking CAMRA was a positive campaign that stood *for* something, not against it, and the reaction from the public was positive. Former National Chairman and entrepreneur Chris Hutt says it was 'not about telling the British public that there is a right thing to drink and a wrong thing to drink, it's about the fact that the public should have the choice, and [we] wanted to keep the choice of being able to drink real ale.' In the early eighties when his career began, brewer Mark Tetlow worked for Courage. He remembers that CAMRA was eventually seen in a positive light by many of the big brewers because they helped them to reinvigorate the market for cask beers. Also, Mark says, the actual brewers employed by these businesses supported CAMRA because they tended to be cask beer drinkers themselves, so they were pleased to see their favourite style of beer being pushed back onto the agenda.

Next steps

Their early legacy was showing people that change was possible.
TIM WEBB, co-author of The World Atlas of Beer

As the Campaign grew, the involvement of the four original founders was varied. Graham Lees moved around the country as a journalist in those early years, juggling his professional life with being national organiser for two years. Eventually he took up a post with the *Hemel Hempstead Evening Echo* which brought him to St Albans. This is how CAMRA's offices came to be based there. Their first paid employee, John Green, was a St Albans local. They installed their new full-time secretary into a rented room above a bicycle shop. The national campaign has operated out of the city ever since.

Graham recalls CAMRA taking up a lot of his time and energy and thinks he probably burned out. At the end of 1974 he dropped out and went to Australia for a year. After this break he was re-elected to the National Executive in 1976. Graham never took up a paid role within CAMRA, only holding voluntary positions on the National Executive. After a further two years he left the National Executive for good.

Michael Hardman was CAMRA's first chairman for two years and then went on to the paid staff as the publications editor and PR officer for a further three years from March 1974. The longest serving of the original founders, his influence is remembered fondly by many who were involved in those first years.

> For a time I worked full-time in the office, which was much enlivened by the presence of Michael Hardman and the frequency of liquid lunches. Often at the end of the day he'd say "I'm going for a swift half. Anyone joining me?" He meant half a gallon. His mate Eric Spragett would turn up and demonstrate his ability to create instant Cockney rhyming slang. "I'm going for a wotser," he'd say. "What's a nice boy like you doing in a place like this: piss."
>
> *TIM AMSDEN, former National Chairman*

Michael eventually returned to the *Evening Standard* as a journalist and also did some work for the BBC. However, the majority of his career, from 1980 until 2007, was spent in PR for Young's Brewery. He is described by veteran pubs campaigner Dave Gamston as 'an exceptional man'.

Jim Makin worked for Whitbread in brewery administration when CAMRA began. Originally employed by Threlfall's Brewery of Salford, it had been taken over by Whitbread in 1967 and the brewery remained operational until 1999. This takeover made Whitbread into the second largest brewing company in the country. As CAMRA grew in size and influence, Jim was warned off from any further involvement with the Campaign if he wanted to keep his job. Bill Mellor says it was incredibly courageous of him to stick in there for as long as he did. As a Whitbread lifer, Jim's pension was potentially on the line.

Bill Mellor's didn't make it far past his ill-fated events organiser role. He went travelling with Graham and his wife, Fran, on an overland trip in September 1974, ending up in Australia where Bill stayed on to work. He was then posted across the world during his journalistic career. In the early nineties Bill wrote a piece about CAMRA for the *Sydney Morning Herald*, much to the surprise of his Australian friends who did not know about Bill's role in the organisation. As he says, '[CAMRA] always invite me back and I'm always happy to go back. They make me really welcome even though my distinguished career as Events Organiser lasted about five minutes.'

What made Bill proud of his part in founding the Campaign was seeing a TV advert with soap opera actors sitting in a pub drinking beer with the message 'less talk, more real drinking'. He realised that the big breweries were on the back foot and had invested in an advertising campaign to disparage CAMRA. It made him think 'Wow, we're winning!'

* * *

When CAMRA came along it looked a bit boorish, student politics meets the rugby club, and I was far from convinced that its obsession with drinking the stuff was ever going to allow it to get to grips with the structural and legal issues that made the industry operate in the way it did.

TIM AMSDEN, former National Chairman

Michael Hardman was succeeded as chairman by author Chris Hutt. Chris had seen an article in a newspaper with Michael and Graham talking about the founding of CAMRA, which inspired him to get in touch and meet them. The meeting was enough for him to join the Campaign. Michael remembers that Chris 'injected a lot of enthusiasm, knowledge, diplomacy, intelligence – he was a true leader.'

Chris saw the Campaign increase by over 10,000 members under his leadership. This was an incredible achievement, but growth at that rate was to create as many problems as it solved for the smooth running of the organisation. In the same year as becoming chairman, Chris also published his seminal work *The Death of the English Pub*. It was a commercial success and ruffled The Brewer's Society's feathers. Chris says they wanted to portray him as 'a know-nothing 26-year-old – I don't know whether they ever called me a Communist or not, but certainly somebody that was politically beyond the pale and really knew nothing about the industry – because how could somebody of that age possibly write a book about the brewing industry?'

However, the book did strike a chord with many readers. Just like CAMRA, *The Death of the English Pub* inspired thousands more people who wanted things to change behind the bar of their local. It is clear that CAMRA was answering a need, not creating it. Chris's book is considered by many early members as one of the most important influences that helped to shape the Campaign. The bleak picture of the industry that it paints evokes a real sense of threat and it acted as a call to arms for the nation's beer drinkers.

The 1974 CAMRA AGM was held at the De Grey Rooms in York. It was an informal affair, with Chris giving his address sitting cross-legged on the table while nominations for the National Executive were taken from the floor. More than 500 members were in attendance and the accompanying beer exhibition boasted six new bars that were open throughout the two days that the convention was being held. This was a huge novelty for the members, who were used to pubs closing in the afternoon. Steve Bury, named as one of the top forty campaigners at the CAMRA 40th birthday celebrations in 2011, managed to drink his way through a whole afternoon and evening with a friend that day, leading to him taking an unexpected dip in the Ouse when stepping out to get some air. He thought his campaigning days were over when he felt something solid above his head as he tried to surface, but luckily it was the overhang of the steps and he was able to drag himself out of the river and stagger back to the 'after party' being held at a local hotel.

Steve wasn't the only one having a good time at that AGM. Tim Amsden remembers the antics of one Brian Sheridan who, after a good session, 'raided the pub kitchen and found a side of beef. The atmosphere at breakfast was chilling when the landlady paraded the remains of the joint, accusing us dramatically of "mu-ti-la-ting" it.'

By the time 1976 rolled around, becoming a company limited by guarantee was the next logical move. Not only had CAMRA undergone a period of enormous growth but because the National Executive were volunteers they needed to be protected from any personal liability should any issue arise. Andrew Cunningham remembers that the constitution for the company was an adapted version of the one for the Armstrong Siddeley Car Owners Club.

People who later became key figures on the National Executive, like John Bishopp, Chris Bruton and James Lynch, supported new chairman Gordon Massey in reorganising the administrative side of the Campaign. Massey's 'Night of the Long Knives' saw half of the National Executive sacked and replaced. They also wrote the Articles of Association for the ratified constitution. In particular it was established how branches would be run and the membership's administration was dealt with, finally bringing CAMRA to the end of its 'shoebox' era.

> It was a very exciting place to be. What impressed me, coming from a serious political background, was the work that went on in CAMRA in those early days ... A lot of very carefully researched reports had been made about the activities of the big brewers which had been presented to government, and I was really impressed by the intellectual drive of the organisation. I found that CAMRA was so far removed from the *Private Eye* stereotype of the man with the big beer belly and big beard falling down drunk all the time.
>
> *ROGER PROTZ*

But not everyone was so convinced about the prevalence of organisational rigour and discipline:

CAMRA was of course the most tremendous fun, if juvenile. I remember sitting watching that Bernard Cribbins film about brewing (he plays all the characters) for the ninety-ninth time, while others in the same row were busy putting bread rolls and vol-au-vents from the buffet lunch into the hood of the duffle coat of a man in the row in front.   *TIM AMSDEN*

Growth continued. There were a lot more branches. More brewers started to pay attention and external commentators like Richard Boston were lending more and more support. The relentless march of keg had been stopped, although in some cases more by accident than design according to Charrington employee Robert Humphreys. He describes his employer as a bit-player although admittedly they were a part of the vast Bass-Charrington empire. He was a district manager looking after thirty-five London pubs and describes how in 1973 they were the only one of the Big Six to still have hand pumps in every bar. This was not because they had a visionary board that had been awoken by CAMRA's messaging, but rather that they had directors so sluggish that they hadn't noticed every other brewer was going over to keg. However, people like Robert could 'see the way the wind was blowing, and the wind was coming from CAMRA,' so they were determined to hang on to and eventually even expand their draught range.

Trade publication the *Morning Advertiser* (MA) initially banned their writers from using the term 'real ale' when it came into common usage, *Morning Advertiser* journalist and, later, *What's Brewing* editor Ted Bruning remembers. The argument was that for a trade publication dealing with brewers of all descriptions, all ale is 'real'. Phil Mellows joined Ted at the MA as a features writer in November 1984 and was also told not to use the term. He still prefers to call it cask beer. 'You might get away with "real ale" in the consumer press thanks to CAMRA's success in getting it into the language,' says Phil. 'Indeed, it was a stroke of genius to come up with that but it's a (very good) marketing strategy, not a definition.'

The real story from Phil's perspective was not the ban on 'real ale', but rather being told not to give CAMRA any positive publicity, or in fact mention them at all if possible. This directive apparently came from the committee of the Society of Licensed Victuallers (LVA) that presided over the MA at the time. While there was some broad support, many pub licensees were hostile towards CAMRA. They didn't take criticism well, particularly those publicans who had spent decades working behind the bar. They may not have wanted to bother with the hassle of keeping cask-conditioned beer, but they wanted to be told their business by the young upstarts from CAMRA even less.

It wasn't just the national campaign that rubbed the Society of Licensed Victuallers up the wrong way. In his popular beer blog, John Clarke records an incident which came about after one of the infamous Stockport 'Staggers' pub crawls. A mixed review of the Emigration pub was printed in the Stockport branch's *Opening Times* magazine after the Stagger in 1986. This led to a complaint from the publican being printed the very next month, with a matching complaint finding its way to the Stockport LVA. He persuaded them to 'kick out CAMRA' – or so it was reported in the *Morning Advertiser*. Unfortunately for the LVA, the public were apparently more sympathetic to the CAMRA branch and a judicious amount of backtracking followed.

There were about 100 breweries in the UK when CAMRA first began, and we now enjoy almost 2,000 today. Undeniably, this is thanks in part to CAMRA. According to former National Chairman Tony Millns, what they stood for was not in itself a revolutionary idea. 'Doing something about it rather than crying into your pint of nasty keg beer was the revolutionary act.'

As CAMRA grew unexpectedly huge, the *Morning Advertiser*'s anti-CAMRA editorial policy couldn't last. Phil Mellows remembers the turning point coming in 1990 when he interviewed new

National Chairman John Cryne at the Trinity Arms in Brixton. This was considered a controversial move at the paper. Phil says he 'put to him [John] publicans' objections to the organisation, and I can't remember it being a friendly interview. But it was a breakthrough of sorts.' Ted Bruning saw CAMRA as 'a powerful irritant' to the licensed trade.

By 1980 the larger brewers were all back on board with the market for cask ale. As *What's Brewing* reported in just one example, 'real ale seems to be bursting out all over the Whibread empire these days.'

> In recent months there have been rumblings in the licensed trade to the effect that CAMRA's role – to bring back cask beer – has now been fulfilled, and that it has no business meddling in such issues as licensing and brewery policy. Until such a time as another organisation comes forward to take over the watchdog role on behalf of the ripped-off drinker, this Campaign, and in particular this magazine, will continue to criticise any moves detrimental to the interests of its following, in particular with regard to pricing, choice and quality. Anyone not liking this situation knows what to do about it.
>
> London Drinker, *the London branches' magazine, 1986*

For some it seemed the battle had been won, and CAMRA became victims of its own success as membership numbers began to tail off.

How CAMRA Works

CAMRA is the biggest social club in the country.

NEIL LEESON, Members' Weekend coordinator

THE essence of CAMRA's structure has not changed in fifty years. A National Executive elected at the Annual General Meeting oversees operations centrally. A paid team of staff supports them – although in the early days the paid staff consisted solely of the company secretary, John Green, housed in a rented room above a St Albans bicycle shop.

The national organisation supports a network of regions, which in turn administer local branches: 220 in number at the time of writing. Branches allow every member of CAMRA to have ready access to local campaigning and events.

CAMRA's key business is administered via a network of themed committees. Critics complain that CAMRA has become overly bureaucratic, but an organisation with 180,000 members and an annual turnover in the region of £16 million has a lot to administrate!

National Executive

The National Executive (NE) is made up of twelve individuals. The voluntary positions are elected annually by members. Usually candidates come up from the branches or regions. It is rare for someone who wasn't previously involved as a member to be successful in seeking election to the National Executive.

The work each NE member undertakes is varied. As a new member of the executive, incumbents are given some time to learn the ropes without specific duties being placed on them, but then an area of responsibility is allocated. In such a huge organisation with varied projects and campaigning interests these special responsibilities can be quite diverse.

A governance review was concluded in 2019 which proposed a new committee structure. This was implemented at the beginning of 2020. There are committees for campaigning (covering Pubs & Clubs, Awards, and Real Ale, Cider & Perry), finance, people (Volunteers & Membership), events, commercial and publishing, branches, and then a small number of advisory groups below these such as the fundraising Games & Collectibles Committee, Brewery Liaison Advisory Group (BLAG) and the Technical Advisory Group (TAG) who set the technical definitions for CAMRA's campaigning.

During her tenure on the NE, Christine Cryne instigated a culture of consultation within CAMRA, including members, branches and committees in decision making on strategy and offering support and training so everyone could get properly involved. The result of this was for Christine to be made the first Volunteer Director, overseeing a new training strategy for volunteers, and a Volunteer Charter which enshrines values of equal opportunities and mutual respect. While it is applicable throughout the organisation, it is perhaps most relevant at beer festivals. Huge numbers of CAMRA members volunteer their time over a number of days to make the events successful. This astounding commitment of volunteer time is a fundamental part of CAMRA life and it is vital that each one of them knows they are valued and respected.

Former National Chairman Dave Goodwin first got involved with his branch at Leicester in 1980 and after a few years started to help out with national committees. He was elected to the NE in 1989 and held positions there until 2004. He remembers that there were a lot of meetings to attend, which meant that it was easy to get to know your fellow National Executive members, but the depth of the commitment only really sunk in for some people *after* they had been elected, rather unfortunately. He once calculated that with his National Executive work, meetings, preparation and festival volunteering he was spending around fourteen hours a week volunteering for CAMRA – and he did this for over fifteen years. 'If you're on the NE and have a full time job then the rest of your time is sleep.'

*　　*　　*

Motivations for serving on the National Executive vary as much as those for joining CAMRA in the first place. Long-serving NE member Gillian Hough came back to serve a second term on the executive after a decade's break in 2018 because she wasn't happy with the direction the organisation was taking. She wanted to volunteer to help bring it back on course because, in her view, 'the members' voice was being left behind.'

Members of the National Executive also have unique opportunities to build an amazing CV through their association with CAMRA, opportunities that no other organisation could hope to replicate. A term on the NE gives the chance to lead the way in liaising with government on policy and strategy, organise huge events attended by thousands of people or take a hand in overseeing a budget of millions of pounds. Former *Good Beer Guide* editor Jeff Evans noted that his personal involvement led to him acting as a spokesperson for CAMRA on breakfast television, TV news and radio.

Andy Beaton held a range of roles within CAMRA. By going to conferences and making speeches he was able to develop his public speaking prowess. In particular he remembers making a speech at the April 1985 AGM at the University of Southampton. A motion had been put forward to withdraw financial support from Ma Pardoes home brew pub in Netherton, Dudley. It was one of the four remaining original home brew pubs that existed when CAMRA was first formed. Andy proudly recalls getting 'something approaching a standing ovation' from the AGM because there was such strong support for his petition. He said that the pub was a Black Country institution that could already have been lost to one of the predatory large breweries had CAMRA not stepped in previously. Happily, in the end the action was a success and the meeting voted to continue supporting the brewery. Andy is really grateful that the new skills he gained with CAMRA opened up opportunities in other areas of his life. His new-found confidence helped him later, when he took an adult teaching qualification so he could run training courses at work.

Current National Executive member Sarah Crawford is proud of chairing a parliamentary reception at the Scottish Parliament at Holyrood when she was a Regional Director. Giving a speech to thirty MSPs is not something she would have been able to do five years earlier, but she learned public speaking skills as well as building her confidence by being a Regional Director.

Standing for the National Executive involves putting forward a personal statement that is printed in *What's Brewing* and made available online via the CAMRA online forum 'Discourse'. Recently there have also been candidate interviews printed in the *Morning Advertiser*, bringing CAMRA's internal election processes to a broader public. The most public interest seems to have been generated by Bradley Cummings of craft brewing upstarts Tiny Rebel, who stood for election in 2018. Brad notably adapted the 'Vote for Pedro' shirt from the film *Napoleon Dynamite*, creating a point of interest for younger CAMRA members by using the contemporary popular reference point, setting himself up as an underdog just like Napoleon's friend Pedro in the film.

Ash Corbett-Collins, the Commercial & Communications Director, was also invited to conduct page-long interviews about why he should be a National Director and gave interviews to the BBC and other platforms during his election.

National Chairmen

> First I am a member of Burton branch, a member of
> their committee and active in the branch and secondly
> I happen to be the National Chairman. I am a grassroots
> member just as much as anybody else.
>
> *NIK ANTONA, current National Chairman of CAMRA*

Leadership of CAMRA lies with its National Chairman, who is elected by their fellow National Executive members. Founder Michael Hardman was the first and a line of sixteen further illustrious names have followed in his footsteps since. The chairman's role consists of coordinating the voluntary National Executive as well as the Chief Executive and the paid staff team. It is a facilitatory role to make sure that each individual volunteer in CAMRA can focus on their own area of responsibility without any impediment.

A good National Chairman has the ability to significantly shift the direction of the organisation for the better. A former chairman himself, Dave Goodwin commented that he considered Tony Millns to be one such individual, modernising the organisation and moving it forward dramatically in a relatively short space of time. Tony was chairman from 1982 to 1985 and Dave remarked that he had done a lot to tackle the 'old image of blokes in jeans and sandals,' and had introduced 'a more modern image of a campaigning group' that was still evolving. While these stubborn old stereotypes about members prove hard to shift, the early 1980s were a time of great change for the Campaign, seeing it become more financially sustainable and more professional in its activities thanks to a series of dedicated national chairmen and National Executive members.

On 13 April 2003 Paula Waters was confirmed as the first ever female National Chairman at the Exeter AGM. She always referred to herself specifically as National Chairman, just like her predecessors, rather than making any changes to the title because of her gender. 'When I reached pub-going age in the late seventies my Pomagne and Martini drinking friends were amused by my preference for Vaux Double Maxim,' she was quoted as saying. Her involvement with the national campaign was motivated by a desire to encourage more women to drink beer. 'One of my biggest ambitions as chairman will be to convince them to try it and realise that the diversity of tastes available leaves wine in the shadows,' she said in *What's Brewing* when she was appointed.

Paid staff team

One industry insider describes the CAMRA staff team as 'some of the most effective lobbyists in the pub sector'. Since the days of the first employee, John Green, their number has grown and their professionalism and expertise has helped to give the organisation a steady rudder in the turbulent waters of real ale campaigning. Having recently undergone a governance review, their structure is now based around divisions under a senior leadership team: campaigns, communications, commercial, and support.

In February 1974 John was installed in a four-room office at 94 Victoria Street, St Albans, above a bicycle shop. From there the team gradually grew, encompassing new specialisms like membership, publications, finance, and campaigns. Finally they needed more space and were able to afford a converted house at 34 Alma Road, which they moved into in 1978. As the team's expansion continued over the years they hoped to extend the building. However, planning permission could not be obtained so they instead moved into offices at Hatfield Road, in a relatively spacious converted car showroom. This move took place in 1995 and was clearly relatively futureproof as the team is still located there.

Mike Benner became the first Chief Executive in March 2004. As with all of the paid roles in CAMRA, the intention was to provide support to the National Executive, to help them become more effective and efficient. The Chief Executive is responsible for managing and leading the paid staff, as well as supporting the National Executive in delivering their strategic goals. Mike Benner was at the forefront of campaigns opposing the beer duty escalator and planning reforms to benefit pubs. It's not unfair to say that the present Chief Executive, Tom Stainer, is occupied with much the same issues, although with the added complication of a global pandemic thrown into the mix.

The paid staff had grown to a nearly fifty-strong team assisting the National Executive in the running of a £16m organisation by the time the government announced a UK-wide lockdown in March 2020. Undoubtedly, there will be some contraction as the organisation has lost revenue and membership recruitment opportunities through the loss of events like the BBC Good Food Show, and, of course, the Great British Beer Festival (GBBF) and other beer festivals. Early estimates are that the staff team will reduce in size by around 25%, and it is too early to assess the overall financial impact of the lockdowns on CAMRA.

The regions

In order to allow it to be administered more effectively, CAMRA has split up the UK into various regions, which in turn are made up of individual local branches. Regions are overseen by their respective Regional Director (RD). These volunteers stand for election in their region and are signed off by the National Executive. They act as a go-between, passing information and comment between the branches and the National Executive. This is always happening informally, but there is also a Branches Committee where all sixteen regional directors meet on roughly a bi-monthly basis. The Regional Directors and the National Executive liaise at four NERD weekends held through the year.

The regional structure is considered crucial in getting the voice of the ordinary member to the ear of the National Executive. Regional Directors spend a lot of time attending branch meetings to make sure they know what the local members want. Some areas are much more geographically dispersed than others, making it more difficult to give adequate coverage. Sub-branches may thrive and fill the gaps, but in the early days the Regional Directors had to take up the slack for jobs like researching possible entries to the *Good Beer Guide*. Andy Beaton, a NE member in the late eighties, remembers visiting Herefordshire with Great British Beer Festival organiser Tim Webb to visit a few pubs to increase the coverage. It wasn't the most robust methodology for researching the GBG, but it was better than missing out Herefordshire entirely.

Scotland and Northern Ireland are counted as a single region for the sake of administration, but each has its own rich CAMRA history. Scottish CAMRA was first established way back in 1974. The recent Scottish and Northern Ireland Director, Sarah Crawford, points out there are many specific needs and challenges that face the eleven branches there. Many areas are quite rural so they need different resources and support compared to metropolitan centres like Edinburgh and Glasgow. In particular there are a relatively significant number of members located on the islands who need attention, not to mention the fact that the Highlands branch is the size of Belgium! Terry Lock recalls that for Scottish branch meetings you might head out on a Thursday and not get home until Sunday because you had to travel so far. However, the benefit of this was that it cemented the relationships of the members, who spent more time together and made each meeting more of an anticipated event.

Former Regional Director and NE member Dave McKerchar spoke, before he sadly passed away in April 2020, of how the Campaign had important work to do in his home region. He remembered his eyes being opened to real ale by a pub in his hometown changing hands to Maclays of Alloa. The beer they served included McEwan's Export and Younger's IPA. They were keg beers on an electric pump, but quite tasty to him nonetheless, and 'didn't make you belch, which was a good thing.' Dave wanted more of this 'good stuff' but you couldn't get real ale anywhere, except for a handful of pubs in Glasgow and Edinburgh. Little by little the early Scottish campaigners got through, mostly by persuading landlords, literally one at a time, to start serving real ale.

The experience of Sarah Durham as Regional Director for London was very different. There are a lot of London branches, but they can all be easily reached to attend meetings due to the excellent transport links. This was in sharp contrast to when she later moved to the Central Southern area, where there would be hours of driving to get to meetings, which took the shine off the role somewhat.

Sarah also reminisces about the organisation of the London Drinker Beer Festival (1985–2018) where there would be enormous group meetings in the pub. Anyone who was a member in the region could just turn up and all branches sent representatives. In the early 2000s these already chaotic meetings would suffer further disruption from the then National Chairman, Dave Goodwin, and his predecessor, John Cryne, who would come along to sit in the middle of the room and talk loudly until she had to warn them, 'Would the National Chairman and the previous National Chairman like to take their conversation elsewhere so we can have the meeting?' The pair of them were dangerously disruptive influences, acting as if they were in charge, according to Sarah.

Branches

Like a vast circulatory system, CAMRA's branches are the life-blood of the Campaign, allowing the organisation to tap into the combined skills, time and expertise of nearly 200,000 dedicated and passionate ale drinkers around the UK (and one or two a little further afield). Branches are local groups of CAMRA members with an elected committee. They have five stated purposes: campaigning, promotion, enjoyment, participation and fundraising.

In the early days, the procedure for starting a new branch was to apply to the NE then hold a modest 'Testing Support Meeting' with a minimum of twelve people. This would be followed by an inaugural meeting of at least twenty-five to show that local support existed. These meetings would be promoted in *What's Brewing*, as they still are today. Former chairman Tony Millns emphasises that the National Executive kept a watchful eye on who was proposing new branches. In his time, the early eighties, CAMRA was still a relatively small family and so it was easy to check that proposals to start a new branch came from a safe pair of hands. 'A group of complete plonkers wanting to set up a drinking club and expecting loads of money from the national organisation to support their beer drinking would quickly be shown the door,' according to Tony.

The first CAMRA branch is often claimed to be the Hertford-shire branch (now South Hertfordshire), with the first branch meeting being held on 20 November 1972 at the Farriers Arms with some thirty people in attendance. The Farriers Arms meeting is even commemorated with a blue plaque on the pub. It was the only pub in St Albans serving real ale at the time and was where secretary John Green recruited members before the Campaign could afford to rent him an office. South Hertfordshire veteran activist Steve Bury remembers it being 50p to join then, when a pint of beer would set you back about 12.5p.

Unfortunately for South Hertfordshire and for the Farriers Arms, Chester and South Clwyd is the oldest branch. Hudders-field was formed next and Hertfordshire is actually the third, according to CAMRA founder Michael Hardman.

Many more branches were founded in the following years, rising steadily to the 220 that exist today. Derek Moore founded a branch because he had the modest ambition of being able to walk to a pub that sold real ale in his local area. He had been disappointed to find only one cask ale outlet in the entirety of his home county of Renfrewshire. Already a CAMRA member, he had to travel across to the Glasgow branch for meetings and good beer so he was inspired to start a branch of his own.

Derek roped in all of his pals so he could meet the minimum tally for a new branch, making them all take out joint memberships so that their wives, friends and partners would also be counted. He recalls that most of his friends weren't the least bit interested in real ale at the time, but many of them later became diehard aficionados. The inaugural meeting of the Renfrewshire branch – also attended by Glasgow members who were there in support – was at the Masonic Arms, now Callum's, in Johnstone. Callum's was an early success of the Renfrewshire's campaigning activities and still has five hand pumps to this day.

Naturally, branches vary in how active and engaged their committees and members are. Andrew Cunningham, an early branch chairman who did a lot of work with the foundation of the various London branches, remembers that in the mid-seventies it would not be uncommon for over a hundred people to attend any given branch meeting, and branch committee seats were hotly contested.

This level of enthusiasm would appear to be somewhat diminished in the current era. To pick out a couple of arbitrary examples to illustrate: the chairman of the Stockport and South Manchester branch, John Clarke, is pleased to have some 1,600 members in his branch, and of those, around 100 people attend the meetings, work on the branch magazine *Opening Times* or work at the beer festivals; Shawn Collier, former chairman of the Leicester branch, reports around 1,950 members, with some 120 taking an active role through the year. Only 3–5% of members per branch, less than in these examples, being active is seen as the norm by the central organisation.

*   *   *

The actual feel and smell of a brewery is something very evocative.

IAIN LOE, former Research and Information Manager

Branch activities can vary greatly, but one thing they have in common is going on brewery or pub trips. Graham Wallen went on a trip organised for Bedford branch in around 1975. One Saturday morning they visited Paine's Brewery in nearby St Neots. Graham and his father-in-law joined the group visiting the old traditional brewery site, a moderately imposing building in the centre of town, which had been rebuilt in the early twentieth century following a fire. Graham vividly remembers the central archway through which the staff and drays entered the site. He also recalls enjoying the trip, especially the generous hospitality bar and chatting with the brewer:

> It didn't seem as if we were in there that long. When it was time to leave we spilled out into the yard, only to find the gate man had clocked off and locked the gates at half past twelve. Oh no! Locked in the brewery. What do we do now?
>
> We moved back into the bar while the brewer went into the office to find the phone number of someone to come and let us out. I can't remember the next bit clearly, but we either sat there calmly, or opened a few bottles.
>
> It put me off brewery trips for a while after that.
>
> It's too risky.   *GRAHAM WALLEN*

Another important part of branch campaigning is producing local publications. Geoff Strawbridge, the Pubs Officer and Regional Director for London, remembers how individual branches sought to keep lists of pubs serving real ale, and publishing them from time to time as local guides. From the late 1970s a *Real Beer in London* guide was published and later updated, which has since blossomed into a whole series of comprehensive pub guides spanning Greater London.

Much of the leg work of keeping a check on the content of these London guides was undertaken for some thirty years by Roger Warhurst, who published updates in the 'Capital Pubcheck' feature in the *London Drinker*, the branch magazine which spans all of the London branches. You can imagine the vast numbers of changes of names, ownerships and beer ranges that took place, as well as closures and demolitions, but Roger assiduously kept up with the demanding task. This is just one example of the incredible tenacity of CAMRA's members, who commit vast amounts of time and energy on a voluntary basis for the cause they love.

The Capital Pubcheck came to be replaced in September 2013 by WhatPub, a website which allowed all of the information submitted by members about pubs around the country to be compiled electronically. Geoff Strawbridge considers WhatPub to be one of CAMRA's greatest achievements. More than 150,000 volunteers have contributed to the online pub guide. It goes much further in detail than the *Good Beer Guide* publication. By virtue of being online it is able to accommodate a much larger amount of information. It continues to be an evolving resource, with the ultimate aim being the mammoth task of having an accurate listing for every single pub in the country.

Another astonishing achievement of the voluntary committees of the Greater London branches is the *London Drinker*. This is an exceptional branch magazine in a number of ways, but not least in its circulation. Some 27,000 copies are distributed by hand to local pubs by local volunteers. Additionally, a box of approximately 100 copies is delivered to each and every Wetherspoons pub in Greater London. This gives the *London Drinker* a total circulation in the region of 50,000 – more than some national newspapers. Edited by Tony Hedger, the London branches continue to release the magazine on a bi-monthly basis, just as they have done since 1979.

Beer writer Matthew Curtis thinks CAMRA's biggest issue is inconsistency across the branches: if one branch does or publishes something inappropriate this is taken as a reflection of the organisation as a whole. This was particularly well illustrated in 2018 when the crossword clues in one branch magazine were circulated on social media because of their outdated racist and homophobic language. As soon as the problem was brought to the attention of the national team, they issued a public apology immediately, but it would have been impractical for them to do anything further. With 220 branches it simply wouldn't be possible (or particularly democratic) to police all branch content before it was published. The organisation has to rely on its membership to exercise common sense.

Brewery Liaison Officers

CAMRA's first attempt to break down some of the initial suspicions that brewers had towards them was to allocate every brewery to a branch as a way of ensuring they stayed in touch. This didn't work as no one was taking responsibility, so they moved instead to allocating each brewery to an individual: it was the birth of the Brewery Liaison system. This was aimed at breaking down barriers and establishing a platform for dialogue so that branches could work together with breweries for mutual benefit.

Of course, when the system first developed, no one could anticipate the huge explosion in brewery numbers, so it is now much more of a commitment to find a willing Brewery Liaison Officer (BLO) for every single brewery, who then feeds into the central Brewery Liaison Advisory Group (BLAG). Some particularly enthusiastic individuals take more than one local brewery under their wing. John Cryne, for example, was BLO for Charles Wells when he lived in Bedford, and has also acted as BLO for Fuller's. He is currently the BLO for Moncada and Gorgeous Breweries in North West London.

At Three Brothers Brewing in Teesside they are quick to sing the praises of their BLO, who supports them at events and really bangs the drum for their business. It shows that when breweries take the time to interact with the support network that CAMRA has put in place it really pays dividends, as they have CAMRA members from across the Teeside area who support them.

Local beer festivals benefit from engaged brewers that are keen to get involved and perhaps even help with the logistics.

Brewers gain from the opportunity to promote their brand to festival goers. They also get the support of their branch when there is a threat to the business, as well as being around to help them celebrate good news. The two-way communication helps to establish what beers each brewery is producing, how these styles are categorised, and, ultimately, which, if any, might be suitable to be put forward for the Champion Beer of Britain competition.

Smaller breweries value the active branch members who give them the most direct and visible support and say they find that the work of the national organisation impacts on their businesses much less. This is perhaps understandable for a consumer organisation, but does show that the part CAMRA played in securing, for example, the Small Brewer's Duty Relief in 2002, is perhaps no longer well remembered by everyone in the industry, despite the ongoing debate that surrounds the relief.

Two-way communication is vital to the success of the system: the responsibility doesn't just fall to the shoulders of the BLO. One CAMRA volunteer remembers being completely cold shouldered by both breweries they were tasked to represent, Guinness and Anheuser Busch. That is until the former wanted to launch a new beer and thought the BLO's successful local beer festival would be a great place to do that. Needless to say, on that occasion it was Guinness who found their calls weren't being returned!

FUNDING THE CAMPAIGN

Finance

The early Campaign did not have a great relationship with financial stability, but to begin with that wasn't a huge problem. It was easier for early National Executive members to keep the organisation afloat than the job of administering a multi-million pound organisation is today. Journalist Terry Pattinson was treasurer in early 1973 when the bank threatened to foreclose. Each member of the NE threw in a fiver to make CAMRA solvent again, which kept the wolf from the door for a little longer.

Steve Bury remembers his branch running car boot sales in the garden of the Crooked Billet in Colney Heath to raise money to make publicity materials to promote local breweries, as well as making badges to sell. They included memorable slogans such as 'DD [Double Diamond] is canine pee' and the famed slight against Watneys: 'closer to water than a couple screwing in a punt'. But these activities were not going to be enough to sustain a nationwide campaign.

According to early chairman Chris Hutt, the most difficult thing for the Campaign in its infancy was the cost of administering each membership. Every new member was promised twelve copies of *What's Brewing* posted to their home address each year. Unfortunately, at the beginning nobody had thought of it in those terms, and the subscription fee didn't even cover the costs of printing and posting, let alone contributing anything into the kitty for campaigning. This meant that keeping up their obligation to produce a magazine monthly quickly became a very difficult burden even in the most successful years.

By the early 1980s the Campaign was at a low ebb. They were victims of their own success. People saw the retreat of keg beer and experienced the increasing ease of obtaining real ale. New microbreweries were cropping up around the country now that a market for cask ale had been tested. All of these signs were taken to mean that CAMRA had done its job. Membership nosedived, putting huge pressure on the organisation's finances. Numbers dropped to some 15,000, having previously surpassed 30,000. Dave Goodwin remembers how hand-to-mouth they were then, with the cheques for staff pay being signed and distributed on a Friday, but the last one to the bank would invariably find no money left.

In 1983 Tony Millns became National Chairman. He had become known in CAMRA for helping to run the Cambridge Beer Festival, which was a fantastically popular and profitable event for the organisation. In fact, it was so successful, Tony contends, that it was practically bankrolling the rest of the Campaign at the time. Tony could see how unsustainable the national organisation was and realised that he would have to roll his sleeves up and get stuck in if he wanted to see it change. He was joined in this work by people like John Cryne, who had a finance background and later worked for PricewaterhouseCoopers.

John was the Finance Director before being voted National Chairman by his National Executive colleagues. The hand-to-mouth existence was really limiting what it was possible to achieve in terms of campaigning. Some unsuccessful publishing ventures did more damage to the balance sheet, generating huge print costs with no income following on from sales. The difficulties fostered suspicion between the branches and the central organisation. Branches were raising good money from beer festivals and felt like it was going straight down 'the black hole of St Albans'.

The new National Executive dream team of 1983 onwards put the price of membership up by a significant percentage. Now it didn't just cover the costs of the member perks but also generated a small surplus. The computerisation of the membership system soon afterwards allowed members to be moved from standing orders to Direct Debit, it gave a much better retention rate and allowed the price of membership to be changed. These changes made the Campaign more stable and allowed them to buy the property at 34 Alma Road, which they had moved into a few years earlier.

CAMRA (Real Ale) Investments Ltd

When CAMRA Investments was incorporated in 1974, the Campaign was at the zenith of its extraordinary rise to prominence on the beer scene, but had not yet been accepted by the brewing industry. When members put up nearly £200,000 to form the company, this helped to convince brewers they were facing a real phenomenon and not one dreamt up by a bunch of Fleet Street journalists in search of a story.

CHRISTOPHER HUTT in What's Brewing, *September 1980*

One idea tabled to further the aims of the Campaign was to create an independent investment company that allowed members to join together to buy pubs which would be run as proper free houses and so demonstrate their confidence in real ale. This would give the pubs the opportunity to provide more choice and make it possible to save endangered ones. CAMRA (Real Ale) Investments, also known as CAMRAIL, was voted through by the National Executive after Chris Hutt had already stepped down. He and Chris Bruton were engaged to implement the idea in 1974. Chris Hutt was taken on in June 1974, originally with a three-month contract, and charged with launching the public company. Shares were floated at £1 each in 1974.

CAMRAIL's holdings grew quickly to five pubs. The first pub to be purchased was the White Gates Inn in Hyde. There was controversy amongst the membership when it was eventually sold on to Samuel Smith's in 1979. The decision to sell to a brewer rather than as a free house was not well received in some quarters. CAMRAIL's statement said that the Sam Smith's offer 'was by far the best, they do brew a real ale and are conservation-minded in their treatment of their pubs,' so there was at least a principled argument behind the sale.

The Nag's Head in Hampstead was opened in 1975. It had previously been run by the first recorded landlord of colour in London prior to the 1965 Race Relations Act, according to research done by the Indian publican's own daughter, Barbara D'Gama. The Old Fox in Bristol was bought from Courage, also in 1975. The Eagle Tavern in Leeds is a 200-year-old pub that opened under CAMRA Investments in 1976 and is now part of the Sam Smith's chain, while the Salisbury Arms in Cambridge was bought for £22,000 and thereby saved from conversion to residential use by Whitbread.

CAMRA (Real Ale) Investments PLC changed its name to Midsummer Inns in 1983. In 1985, when it owned a total of ten pubs, it was taken over by Swithland Leisure, run by Midlands entertainment entrepreneur Adam Page. Chris Hutt went on to found his own pub company, Unicorn Inns, which was sold to Moorlands for £16 million in 1996.

CAMRA Members' Investment Club (CMIC)

> The Club invests in a variety of stocks and shares (quoted and unlisted) in companies operating in both the production and retailing of real ale and allied trades including large and small breweries, pub owning companies and property businesses operating in the pub sector. *CMIC website*

At the instigation of Neil Kellet, a group of members proposed investing their own money into the industry at the 1989 AGM in Aberdeen. This grew into the CAMRA Members' Investment Club, which is still in operation today and is one of the biggest investment clubs in the UK with more than 3,000 members and assets valued at some £17 million.

While the club is operated under the best financial industry practice, it is sympathetic to CAMRA's aims. This means the club provides a safe home for the shares of family and regional brewers. They helped to keep Wolverhampton & Dudley (renamed as Marstons PLC in 2007) out of the clutches of Pubmaster, who made an undervalued bid for the brewery in 2001.

In 2003 a proposal was made at the Investment Club's AGM to use £50,000 of club funds to buy shares in McMullen who were fighting to stay trading as a vertically integrated brewer and retailer. The brewery had previously been criticised by CAMRA in 1997 and 1999 for use of the cask breather in their pubs, but the decision to invest was still carried. The intervention of the Investment Club appears to have had a positive effect as McMullen remains a successful brewery to this day.

CAMRA's shareholdings

The Campaign itself built up a holding of brewery shares in order to access their AGMs. Neil Kellett was a Manchester-based accountant and CAMRA's first auditor. His firm went on to audit the accounts for many years. He thought that it would be helpful for CAMRA to have access to decision making at the board level when it came to brewery takeovers, and perhaps even swing the odd vote in favour of keeping a brewery that would otherwise be lost. It was also thought to be a good idea for members of the Campaign to feel a sense of ownership over the breweries whose beer they drank.

What's Brewing in January 1974 records that the proceeds of the CAMRA 140 Club, a fundraising lottery, were invested in eight brewing companies so that the NE could attend and vote at shareholders' meetings. A stake of just under £50 was acquired in Allied Breweries, Grand Metropolitan, Whitbread, Imperial Tobacco, Scottish and Newcastle, Marston, Thompson & Evershed Ltd, Bass Charrington and the Whitbread Investment Trust.

These holdings slowly built up until they provided the Campaign with a useful source of dividend income. However, they can only hold so much interest because CAMRA needed to demonstrate clear independence when the invitation to become a super-complainant came along in 2002.

The Enterprise Act (2002) designated the bodies that could make 'super-complaints' on behalf of the large body of consumers that they represent. This is a particularly rare status, and you can count on both hands the bodies, such as the National Association of Citizens Advice Bureaux, who have been awarded it. CAMRA was added to this list in a 2004 amendment. The status means they can make a complaint to the Office of Fair Trading if some part of a UK market for goods and/or services is significantly harming the interests of consumers. CAMRA's shares were run down to a token level and the CMIC was given first refusal to buy them to meet the requirements of CAMRA's new responsibilities. Super-complainant status puts a significant onus on CAMRA to retain its independent voice and to truly represent the voice of its members, the consumer. It has proved an important way into being heard by regulatory bodies on matters of takeovers, closures, monopolies, etc.

Former Finance Director Ken Davie notes that 'CAMRA is not permitted to hold any large shareholdings because of its super-complainant status.' In 2004 this caused some controversy as some branches held shares from before CAMRA finances were centralised and didn't want to give them up. Just like the national organisation, it was seen as a way to have influence at brewery board meetings, but they were told they must dispose of them. There were a couple of situations where the branches refused to transfer or sell their shares. Resolving these issues took years in some instances and fuelled some degree of tension between the national organisation and the branches. Even when a matter was made the subject of published CAMRA policy, branches might choose to ignore it.

CAMRA has invoked its super-complainant status only once and that was in 2010 to complain about the beer tie. Unfortunately, upon investigating the complaint, the Office of Fair Trading's report found insufficient grounds to investigate the pub companies under either the Competition Act 1998 or the Enterprise Act 2002. It was held that 'beer ties do not adversely affect the number of beers available to the end consumer or contribute to artificially high prices.'[3]

Having a seat at the table doesn't necessarily mean the Campaign can effect real change, even where it wants to, as the recent sale of Fuller's to Asahi showed. The CMIC was not able to vote the sale down despite their several million in shares in Fuller's.

MEMBERS

CAMRA's greatest strength has always lain within the ranks of its membership. No other organisation I can think of has ever had such a broad appeal to people at every point on every spectrum of society, bringing people together who would never otherwise have even passed the time of day with each other; people of all ages, background, financial circumstances, occupations, educational backgrounds and even religions. So refreshing. A common cause that united everyone regardless.

3. www.lexology.com/library/detail.aspx?g=b4e8c174-6597-479b-91f5-03f7ae70d88f

> We had within our ranks the most experienced, highly
> qualified and highly skilled people in every field, ready,
> willing and able to play their part. For that reason and
> because of our limitless energy and enthusiasm the
> Big Breweries found that they'd totally underestimated us
> and ultimately were beaten.
>
> *JAMES LYNCH*

Initially recruited from the friendship groups of the four founders, the membership of CAMRA expanded exponentially because of the publicity the Campaign was generating. In the early days, branch members would also walk from pub to pub selling memberships and promoting the idea of CAMRA to the uninitiated, one neophyte at a time.

An infamous early CAMRA recruiter was John Bell. He is remembered for his bold personality and virtually forcing everyone in a pub to sign up, says Cambridge pioneer John Bishopp. John had been helping out a friend to run a pub in South Cambridge at the time and this was how he discovered the Campaign. John Bell must really have had the gift of the gab, as not long after John Bishopp met him in 1973 the inaugural meeting of the Cambridge branch was held; John Bell had managed to recruit enough people to start a new branch! Initially, some publicans were sceptical of the activists in their midst, but as the Campaign picked up momentum it was clear they were good customers who encouraged even more good customers to visit pubs that served a quality pint. Supporting them was good for the bottom line.

Dave Goodwin, a former National Chairman, remembers trying different things to get people to sign up at the Great British Beer Festival membership stand. In particular he recalls one potential member stalling, claiming a cash flow issue. The tenacious volunteers were trying every trick in the book to persuade the man, until Dave walked over and offered life membership. This had been introduced by Stuart Sturrock of the Leeds Branch at the 1981 AGM. Dave simplified its description: '*you* give me your credit card, *I* take a load of money and *this lot* will never bother you again.' That was enough to convince the chap, who liked a peaceful life. Dave was also known to offer life membership renewals to the unsuspecting. They apparently do everything a life membership does, but can also be taken on to the afterlife. According to Dave, 'there are several members already up there enjoying their beer. It's a really good deal because it lasts forever!'

A short piece by North Midlands area organiser Peter Linley featured in the January 1974 edition of *What's Brewing* and looked at the types of people who were joining CAMRA. It is worth reproducing in full as it gives a good impression of the way that the organisation was rapidly and democratically growing in its early years:

> As we all know, CAMRA is now moving from its original public image of a gimmicky joke into a well respected, serious consumer organisation, and it may well be of help to members who are not attached to a branch to know what they can do.
>
> It is important to get your own philosophy on the subject completely right. I think members fall loosely into three categories:
>
> - Fee-paying members of a "union" who look to the National Executive for leadership. These people will enjoy similar privileges and benefits as members of the large trade unions and professional institutes where the body of the membership is non-active.
>
> - The socially orientated members who want to pay their subscriptions, hold regular social events with friends in the area and occasionally for subdued publicity in the manner of entertaining and visiting friendly brewers and landlords.
>
> - The militantly orientated group which supplies the main bulk of the expansion of CAMRA in the regions and gives massive support to the national protests.
>
> CAMRA members come from all walks of life and there is nothing to be ashamed of in being part of any of the above

groups, though it is preferable that CAMRA is weighted towards the last two, since time is not on our side.

The best contribution that the first group can make is to donate more in their annual subscriptions than the current 50p as CAMRA needs funds urgently.

I would like to reassure members who are worried about CAMRA activities being bad for their own careers and ambitions. I am a college lecturer and it has been my privilege to be on two very large CAMRA gatherings. The behaviour on both occasions was noisy but exemplary in all respects, and as the recruitment of doctors, accountants, solicitors, teachers, policemen, carpenters, factory workers and labourers continues, I am quite sure that public goodwill will not be eroded. It is therefore important that on national demonstrations we all stand up to be counted, for in this way our influence will be strongest. In other words, the 600 who were at Stone could become 6,000 at Barnsley, and if a really big battle takes place with Ansells, we might consider hiring Villa Park for the 60,000 demonstrators.

Membership records were famously kept in a shoebox under Graham Lees' bed at first, and things did not get much more organised, even when membership numbers had skyrocketed. Tony Millns, whose eight-year tenure on the National Executive began in 1980, worked with fellow NE member Pat O'Neill on a computerised membership system. Pat worked for IBM as a Senior Systems Analyst at the time, so CAMRA were relatively early adopters of this technology, requiring a huge mainframe at the cost of around £30,000. This meant doubling their existing debt, but Tony was determined to push it through and managed to persuade the bank to lend them the money. 'The manager must have been a member,' he muses.

By 1984 they finally knew who their members were and where they were. At a stroke they were able to send out reminders and special offers to members. A printer ran off the system, so they were no longer reliant on the arcane metal plates of the addressograph for mailings, which had been used since the summer of 1974. This consisted of a metal plate manually embossed with each individual's details, fed into a printing press to print address sheets for sending out *What's Brewing* and other mailings. It was already so ancient that when it catastrophically (and regularly) broke down, it took at least a week to have new parts engineered for it, by which point Tony would be receiving endless late night phone calls from members asking 'Where's my fucking *What's Brewing*?'

Having better control of member information meant better control of Campaign finances. Under Tony's leadership they put the subs up from £5 to £7 – a 40% increase that was pivotal to securing CAMRA's shaky financial health.

*   *   *

Reasons for joining CAMRA are as diverse as the members themselves, but there are some common themes, not least support for their campaigning aims. Master trainer and former GBBF organiser Christine Cryne likens her CAMRA membership to that of organisations like Friends of the Earth or Greenpeace. You are likely to join because you want to show your support for them, unlike institutions like the National Trust that are more benefit driven.

Some people make a Damascene conversion to real ale simply because of its quality. Chairman of the Pub Heritage Group, Paul Ainsworth remembers meeting a friend in 1979 at the Greene King-operated Cambridge Arms in Cambridge. His friend was drinking Abbot Ale, 'which in those days was arguably a better drink than it is now. I could see that he was enjoying his drink more than I was enjoying my lager.' This was the first time Paul had considered there might be something to this real ale thing after all, having dismissed it when friends recommended it previously. He decided to try a few pints, became accustomed to the taste and the lightbulb went on for him.

Within a matter of weeks he had joined CAMRA and in early 1980s he had a new colleague at work in the form of National Executive member Tony Millns. Tony took Paul along to the Cambridge branch meeting where he was swiftly co-opted into the vacant role of secretary. When Tony was made National Chairman in 1982, he also invited Paul along to act as secretary to the National Executive as the previous post holder had resigned. Having no reason to say no, Paul agreed to participate. Such is the way many volunteers are co-opted.

It was something of a baptism of fire for Paul's first national meeting in Liverpool. The local branch organised all the accommodation and as CAMRA was short of money they were expected to minimise expenditure. This meant that Paul, Tony and another member, Rob Walker, were inadvertently booked into a 'rather seedy looking property round the back of Lime Street Station' where the exotically dressed ladies abroad thereabouts made it pretty apparent that their B&B doubled up as a bordello. Being rather innocent young men, they locked themselves away in their rooms, and little did they expect that they would also be served breakfast in bed by a glamorous lady in the morning!

For some people, attending branch meetings can be the only social contact that they have, creating a vital link in the community to combat loneliness and encourage intergenerational friendships. With the rise of the internet, CAMRA's members are now able to socialise virtually as well as face to face. This online provision started with the CAMRA forums set up by former NE member Brett Laniosh, first as a Yahoo group and then moving to its own server. Now CAMRA Discourse is a dedicated message board which helps members who perhaps cannot reach branch meetings as often as they'd like to still get involved and share information.

Undoubtedly, establishing lifelong friendships is the real joy of being part of CAMRA for many people. Some of the relationships even bubble over into something more. The Great British Beer Festival has a bit of a reputation for acting as a dating service for volunteers. Brewer David Sanders met his partner of 16 years working at the Bières Sans Frontières bar. Sarah Durham would bring all of her family along to work with her and in the end she and her sister both met their husbands there. Denny Cornell-Howarth's husband went down on one knee in front of 1,000 of her friends and proposed at the volunteer party at the end of GBBF. What he hadn't realised was that the back of his t-shirt read 'I volunteered to serve' – the volunteer staff slogan that year.

As CAMRA reaches its fiftieth anniversary, there are increasing numbers of examples of membership being kept in the family. Gill Keay organised the second oldest regular festival after Cambridge, the Kent Beer Festival, from 1974 until 2014. She had visited Cambridge and wanted to replicate it, finding a nice site in the middle of Canterbury in a park. In forty years of festival organising, Gill saw many people meet their partners and later bring their children along. One year she remembers the treasurer bringing four generations along to the Kent festival when she became a great grandmother.

Carl Brett followed in his father's footsteps in first becoming Deputy Regional Director for the East Midlands, before moving up to his current post of Regional Director. Steve Russell volunteered at the Great British Beer Festival Winter 2020 in Birmingham. Having been a member himself for five or so years, he bought his son CAMRA membership last year. Steve has been a regular attender at the Birmingham Beer Festival since his three sons were old enough to drink, and also volunteers at his local branch festival in Tamworth. However, this was the first time that father and son had volunteered side by side at one of the bars.

Even founder Michael Hardman was renowned for developing love interests through his beer connections. When he went into PR for Young's brewery, one of his first jobs was to entertain the local press in a pub. He spent quite a lot of time with one individual in particular on that day, and four weeks later he married her! No one believed they'd get married so quickly, but forty years later they were spending their anniversary in Hampshire in a little pub with a great selection of beers that Michael could enjoy, although his wife doesn't drink beer.

Michael is the first to admit, however, that the picture was not as idyllic as it first sounds. 'CAMRA has led to a lot of divorces. Mine was one of them. My second wife and I split up after all my CAMRA business, not entirely because of CAMRA but because she didn't see me … I might have been womanising or going to football matches, but I was doing neither, I was going drinking and having meetings.' It goes to show how enormous his commitment to the Campaign was: nothing else mattered for several years, and every friend was also a member of CAMRA.

*   *   *

As well as campaigning and camaraderie, joining CAMRA gives an unparalleled opportunity to learn new skills as well as putting old ones to good use. This has been particularly important to younger participants over the last decade or so since the global financial crisis, where entry into the workforce has become considerably more challenging for new starters without experience. Now a member of the National Executive, Ash Corbett-Collins was keen to work in marketing or communications in his early career and by getting involved with CAMRA he was given opportunities to work on social media, work with the branch membership and to help organise the beer festival. Every opportunity he showed an interest in he was welcomed along to, being given guidance on how CAMRA would do things and receiving training where needed, but otherwise readily encouraged to try his hand at learning new skills.

Vale of Belvoir branch member Ed Taylor's favourite memory of his time with CAMRA was being invited to present his branch's Pub of the Year Award in 2018. This saw him give a speech to a packed house for the winning pub, the Geese & Fountain in Croxton Kerrial, Leicestershire. His speech was also broadcast on social media and he felt quite honoured to have such a large and attentive audience.

Brewery manager Stephen Boyle describes how much he loves the knowledge and experience that is evident in the room when he gets the chance to associate with his local branch. Stephen thinks they are so inspirational because there is no ulterior motive – there's nothing in it for them except good beer. CAMRA members don't have a commercial interest or followers to keep happy. Their opinions are based on years of experience rather than what they've read or been told. And as an industry professional, this is really what Stephen values.

The current CAMRA Learning and Discovery Manager, Alex Metcalfe, says he encourages people to get involved beyond the branch level, because once they do they can increase their knowledge and use it to help shape the Campaign. Alex believes that making drinkers feel empowered to make informed decisions will be a particularly important direction for CAMRA in the future.

Milestone members

In 2001 student Laura Craft got more than she bargained for when signing up for CAMRA with her boyfriend at the York Beer Festival. She had unwittingly become CAMRA's 60,000th member. The next thing she knew she was being photographed for *What's Brewing* and the local paper and was later treated to an all-expenses-paid trip to the Great British Beer Festival. She enjoyed being a bit of a media star for forty-eight hours, and as a poor student, loved the free trip to London with her boyfriend.

The pair had met less than six months earlier at the Cropton Beer Festival in North Yorkshire. Today, the couple are happily married and Laura works for a mental health charity. They are still attending beer festivals as well as being active branch members. Laura says being a part of CAMRA has been a great way to meet people when moving to a new area. This was especially true in rural areas where joining a new branch helped them to get involved with their local community. A lot of activities CAMRA does in smaller places are linked with local charities, businesses and civic societies.

As part of the fortieth anniversary celebration in 2011 the membership voted for their list of the Top 40 campaigners. It was an opportunity to thank some of the most dedicated of the dedicated for their tireless service, many of them having committed decades to the organisation.

Sadly a quarter of the list are no longer with us to enjoy CAMRA's golden anniversary, including celebrated activists like the first female National Chairman, Paula Waters, and pioneering beer writers Michael Jackson and Richard Boston.

Alan Risdon is fondly remembered for attending the award ceremony, firstly because he always wore clogs, and secondly because he had to sneak out of his nursing home to be there. He had been expressly forbidden from attending by his carers. Let the record show that he said 'bugger that' before effecting his escape.

The 40 Top Campaigners, half of whom have kindly contributed their stories to this book, were:

Paul Ainsworth	Mark Haslam	Bill Mellor
Bill Austin	Martyn Hillier	Greg Mulholland
Richard Boston	Chris Holmes	John Norman
Alistair Boyd	Marc Holmes	Barrie Pepper
Chris Bruton	Chris Hutt	Roger Protz
Steve Bury	Michael Jackson	Alan Risdon
Christine Cryne	Lynda and Stuart	Andy Shaw
John Cryne	Johnson	Michael Slaughter
Andrew Cunningham	Rhys Jones	Colin Valentine
Graham Donning	Dan Kane	Paula Waters
Peter 'Spyke' Golding	Neil Kellet	Tim Webb
Dave Goodwin	Graham Lees	Steve Westby
Joe Goodwin	Jim Makin	Simon Wiseman
Michael Hardman	Tim Martin	

The Old Soaks

The founders and first wave of members are septuagenarians or older now. Being the instigators of a movement that is now celebrating half a century means that their long friendships are regularly celebrated and deeply treasured.

The inimitable Frank Baillie is one such early member who is sadly missed, having died at the age of 92 in 2014. He was famous for writing *The Beer Drinker's Companion*, which was published on 1 January 1974. It was the first book about the availability of beer, rather than the brewing of beer. Frank had carefully researched and compiled every beer produced by every brewery in Britain – some 1,000 products made by close to 100 companies. His research had been incredibly pioneering, particularly with the bigger brewers being relatively hostile to outsiders who took an interest in them. 'He was our guru really, in the early days,' Michael Hardman remembers.

Happily, many other early campaigners are still active within CAMRA, although on the whole they tend to have stepped back from the national platform and focus their energies on the branch level.

The so-called 'CAMRA Pioneers' hold regular reunions for people who have been involved since the 1970s. There is also a more informal group of friends who have come to be affectionately known as the Old Codgers, the Old Soaks, Old Folks or sometimes Silly Old Farts, depending on who you talk to. They are facilitated by Richard Sanders, aka Colonel Sanders. Richard has organised a visit for the gang to watch a test match at Trent Bridge since the 1970s. Clearly the moniker for the group must have arisen later as they weren't particularly old when this began. They always used to book an extra seat for the beer barrel, according to John Bishopp. It's a great shame they are no longer allowed to BYOB (bring your own barrel).

CAMRA and cricket seem to have a long and happy association Perhaps it is because they are both concerned with quintessentially British pastimes. Roger Protz evocatively describes how there is something about the way Sunday afternoon cricket was organised that meant it lent itself also to the enjoyment of real ale. He talked of the umpire calling out twenty overs at 6pm which meant you had one hour left of the game, and in those days the pubs didn't open until 7pm on a Sunday, so it was wonderful timing – you'd finish the game, get changed, go to the pub and have a few beers.

Gill Keay, organiser of the Kent Beer Festival, also runs the members-only Kent Cricket Tents. This CAMRA hospitality tent at the Kent County Cricket ground operates in aid of charity and the cricket players' benefit, so they ask brewers to donate beer and then sell it to CAMRA members. It has been running since about 1983 and now they are joined by about 300 guests each time. Members from all over the country visit the tents while Kent play other sides throughout the season, and they have had more than their fair share of famous cricketers visit them over the years. In particular Gill remembers David Gower falling off his seat outside the tent one year, although we couldn't reach Mr Gower for comment to find out why!

The Members' Weekend

Each year, a weekend is held for members incorporating the annual general meeting and a conference. It is celebrated as one of the key dates on the social calendar and gives a welcome opportunity to meet up with old friends, discuss policy, visit recommended pubs and breweries in the area and socialise in the members' bar. These days some 1,000 members attend the event each year, although in 2020 the weekend was cancelled and the AGM was recorded online for the first time due to the Covid-19 outbreak

CAMRA member Roy Lewry remembers a very early beer exhibition combined with the 1975 AGM, which was held at Nottingham University. The members' bar was a relatively small affair to begin with, but was really quite a novelty. Roy and three friends went up to Nottingham from London having secured accommodation at the Halls of Residence. The AGM was scheduled for around 11am on the Saturday, so they gathered for breakfast in the refectory, where the beers were also set up ready for the exhibition. The AGM was prepared in an adjacent hall, but with no chairs provided. The chairman declared that the beer festival would only commence when the AGM business had been completed: 'Records may show this must have been one of the shortest AGM's ever and, as a means of stopping endless waffle, this was to be wholly commended.'

Roy is not the only one who has found that enthusiasm for the serious business of the AGM wanes when a beer exhibition and the exploration of local pubs beckon. Chris Holmes, CAMRA's fourth National Chairman, has attended every AGM except two in forty-five years, but happily admits that nowadays he doesn't bother going to the meeting, instead he takes the opportunity to meet with friends, whom he only sees once a year, and visit the local pubs with them. What more noble purpose could there be in a membership organisation devoted to beer?

Neil Leeson is the current Members' Weekend Coordinator. This voluntary role consists of finding venues for each year's event: somewhere suitable for hosting the AGM, the members' bar and a lively programme of fringe activities and workshops on various subjects. This can include everything from informal beer tastings to sessions on how to look after cask ale, cider and perry properly in a commercial environment. The weekend is vital to the ongoing health of the organisation as it gives every member the opportunity to help shape the policy of the organisation in a way that is not attainable at a branch level.

CAMRA discounts

[Brewing cask ale is] back breaking work and as much of an art as a science. The fact that the general public still doesn't understand that has to go down as a failure of CAMRA [...] They need to make people love it, understand it or at the very least respect it.

MELISSA COLE, beer writer

One of the headline reasons for joining CAMRA, but also one of the mostly controversial issues within membership circles, is the CAMRA discount scheme. Available discounts fall into two categories. Firstly, there are ad hoc local arrangements that pubs offer and will predominantly be used by branch members who live in the area. These are nothing to do with the Campaign as an organisation, although you will often find a listing of discretionary discounts printed in branch magazines to keep members informed. Secondly, there is the set of printed vouchers that are issued to each member when they join and which are then reissued annually.

The chair of the Rochdale, Oldham and Bury Branch for over twenty-five years, Peter Alexander, says that the local discounts are the ones that matter. In his area there are thirty or forty pubs that voluntarily offer discounts and he sees anecdotally these are the ones people value, and a lot of older members really appreciate any discount scheme because they are on a lower income. Peter sees genuine benefits to individual consumers from the discounts schemes generally.

The formal discount voucher scheme was first suggested at a marketing meeting in 2008 by CAMRA's Head of Marketing Tony Jerome. A successful beer and pub marketing professional, Tony led the way on several important campaigns, including the Cyclops system of classifying beer by smell, taste and appearance. The vouchers each currently give 50p off a pint of cask ale at a select range of venues and individual members receive £30 worth of vouchers to use each year.

When the scheme was first introduced the vouchers could only be redeemed in Wetherspoons pubs. This led to a great deal of criticism, with CAMRA being seen as cosying up to Tim Martin's brand, particularly at the expense of small brewers and freeholders. Nottingham brewery Castle Rock made a big deal out of accepting the vouchers themselves in an attempt to lure CAMRA members to their pubs instead. Castle Rock founder and former National Chairman Chris Holmes said supplying the Wetherspoons-exclusive vouchers was a conflict of interests, 'like a manufacturer of washing machines doing a deal with *Which?* magazine'.

Chris put forward motions against the scheme at two AGMs, but believes it didn't get past the National Executive as the vouchers were attracting more members – which they were intended to do. Christine Cryne says that keeping the membership numbers high is ultimately important for giving CAMRA the weight to go and talk to MPs. Veteran campaigner Steve Bury agrees, and sees that for every 'armchair member' who is initially attracted by the discount there is a potential real ale activist waiting to be unleashed. When they redeem a voucher, they might get more interested in real ale and be more likely to come to events or meet other members. And for some people on lower incomes, the vouchers may well make the difference that allows them to enjoy an occasional pint of real ale in a pub.

On 1 July 2019 the voucher scheme was widened to be valid in a range of venues: some 1,500 new pubs joined the scheme. They were mostly pubs in big chains, but fifteen of them – admittedly just 1% of the new entrants – were independents that have chosen to accept the vouchers too.

The main criticism of the voucher scheme is the perception that it devalues cask ale – the very thing the Campaign was founded to protect. For writer Melissa Cole, cask is already sadly undervalued by consumers and the scheme is not helping the public to understand the skill that goes into creating and keeping a good cellar.

The most vocal detractors of the discount vouchers tend to be (quite understandably) the brewers themselves. Bradley Cummings, co-founder of Tiny Rebel Brewery, stood for election to the National Executive in 2018 with his opposition to the scheme as a key part of his manifesto. He lost out on a place on the NE by only a 0.8% share of the vote, so there was a good deal of support for his manifesto commitments amongst the membership.

In February 2020 Yorkshire brewers Brass Castle and 140 other members of the industry signed an open letter to CAMRA urging them to reconsider their policy on the promotion of discounting real ale and the distribution of vouchers to their members. Vale of Belvoir member Ed Taylor remarked that he has discussed this issue with the Brass Castle team a lot on the CAMRA online forum, Discourse, and can see the problem in having a hard core of members who want their pint to be as cheap as possible. However, he also makes the interesting observation that several of the brewers who signed the open letter actually supply the pub chains that they complain about, or even supply beer to the supermarkets, so they must already be offering their real ale at 'a crazily low price' by choice. Since these places actively undercut free houses, it could be seen as a little hypocritical to criticise CAMRA's discount vouchers.

*   *   *

In 2010 feelings of resentment about CAMRA members demanding discounts bubbled over online. Food and drink writer Pete Brown had discussed 'CAMRA's noxious culture of entitlement' on his blog, causing a public disagreement between himself and Roger Protz.[4] Pete had been writing about beer for some ten years already when he penned this post, observing an 'old guard' of CAMRA members locally who came across pretty badly in pubs, demanding good treatment and threatening a pub's place in the

---

4. https://www.petebrown.net/2010/05/04/camras-noxious-culture-of-entitlemen

Good Beer Guide if they didn't get it. In retrospect Pete knows that this would be a tiny proportion of the membership and that it is unfair to tar the whole of CAMRA with the same brush. Roger, a long time CAMRA stalwart, had been present on the occasion Pete was describing, but didn't agree that anything particularly out of line had occurred as he didn't recall anyone asking for particular special attention.

The disagreement between the two was purely in print, and not the last time they would have a war of words on paper, although they are known to get on famously in person. Pete actually joined CAMRA shortly after writing the noxious culture post because he already felt more aligned with the direction in which CAMRA was moving than he had previously, despite his misgivings about a small minority of members.

Former chairman Dave Goodwin says that in the past hospitality from breweries was common, which could have fed the perception, but sees an attitude of entitlement as a more recent issue:

> One of the problems we've got is that a large proportion of our members now just treat it as a beer drinker's club. They get discount vouchers on their beer and they look for discounts from breweries and pubs and that sort of thing. Years ago, if you were a member and you went to a brewery you might expect to receive a whole load of hospitality. You might expect to get a load of free beer, probably a buffet or something like that and probably expect to take away a few packs of bottles of beer with you when you leave. These days most breweries, except the very big ones, are not able to do that. They'll show you around the brewery but if you want a beer, you have to buy it from their bar [...] We should no longer expect a load of freebies when we visit a brewery. It was almost taken for granted back in the 70s, 80s, even into the 90s when most breweries were reasonably large businesses.
>
> *DAVE GOODWIN*

DIVERSITY IN CAMRA

People have got this perception of CAMRA, the old perception of beardy white guys in sandals. Unfortunately we have got some people within the Campaign who are quite happy to play to that image. We need to get outsiders looking in at CAMRA and thinking "they know what they're talking about, they are moving forward, they are with the times." Create a positive image for the public.

MARK PARKES, GBBF Winter organiser, 2020

Some might say that CAMRA has an image problem. Its membership is often depicted as a legion of old men with beards who wear sandals. One old campaign leaflet pleads desperately with the reader that real ale is 'not an old man's drink'. Where these stereotypes originated is something of a mystery. Beer writer Lynne Pearce was pretty clear in her *What's Brewing* column at the turn of the millennium that she blamed 'freeloading media hacks' for the pot-bellied stereotypes.

The first caricature may have been put out by *Private Eye* and anecdotally there is certainly a strong feeling that the press actively single out people who fit the preconceived notion of a CAMRA member to photograph when they visit Campaign events in the present day. The light-hearted ribbing continues in *Viz* comic with Davey Jones' 'Real Ale Twats', who were first created in 2001 and inspired by the Half Man Half Biscuit song *CAMRA Man*.

The current GBBF festival organiser, Catherine Tonry, thinks the real irony about the stereotype is that the very people who might fit this description now were originally the vibrant, energetic young men that started the Campaign. Roger Protz speaks highly of erudite men like Chris Hutt and Dr Chris Bruton who were pioneers in the organisation, doing an enormous amount of intellectual work to pitch CAMRA's arguments to the world.

Catherine says she recognises herself in those strongly opinionated and idealistic twenty-somethings: 'They have grown up with the Campaign – they were radicals when they started.'

Former twenty-something radical Michael Hardman is unequivocal: 'We weren't oddballs in any way or a refuge for people who didn't fit in – just people who wanted a decent pint.'

While some stereotypes may have relatively little foundation in reality, it is undeniable that CAMRA has always attracted more than its fair share of white males. CAMRA is an organisation founded by white men, who have since become old white men. The membership's average vintage has steadily crept up from around twenty-five to fifty-six. A Young Members Advisory Group was started to ensure that the opinions of young people were being heard across the Campaign. Initially this was perceived with some scepticism. Writer and CAMRA member Adrian Tierney-Jones described the Young Members Advisory Group as being a bit like trendy sixties' vicars trying to be down with the kids.

You can see his point when you read about the 'formal launch of its Under-26 Task Group and the appointment of a chairman and secretary' in *What's Brewing* of December 2000. It couldn't really sound more stuffy and middle aged. At least most of the members of the committee were actually under twenty-six. They ran Bar 18–30 at the Great British Beer Festival to encourage more young attendees, and it certainly seems to have met with some success as it was reported that more than 50% of the evening session festival goers in 2000 were under the age of thirty-five.

*   *   *

Beer writer Emma Inch thinks that beer as an industry has issues with perceptions and stereotypes, and that it isn't just CAMRA's problem. Beer can be seen as male dominated and white, and real ale in particular is thought to attract people of a certain age while the young things supposedly drink funky craft beers.

More exclusionary, says Emma, is the single-minded pursuance of the definition of real ale. When judging for CAMRA at local festivals she has heard volunteers on the panel discrediting a beer by saying they couldn't drink a pint of it. This leads her to wonder, is that the criteria? The idea that real ale has to be exclusively enjoyed in pints is exclusionary. Not everyone wants to be a volume drinker and not all real ale has to come in a pint pot. Emma believes that CAMRA is so big now that it has the power to change these sorts of discourses around beer, so it's quite exciting to see how it will wield that power in the future.

A humorous approach to member stereotypes that had a serious undertone took place in 1989. A very unusual motion was put to the Aberdeen AGM by John Kelly and passionately seconded by Alistair Boyd of the Glasgow branch. The motion was that 'being fat is not incompatible with CAMRA membership'. It was a response to a *What's Brewing* front cover image which featured Alistair and the then *Good Beer Guide* editor, Andrea Gillies. Alistair was holding a pint and sporting a not inconsiderable waistline, which had sparked some controversy. Some parts of the Campaign were keen to distance themselves from pictures of fat men with beer guts and beards. Alistair was the first to admit that this description fitted him to a tee, but that everyone should be included in the Campaign regardless. Therefore, he felt it needed to be confirmed that being fat was 'allowed'. It was all very tongue in cheek, not least the amendment proposed to replace 'stout' for 'fat' so as not to encourage a slovenly impression of membership. Behind the giggles there was a serious point, as Dave Goodwin said, 'What we don't want is a stereotyped image.'

One area where CAMRA could do more work in the future is welcoming people with disabilities. The *Good Beer Guide* included a wheelchair symbol to indicate physical access for disabled people from 1980 after a motion was put forward by Christian Muteau at the 1979 AGM, but there doesn't appear to be anything else that CAMRA has arranged for disabled people. Billy Tipping, a CAMRA member with a disability himself, can see merit in having a disabled members caucus. In particular there are problems around some of the nicest pubs being older buildings, which may limit their accessibility, while newer pubs with good facilities may not respect them. Billy has seen accessible toilets used by publicans as convenient ground floor storage spaces for example. This could be another great frontier of CAMRA campaigning as the organisation seeks to help pubs to increase their audience as widely as possible.

Women in CAMRA

> I spent 20 minutes on the phone trying to convince the female reporter from that most liberal of newspapers, the *Guardian*, that it really wasn't that unusual for a woman to choose a pint of real ale and not something pink, sweet and fizzy served with a cherry floating around in it. I then had the same conversation with the woman interviewer from Radio Five Live, who confessed to having drunk a pint once "with dire consequences". She really ought to get out more.
>
> *LYNNE PEARCE, writing in the 2001* Good Beer Guide

As we have seen, the Campaign was socially diverse, but relatively male-dominated in its membership, so the founders celebrated the arrival of members like Gillian Keay, née Knight, who were the pioneers of the 'top class women' who have joined CAMRA over the years. Unfortunately, female members didn't always get the respect they should have been able to expect back in the 1970s. One early CAMRA poster featured a woman with a short skirt seated on a bar stool saying 'I like mild and I like the men who drink it', which pretty much speaks for itself.

Roger Protz recalls the trouble Margaret Clark-Monks experienced at the first CAMRA AGM he attended in Brighton 1976. She was later to become the second woman to be elected to the National Executive in 1977 and served until 1984. When she walked out to the microphone she was greeted by one audience member wolf whistling and someone else calling out for her to 'give us yer phone number'.

Thankfully both CAMRA and society at large have, mostly, moved on from this lazy, thoughtless sexism. The dynamic and inspirational women who have taken an active role in furthering the aims of the Campaign have surely helped attitudes to change. Although the first woman to be elected to the National Executive was Cecily Longrigg in 1974–5, the major landmarks for women in the Campaign were arguably the appointment of Andrea Gillies as the *Good Beer Guide* editor in 1989, then 1992 when Christine Cryne became the first female GBBF organiser, and finally 2004 with the election of Paula Waters as the first female National Chairman.

Paula held that position for six terms, then, in April 2018, Jackie Parker became the second female National Chairman. CAMRA continues to try and make women feel more included, both as potential and actual members. Christine Cryne has seen that when she leads beer tastings that are paired with food the proportion of women attending increases, so there is an argument that this sort of approach helps. This is similar to the angle that the esteemed writer Susan Nowak took when writing her column for *What's Brewing*, mainly focusing on how beer complements food.

Christine themed her first GBBF in 1992 – the first in a central London location and the 'coming of age' festival in CAMRA's twenty-first anniversary year – as 'Women and Beer', though sadly the theme didn't appear to have warranted a single mention in *What's Brewing* either before or after the festival. Clearly the equality agenda needed time to become established.

Christine says she 'never had such a feeling' as opening her first festival, although the problem with being the first female organiser was the amount of daft questions she got from the press: 'does she drink pints?' and 'how many does it take to get drunk?' being the most common ones. The condition of the beer was held to be the greatest triumph of her festival after the near disastrous breakdown of the air conditioning in the previous year.

At that same festival Denny Cornell-Howarth was the technical manager and when questioned about CAMRA stereotypes by reporters she told them, 'it's really hot here at GBBF so I am wearing my sandals, I'm not the smallest of people and I haven't shaved this morning,' taking on the fat, bearded sandal-wearing image head on. 'We are people, we are CAMRA members and we can all quite equally do the same job. I can chuck an 18 barrel of beer about (or I used to before my knees gave way) as well as the best of them,' Denny says.

She is not the only one who slightly resents women in CAMRA being perceived by journalists as a rare and exotic species. Sarah Durham remembers an interview at Sky when she was in her twenties and London's Regional Director. The interviewer exclaimed that they were expecting some middle-aged woman twice the size of a house and Sarah wasn't that. She gradually became accustomed to having to reassure people that she really was the CAMRA representative when turning up at a pub to give out a certificate or give an interview.

In February 1993 APPLE committee member Sara Hicks struck a landmark blow for equality after she was refused service of a pint at Ye Olde Cider Bar in Newton Abbot, Devon. Landlord Richard Knibbs held a twenty-two-year-old rule of not serving pints to women. *What's Brewing* reported that he believed 'women cannot handle pints of strong cider,' and remained unrepentant about his actions, saying, 'it's off-putting to see ladies drinking a pint. We have nice goblets for ladies to use but she refused.' He was quick to point out that he had offered her two halves instead of a pint. What a gent.

Sara threatened legal action and Knibbs lifted the ban as well as paying £500 towards her legal costs in an out of court settlement. He also had to promise to pay £1,000 damages if he was found to discriminate similarly in the future: something of an empty gesture as it was quite clear that she was barred from the pub. Sara's only regret was that it was such a good pub, which unusually had a licence only to serve cider and wines.

Interestingly, it was recorded in the *London Drinker* by Martin Smith that one pub at least, Watneys' Antler in Brixton, actually refused to serve anything *less* than a pint, to anyone, as halves were considered too cheap.

Beer writer Melissa Cole has long had a reputation for championing women in the beer industry and doesn't think that gender equality has entirely been cracked by CAMRA just yet. She began her career in 1999 working for the *Morning Advertiser* where she regularly contacted CAMRA looking for opinions on the story of the day. Even then it still came across to her as a bit of a boy's club and it was not unusual for her to be handed a 'ladies' glass' upon entering a CAMRA festival, even as a member of the trade press.

Sometimes, though, CAMRA can't do right for doing wrong. In 2001 they launched a campaign to attract more women after undertaking research which showed 22% of women didn't drink cask ale because they didn't feel it was promoted to them. Their campaign used Ninkasi, the Sumerian goddess of beer, as its figurehead. This included a 60-foot banner at the Great British Beer Festival along with 'live appearances' by a costumed actress and life-size cutouts. There was also a range of leaflets and promotional material sent out to pubs around the country. Unfortunately, as the *Guardian* pointed out, the costumed actress looked rather like 'the Lara Croft of real ale'[5] and was perhaps more likely to titillate men than attract new female members – a pretty spectacular backfire of the promotional campaign's intention.

Ethnic diversity

CAMRA is a very white organisation, a trend which seems to be mirrored more broadly in the beer industry. In the summer of 2020, as Black Lives Matter protests were sparked globally following the murder of George Floyd by police in Minneapolis, an opportunity arose for CAMRA to put out a statement for the first time on matters of racial inclusivity and privilege.

5. https://www.theguardian.com/business/2002/aug/04/theobserver.observerbusiness

A sensitive and thoughtful statement by Nik Antona was released on 10 June 2020 across social media platforms:

> The Black Lives Matter Movement has touched every part of society – including the world of beer. It demands attention, reflection and strong voices of support if we are to make beer, brewing and pubs a more inclusive and welcoming place for everyone.
>
> Beer is for everyone, not a privileged few. Everyone in the industry needs to recognise the offence certain material – whether pub names and signs, or beer and cider names and marketing – causes and how that material excludes some members of the community. The first step is changing those names, signs and symbols to ensure pubs and beer are welcoming to all.
>
> We've seen what an impact sexist advertising and marketing has had on the gender divide in the beer world, and the strides today's brewers and publicans are making to turn this around. This same solidarity and support should have been made a long time ago for people of colour. We encourage everyone within the industry to stand together to oppose all forms of discrimination and use this movement to educate, reflect and improve the beer world for all.[6]

Nik's statement is reproduced here in full to give an opportunity for accountability, for CAMRA to be able to materially demonstrate how the sentiments set out in this statement were later followed up. There was a surprising amount of negativity in the public response to the statement, given that the overarching sentiment was 'beer is for everyone'. CAMRA's social media team had to add a qualifying comment that they would 'be removing and reporting any inappropriate language or attacks on other members, as well refer them to our disciplinary committee. This type of behaviour has no place within CAMRA.'

---

6. https://www.facebook.com/campaignforrealale/photos/a.392070239862/10159652579824863/?type=3&theater

LGBT+ friendly

In July of 1995 Billy Tipping wrote a letter to *What's Brewing*. He had realised that he was leading two lives – either going out with people who were interested in real ale or going out with friends on the gay scene – usually to places where there wasn't any real ale. His letter was a call to other gay real ale drinkers to see if they wanted to form a group. He was sure he couldn't be the only one.

Billy invited all those who had expressed an interest to meet at the Central Station pub near King's Cross. Although Billy had been in the pub in advance to make the arrangements with the landlord, the pub was actually shut on the allotted day, so they had to use the upstairs bar instead. It didn't serve real ale so that was a bit of a disastrous start.

Seven people came along to that first meeting and the Lesbian and Gay Real Ale Drinkers group (LAGRAD) was born. The group has no formal membership, but there are iterations around the country – including London, Brighton and Manchester. They put on informal events and have Facebook groups for discussion and organisation.

When he started LAGRAD, Billy's intention was to popularise real ale in gay pubs. For some reason, the gay scene seems to be one of the last bastions of resistance to the hand pump. Billy was repeatedly told he was flogging a dead horse. Gay real ale drinkers were avoiding the gay scene specifically because there was no quality cask ale. Eventually he was persuaded to change his emphasis from availability of beer on the scene to focusing on the people themselves, and started to organise pub crawls.

In many respects this was a huge step for Billy and the early members of LAGRAD. Billy himself had come out in the early eighties, at the age of 23. This was after he had joined CAMRA and still a time when being gay was not seen as acceptable by the majority of society. It was particularly difficult for a group of gay people to visit a straight venue – it simply wasn't always safe. However, by the mid-90s, things were beginning to improve and it was becoming easier for people who identified as gay to go to a pub together and feel safe. It seems likely in this sense that LAGRAD had developed as soon as it possibly could have and now the informal collective boasts several hundred members up and down the country.

The Great British Beer Festival 2019

[I appreciated] the work they did to make this year's GBBF NOT a douchebro-dominated retrograde cask-is-holy-grail dystopia. This year has been a long time coming and it's thanks to the strong voices in the industry that the old backward stereotypes have been *nearly* defeated.

Michael @bringonthebeer on Twitter

The Great British Beer Festival in 2019 was a seminal moment for diversity in CAMRA, where they made a genuine and whole-hearted commitment to inclusivity and representation. Organiser Catherine Tonry proclaimed in her opening remarks that 'diversity has defined this year's festival'. This was a far cry from previous years, where the festival had been criticised for being unwelcoming and cliquey – the implication being 'if you drink lager, like me and 95 per cent of Britain's beer drinkers, you can fuck off', wrote beer writer Pete Brown in 2006.[7]

Catherine's rallying cry for inclusion appears to have really struck a chord with commentators. Writer Emma Inch remembers the 2019 festival fondly, saying that from the moment she walked in it felt different to other years. The charity Stonewall's rainbow lanyards were being worn by volunteers to highlight that the LGBT+ equality charity was the main charitable partner that year. Pride flags were dotted around the venue. Although Emma admits that although she is not the sort of person to be particularly bothered by being in a male dominated environment, she still felt that CAMRA was making a clear statement, inviting people to come in and to feel safe.

---

7 https://www.petebrown.net/2006/08/06/great-british-beer-festival-is-i

The action that was most widely reported on during that year's festival was the banning of beers with offensive names or artwork, after a YouGov survey showed that women were actively boycotting beers that reflected out-of-date and discriminatory attitudes. National Director Abigail Newton said, 'consumer organisations like CAMRA have an important role to play in making women feel more welcomed within the beer world. We have already been refusing to stock sexist beers at the Great British Beer Festival for several years now, but this is the first time we've made such a bold statement.'

Melissa Cole was called in for a few days of interviews on the subject at the festival, which she found 'absolutely astonishing'. She saw a 'strong demonstration that CAMRA has never made before in such a public manner. They used their showcase of the year to say we are an inclusive organisation and that was such a tremendous step forward. I was incredibly proud of the way that it was handled, the fact that there was no prevaricating, no pandering to any members who didn't like it – get on board or get out of the way.'

Melissa thinks that this made some parts of the craft beer community sit up and look at real ale in a different way. There is no turning back from that kind of bold public statement – organisationally or societally – so CAMRA's ongoing challenge is remaining relevant. It's not just about survival, they need to represent everyone to get more support for their aims, and because it is the right thing to do. There is a suggestion that the beer industry, and by extension CAMRA, could act as a vehicle for social change.[8] The British Guild of Beer Writers Beer Writer of the Year 2019, Jonny Garrett, talks about the approachability of the industry being one of its biggest problems, which is counter-intuitive because beer is an approachable drink. He feels that CAMRA had spent too long only talking to middle-aged white men and now they have started a lot of positive new conversations.

8. https://vinepair.com/articles/beer-festivals/ Lily Waite

(L-R) Michael Hardman, Bill Mellor, Jim Makin and Graham Lees on the trip to Ireland in March 1971 where they came up with the idea which would ultimately grow to become CAMRA.

Christmas
& New Year Greetings
from
CAMRA

Whether in city bar you sup
Or in village vault you get tanked up
Be on your guard against bad ale
Or you'll never live to tell the tale ...

of CAMRA.

Merry Slutching

The Christmas card produced by Graham Lees and sent to his journalist friends in December 1971, which sparked wider interest in CAMRA.

The first logo for the nascent Campaign for the Revitalisation of Ale.

CAMRA

MICHAEL HARDMAN

is a member of the

Campaign for the Revitalisation of Ale

from 15/4/72 until 15/4/73

Signature of member

CAMRA

JOHN HANSCOMB

is a member of the

Campaign for the Revitalisation of Ale

from 13/7/72 until 12/7/73

Signature of member J. Hanscomb.

Michael Hardman and John Hanscomb's CAMRA membership cards.

The letter to the editor, printed in the *Hemel Hempstead Evening Echo*, penned by John Green, the first paid employee of the Campaign.

A CAMRA member collecting signatures on a petition in the early 70s.

National Chairman Chris Bruton leads a demo against Courage's keg beer policy in London, in September 1977.

CAMRA members in London marching to hand in a petition demanding that Courage brew Old English Ale instead of keg beer at the new Worton Grange brewery, in September 1977.

The membership stand at the 1985 Great British Beer Festival in Brighton.

Members' bar at the 1985 AGM in Southport.

CAMRA members laying wreaths at Whitbread's brewery in Chiswell Street, East London.

The Reading and Mid Berks branch protested with the 'biggest barrel in Britain' as a way of drawing public attention to Courage's plans to stop producing cask-conditioned beer locally.

Alistair, front man for Andrea

YOU have to admire his guts! Stalwart Glasgow CAMRA member Alistair Boyd let it all hang out when press snappers turned up for the Scottish launch of the 1989 Good Beer Guide.

Editor Andrea Gillies refused to be up-staged by the beautifully-balanced Boyd but had to play second fiddle in the girth stakes.

The Scottish launch was just

one stop for Andrea in a breathless dash round Britain to promote her first edition of CAMRA's annual best-seller.

Alistair Boyd took off his corset and joined in with gusto to help boost sales of cask beer in Scotland. *Picture: Glasgow Record.*

● Scots break ranks over S&N: back page.

● Midlands launch row: page 4.

On the 9th January 1988, CAMRA members from around the country travelled by train and foot to rural Shropshire to protest the proposed closure of Wem Brewery by Greenall Whitley.

Alistair Boyd and *Good Beer Guide* editor, Andrea Gillies, at the launch of the 1989 Guide – the image that sparked the infamous Fat Motion at the 1989 AGM in Aberdeen.

Under 26 Membership

A POWERFUL VOICE FOR THE DRINKER

Join CAMRA
The Campaign for Real Ale
The Consumer's Champion!

Despite being founded by young men, the age profile of CAMRA members has steadily increased. CAMRA actively began recruiting younger members in 2000 with the launch of its under-26 membership offering.

Laura Craft became CAMRA's 60,000th member when she signed up at the York Beer Festival in 2001. She says that says being a part of CAMRA has been a great way to meet people.

CAMRA has played a significant role in the lives of many of its members. In 2008, long-serving GBBF volunteer Denny Cornell-Howarth's partner went down on one knee and proposed to her at the volunteer party at the end of the festival.

Photo: Laura Hadland

A volunteer at GBBF 2019 sporting a rainbow lanyard. The festival was lauded for its commitment to inclusivity and representation.

Grassroots Campaigning and Lobbying

In the early seventies the fun part was very, very important.
I'm not really sure that a lot of us thought we would win or
that we stood a chance. But it was a way of protesting and
making our voices heard. Then in the mid-seventies it started
to get serious. *CHRIS HOLMES, National Chairman*

WE have seen how the Campaign for Real Ale was formed and
how it is structured, but what did they actually do? Over fifty
years their campaigning has developed and changed dramatically in style, but broadly speaking it can be divided into three
categories: beer, brewery and pub campaigning. These three categories cover a phenomenal amount of activity, more than can possibly be catalogued exhaustively in this slim volume. It includes
running beer festivals, publishing books and magazines, putting
on mock funerals for breweries under threat, days of protest
outside Parliament and the foundation of groups to coordinate
the interests of beer consumers around the world.

In the early days, when CAMRA had a go at a brewery
about something, the brewery absolutely shit itself.
Veteran volunteer, MICK LEWIS

CAMRA started off as a word-of-mouth campaign. They took
up issues directly – where a brewery was under threat of a takeover from one of the Big Six they would draw attention to it
locally. The more media attention they got, the more people that
joined them as members. Campaigning was very basic and
straightforward initially – they were focused purely on saving

this certain type of beer and improving its quality. Saving pubs simply wasn't an issue because most pubs weren't under threat, but as the brewers got bigger they wanted more pubs in order to have control of the outlets. For CAMRA, the lack of free houses became an issue as the rising number of microbreweries were struggling for market share.

Boots on the ground

They were revolutionary. They were the first.
CHARLIE PAPAZIAN, Founder of the Great American Beer Festival

CAMRA wanted the brewing industry to make a change. During his tenure as the second National Chairman, Chris Hutt tried to get them to listen by making an impact on their sales. At first, quite understandably, the big breweries were not inclined to pay CAMRA any mind. The company that was ignoring them the most, and therefore the company that Chris and his National Executive were the most angry with, was the mega-brewer Watneys. Here CAMRA had a bit of a head start – Watneys Red Barrel was clearly failing to impress consumers as it had already been renamed and relaunched with a tweaked recipe. The fizzier and sweeter Watneys Red was launched in 1971, nearly a year before CAMRA actually began to function as a campaigning organisation.

Such was the awful quality of the product that it was easy to lampoon and ridicule, and sales continued to drop. Journalists like Terry Pattinson put their investigative hats on and demonstrated that drinking two pints of Watneys Red would lead to terrible hangovers, even though the alcohol content was only a relatively light 3.6%. CAMRA were canny in slowly drip feeding their discoveries to the press to score hit after hit against the relaunched product.

Maxwell Joseph was the chairman of Grand Metropolitan, who bought Watneys in 1972. He is said to have told his shareholders at the AGM that sales of Watneys beer had been destroyed by a campaign of 'journalists masquerading as beer drinkers'.

CAMRA's journalistic connections engendered an endless stream of bad publicity which ultimately and irreconcilably damaged sales of Watneys Red. Chris Hutt remembers cheering from the rafters when news of Joseph's complaint got back to them. This was one of CAMRA's first national successes.

One important weapon in the arsenal against keg beer was the acerbic wit of illustrator Bill Tidy and his regular cartoon, Kegbuster. Bill's column of stories from the fictional Crudgington's Brewery in *What's Brewing* started in August 1974 and made the pun 'Grotneys' almost a national byword for bad beer.

Local activists really took the fight for real ale to the frontline, not just encouraging landlords to stock real ale by creating a market for it, but by actively assisting in installing it on the bar. Former Regional Director Dave McKerchar remembered that when he first joined the Campaign they would encourage landlords to take hand pumps with casks on sale or return. The local branch would help with negotiations between brewers and publicans and spread the word about newly installed pumps to potential punters. To the landlords' surprise the cask ale would sell well and it made financial sense to keep it on the bar.

Some licensees and brewers claimed that they couldn't possibly put hand pumps on the bar as beer engines were no longer available to purchase. This was disproved through some solid journalism in *What's Brewing* and gradually a long list of stockists was drawn up. Steve Bury remembers going to visit the Lower Red Lion in Fishpool Street, St Albans, around 1973. They were selling Young's Special bitter on top pressure. He addressed the issue of real ale with the publican, who was a bit cautious of the branch members at first. He thought 'they were long haired hippies encroaching on his nice drinking circle.' But as time went on the branch encouraged people to write to the pub and the brewery to ask them to put real ale hand pumps on the bar. They finally caved in after 365 individual letters. Young's provided the Lower Red Lion's licensee with a hand pump and 'it was the best thing that ever happened to him because the place was absolutely mobbed, he'd never made so much money.' A couple of hundred people came down to drink in the pub on the first day that real ale was served.

Steve also remembers finding a large number of hand pumps and fittings, in an antique shop in St Albans, that were going to be sold as scrap. He and his fellow branch members found a pub supplier with everything needed to refurbish the pumps, and they commenced leasing them out to pubs that wanted to put real beer on again. This allowed them to test the water without committing themselves to the expense. In other pubs the old hand pumps had remained on the bar and just needed to be flushed out and refurbished. The branch developed quite an expertise in fitting and refurbishing the kit needed to serve draught ale.

> Little by little, drip by drip, the brewers started brewing beer again. And it was great when you saw a pub in the local CAMRA newsletter, saying the Red Lion have got a hand pump. That's a win situation. An old real ale pub had put a hand pump back in, or a new pub had put its first hand pump in.
>
> *DAVE MCKERCHAR, CAMRA member*

In January 1973 Courage told the Campaign that they needed their Directors Bitter to sell 20 gallons a week in each of their 200 pubs for it to be 'an economic proposition'. This was in response to General Secretary John Green writing to them after rumours that Directors was to be phased out. 'I was assured that Directors would not go unless demand dropped, so it is up to the drinking man to preserve it,' John said. The brewery had issued a challenge to CAMRA's membership to put their money where their mouth was to make the beer viable. The membership was happy to oblige and Directors is still brewed to this day.

'Coming into the eighties the brewers started to catch on that they could make money [from real ale],' remembers Steve Bury. It started with Draught Burton Ale, which was launched by Allied Breweries, formerly Ind Coope, in 1976. It was 'an absolutely cracking beer' that they put in around 600 pubs. They also launched Aston Ale in Birmingham at around the same time. A bitter went in alongside it on the bar and when other breweries saw the demand they followed suit. Courage, Greene King and others started to brew real ale again and Steve's local brewer, McMullens, also started to convert back to real ale, even though they hadn't finished converting all of their pubs to keg yet. The story in St Albans was being repeated around the country and so the resurgence of cask ale was under way.

* * *

Joules

As well as taking direct action in their local pubs, the early branches of CAMRA were famed for their brewery closure protests – often involving marches around brewery buildings. Founder Graham Lees was at one of the very early protests at Joules brewery in Stone, Staffordshire. 'We started organising public protest marches in towns where breweries were threatened and that expanded the publicity. We knew [Joules] was doomed because the decision to close it had already been made,' he notes. But that didn't stop them from organising a day's march to protest in the town. Andrew Cunningham, who has been a CAMRA member since September 1972, was also at the march, which had been organised in conjunction with the SPBW. He agreed that all of these early organised marches 'were frankly a bit of a waste of time', except for the publicity they generated and the fact that the membership enjoyed them.

Matthew Brown

Andrew recalls that a horse-drawn dray sporting a 'not for sale' board and brass band was sent up from Blackburn to the demonstration against Scottish & Newcastle's bid for Matthew Brown brewery, held on Saturday, 22 June 1985. This was the start of a major CAMRA campaign to 'Keep Matthew Brown Independent' and took place in Edinburgh outside the Scottish & Newcastle head office. The protest was orchestrated by CAMRA and the newly formed Matthew Brown Preservation Society, with support from the local trades unions. Andrew's son thoroughly enjoyed riding the dray horse, but it was decided that it was best his mother not know that the five-year-old had been involved in a protest.

This event was particularly significant as the branch committee were invited to meet the brewery directors at Bannerman's pub in Edinburgh. It was the first time CAMRA members had been invited by the brewery to meet the people fighting the takeover bid from within the business. Matthew Brown was a successful concern and its board was resisting the acquisition. Clearly CAMRA's influence and experience was considered valuable to the board.

The campaign was ultimately unsuccessful and Scottish & Newcastle's assurances to the Monopolies and Mergers Commission in 1985 that the Blackburn brewery was 'sacrosanct for continued brewing purposes' proved to be deeply hyperbolic. At the time it was suspected that the purchase was driven by Scottish & Newcastle's desire for the Theakston's brand, which had itself been taken over by Matthew Brown in 1984. However, in retrospect it appears much more likely that it was the 500 tied Matthew Brown pubs that were the real object of the merger, as the brewing arm was run down relatively quickly. Their Lion Brewery ceased operations in 1991. Theakston's returned to the original family's control in 2004 after the four brothers bought the majority shareholding back from Scottish & Newcastle.

JP Simpkiss & Son

Mark Parkes recalls the end of the fight against the closure of JP Simpkiss & Son of Brierley Hill in the Black Country. It was closed in 1985, the day after it was finally acquired by Greenall Whitley, but the local CAMRA branch were able to give it a good send off. They held a wake at the brewery, complete with a coffin. The brewer told them that he'd been told to ditch the final batch of Simpkiss beer that Greenall's didn't want, and invited the local members to sit in the brewery with him and drink up their last ever mild.

Mansfield

Chris Holmes loved going on brewery protests to meet other members from all over the country. In 1973 the first major campaign that he was part of was protesting against the Mansfield brewery which had stopped brewing real ale and were only brewing keg beer instead. They came within his Nottingham branch's remit at the time. So he organised a survey on the streets of Mansfield, asking the public whether beer locally was worse, the same or better than it had been three years ago. About 90% of Mansfield Bitter drinkers thought the product had deteriorated since the brewery stopped producing traditional beer, which was great PR for CAMRA to put out in the Nottingham newspapers and on local radio. Learning from his national colleagues, Chris also took the time to find out where all the local journalists drank and made friends with them, so whenever he put a story like this out it got great coverage.

Courage

One of the most fondly remembered pieces of direct action taken by CAMRA extended over four years. From 1977 to 1981 they were consumed with the Courage Campaign. The Reading and Mid Berks branch led campaigning against Courage brewery's plans to stop producing cask-conditioned beer locally. They protested outside the head office in London as well as delivering a petition of some 250 signatures from local people and landlords in Reading. The minutes from a campaign meeting in July 1977 suggest that brewery managers were putting pressure on landlords not to sign.

To add the now legendary CAMRA campaigning zing, they next toured the 'biggest barrel in Britain' – supposedly an escapee from the Courage brewery – as a way of getting press attention and introducing the public to the cause. Dave McKerchar also recalls 'Running Rounds on Courage', a relay race around the brewery on a very hot summer Sunday. Writer Roger Protz was also a participant but only did about two circuits before giving up. Others were running for many hours.

Roger is insistent that these actions weren't just mindless stunts. They were well planned, well intentioned and they worked because they got the attention of the media, helping to increase membership and sometimes even saving breweries. The power of the accountants won in the case of Courage. The brewery was closed and the whole operation was moved to London initially, until they built the large new site at Worton Grange in 1980. Courage was merged with Scottish & Newcastle in 1995 and the site itself closed in 2010.

King & Barnes

CAMRA continued to fight, often unsuccessfully, against brewery closures for years to come. In March 2000 Sussex brewer King & Barnes thanked CAMRA for helping its fight to survive Shepherd Neame's £15 million takeover bid. But even when this was reported in *What's Brewing*, caution was urged against premature celebration as 'the brewery's latest move to keep its shareholders on board will set alarm bells ringing.' Sure enough the brewery was bought out and closed by Hall & Woodhouse just five months later.

The Old Bog Society

A slightly more unusual piece of campaigning – of which CAMRA members jumped on the bandwagon (but cannot, in the ultimate analysis, take credit for) – took place in Cambridge in 1979. Greene King had, of their own volition, decided to remove the famed outside loos of the Cambridge Arms, the only Cambridge pub featured in the first edition of the *Good Beer Guide* in 1972. The tale goes that a funeral procession was held for the unsavoury bogs, led by the 'Bishopp of Cambridge' – branch chairman

John Bishopp. A coffin supporting one of the redundant thrones was hoisted aloft by enthusiastic members. Following the procession, the pub landlord, Peter Fagg, formally opened the new indoor loos by cutting a pink ribbon and dispensed free pints of Abbot Ale and Old Bog Society t-shirts.

When interviewed, John was able to verify some elements of this story. There was indeed a coffin, which was used by the workmen to scare the living daylights out of their youngest colleague. One workman was secreted inside and stepped out as the young lad went past. It's not clear from whence said coffin originated. It was certainly draped in black and processed around but John doesn't remember one of the old toilets being involved. Certainly the whole thing was a cause for celebration as the old outdoor toilets, the gents especially, were 'a disaster area'. There was a rat infestation, and an apocryphal tale was that, apparently, a sandwich had been left in there for a full five years. John is also able to confirm that Greene King were the arbiters of the celebration, donating the firkin of Abbot Ale for the afternoon's festivities. John was pleased to have organised the wake as a tongue in cheek activity, which ended up being reported as far away as Canada owing to its novelty.

The Whitbread Tour of Destruction

In 1990 CAMRA released what was to become one of their most successful campaigning t-shirts. It featured the 'Whitbread Tour of Destruction' and listed, in the style of a band tour t-shirt, all the breweries Whitbread had taken over then closed. Mark Enderby remembered particularly enjoying wearing his when he was attending a meeting at a Whitbread pub or office in his role as Regional Director. The t-shirt was so successful they made a copycat for Greenalls, along with anti-Whitbread and anti-Greenalls stickers. He would surreptitiously slap those stickers on the Greenalls brewery wall whenever he passed it on the way home from the pub. It didn't really achieve anything but it certainly made him feel better.

The Campaign matures

> I think it's fair to say that CAMRA grew up. But in growing up,
> we sacrificed some of our edge for greater respectability.
>
> GEOFF STRAWBRIDGE, *Regional Director for London*

The 1980s were an important turning point for CAMRA's campaigning. The Big Six released their stranglehold on the industry and resurrected a number of historic cask-conditioned beers and recipes as their way of showing customers how respectful they were of local products, quality and tradition. Their marketing staff had finally decided to read the room. The big breweries exploited the public awareness raised by CAMRA and by doing so they nearly rendered the Campaign obsolete.

As the former *Good Beer Guide* and *What's Brewing* editor Roger Protz recalls, there was a feeling that they achieved what they had needed to. Real ale was successful again – and they had even coaxed the great London brewery Fuller's back to cask after they had considered abandoning it in the early seventies.

Roger and his contemporaries knew that the fight was not over – the quality of cask beer needed to be preserved and it was important to keep the flame alive. When Whitbread announced in 1979 that in the future a massive percentage of all beer brewed in the UK would be lager, Roger highlighted it with the membership, urging them against complacency that real ale was safe. He knew that the big brewers were focused only on profit and if they could make more money from lager then that's where they would concentrate their efforts, to the detriment of cask. This spirit of eternal vigilance remains strong amongst both CAMRA pioneers and more recent devotees who feel that the battle for cask will never be won, not least since so many pubs and breweries have come under threat because of the damaging effects of the Covid-19 lockdowns in 2020 and 2021.

*　　*　　*

As CAMRA aged and developed, its influence grew and that has changed the emphasis of the campaigning in some instances. Long-term member Geoff Strawbridge complained that the central office function of CAMRA running out of St Albans had become focused on 'public affairs' rather than campaigning. Geoff sees public affairs as being nice to people, while campaigning involves telling people what you think of them, so he believes that this change in attitude has lost them some grassroots support. Mark Enderby agrees, saying that in the early eighties they seemed to be going on brewery marches every few months. As a Regional Director, Mark would turn out to support all the campaigns on or near his patch, such as at Oldham brewery and Higsons.

The closure of Wem brewery was the first to happen during Mark's tenure as Regional Director. He didn't think twice about attending meetings to plan the counter-closure campaign even though it was an hour away by car: 'I believed in ensuring these breweries were saved, or trying to. Sitting back and doing nothing wasn't an option. Even though we knew it probably wasn't going to work we wanted to show support.'

Andy Beaton was also keen on rousing as much support as possible for the cause at Wem. On the train one day he read an article in the on-board magazine about how much Michael Palin enjoyed Wem beer. Andy decided to write to the comedian and actor to ask if he knew the brewery was closing. He received a typed and hand-signed response to the effect that Michael had heard of the Campaign and was supportive of it. Needless to say it was a big boost for CAMRA to be able to attach the household name to their activities.

This was the part of the Campaign Mark Enderby enjoyed, actively supporting the breweries and drinking the beer. Lobbying Parliament seemed irrelevant – to him, it wasn't really 'getting stuck in'. However, others see CAMRA maturing and growing in professionalism as a positive development. John Clarke was pleased CAMRA was getting more slick and professional.

Gone was the slapdash approach and poorly designed publicity materials. As a larger organisation they could now employ the best people with the skills needed to move the organisation forward.

Many grassroots members see a clear divide or progression in CAMRA's campaigning styles from the beginning to the present, moving away from grassroots protest group and becoming a lobbying body. In reality the two elements have been running in tandem almost since the beginning. As a member of the National Executive, Andrew Cunningham was invited to contribute to the shaping of national policy in 1974. Andrew, Chris Hutt and Gordon Massey presented evidence to the Food Standards Committee's investigation into the definition, composition and labelling of beer, which backed up a seventeen-page report submitted by a special CAMRA committee. The government answered CAMRA's call for an inquiry into the description of draught and bottled beers at the point of sale. The success was trumpeted proudly on the front page of *What's Brewing* in May 1974.

CAMRA wanted terms like 'draught' beer to be defined so that they could not be misappropriated and used in a misleading way. The enthusiastic beer amateurs found themselves in front of a rather intimidating panel including two professors of brewing. Afterwards, Andrew received a call from one of the directors at his place of employment. He worked for an industrial supplier to the brewing industry and was immediately concerned that his appearance on the panel was seen as a conflict of interests. On the contrary, his director was also a member of the Food Standards Committee and had called Andrew to tell him that they had expected CAMRA's evidence to be unrealistic, perhaps even extreme, but had actually been impressed to find their presentation to be practical, implementable and sensible. It had taken a very short time for CAMRA to be taken seriously by government bodies. Nowadays, they have their feet firmly under the table, as they annually host their own reception in the House of Commons.

Current National Chairman Nik Antona points out that by the time the Campaign hit the 100,000 member mark, politicians and other external parties were really obliged to take notice of them. Nik thinks that in the late seventies and early eighties fake funerals and marches were a reflection of the political activity that members saw around them in the various industrial strikes that were common at that time. But then the National Executive got more organised and represented a significant chunk of people power. Their consumer-led perspective is valued by policy makers. However, Ash Corbett-Collins sits on the National Executive now and is more cynical, feeling that MPs are quick to pay lip service to CAMRA, or any organisation, where there are votes to be had. This was seen in the debate about taxation on pubs in 2020, where MPs lined up to talk about the pubs and breweries in their area, but at the onset of the Covid-19 pandemic those actively offering support were much thinner on the ground.

Sometimes CAMRA is accused of doing less campaigning, but actually much of their work on the national level is just less visible to commentators. By the mid to late nineties they had certainly become much more integrated within the industry. CAMRA was recognised for twenty-five years of campaigning in 1996 with a special award for outstanding services to the industry at the pub trade's own 'Oscars', The Publican Awards. The citation applauded their contribution, which encouraged more than 300 new breweries to open. Chairman John Cryne was named as one of the *Morning Advertiser*'s pick of the most influential people in the drinks industry in 1997.

However, this broad acceptance of the Campaign does not mean direct action has ceased. Members are still out pounding the pavements to protect their local beers, breweries and pubs, such as their involvement with the successful campaign against the conversion of the historic Old White Lion in Bury in late 2019.

*   *   *

CAMRA got *really* political with a capital P when National Executive member Tony Millns fought a parliamentary by-election at Richmond as the 'Keep Theakstons British/CAMRA' candidate in 1989, aimed at focussing attention on CAMRA's opposition to the takeover bid by Australian brewers Elders IXL for Theakston's owners Scottish & Newcastle. Tony optimistically declared: 'If everyone in Richmond who enjoys a good pint votes for me, I am sure of an historic victory.' In the end he polled an admirable 113 votes, but William Hague comfortably won the seat with 19,543.

Commentator Melissa Cole has watched CAMRA becoming more politically savvy in recent years. Improvements in gathering and using political and industry intelligence have created a more intelligent and better targeted organisation. And she sees this as CAMRA coming full circle over fifty years, from the politically switched on journalists who founded CAMRA to today's usually savvy organisation, particularly in terms of the paid staff.

In-fighting and controversy

With nearly 200,000 members it is not surprising that CAMRA cannot always present a united front. Being pretty niche in core purpose means that where controversy does appear it is usually over the minutiae of beer, which would make an outsider (not to mention a large percentage of members) weep with boredom. In fact, founder Graham Lees finally quit the National Executive in 1977 because of a dispute over just such a technical issue.

The Grand Metropolitan group introduced a new cask-conditioned beer, Truman's Tap Bitter. It had been designed to be served by hand pumps that pushed air into casks to force the beer out. The National Executive deemed that this, and any other beer served by air pressure, could not be considered 'real'.

Unfortunately, they appear to have forgotten, or overlooked, the fact that air pressure was the traditional method of dispensing beer in Scotland. The system had been in use for decades to serve live beer, so naturally Scottish CAMRA members were pretty upset that the vast majority of their beer had suddenly been 'outlawed' overnight. A year-long debate of the issue ensued and the Technical Advisory Group (TAG), who are the keepers of all CAMRA definitions, ruled that using air pressure in dispense wasn't *proper*. Graham thought this was splitting hairs and that it was more important to keep the Scots on board as part of the national Campaign, rather than upset them by ruling against a traditional practice, hence why he decided it was time for him to leave.

In fairness, Graham's view was shared by the majority. The TAG decision was overruled, by an overwhelming vote from the membership, at an Extraordinary General Meeting held in Manchester on 8 October 1977. It was held that beers dispensed by air pressure would be allowed entry into the *Good Beer Guide* if they were recommended by their local branch. The risk of a split in the Campaign, the first to pose a genuine threat to the organisation's future, was much commented on in branch magazines of the time.

One of CAMRA's longest running schisms, the mere mention of which elicits much sighing and rolling of eyes from those who remember it, was about the propriety of the use of the cask breather. The offending article, the cask breather, is a simple plastic valve. Instead of ambient air filling up the space in a cask when beer is poured out of it, the valve allows carbon dioxide to be added instead. Thus the beer stays fresher for longer. National Director Nick Boley couldn't understand why people were calling for pubs that used them to be banned from appearing in the *Good Beer Guide*: 'I've tried to work out the chemistry of why cask breathers were wrong. I couldn't and I'm still scratching my head. Cask breathers are a boon for small rural pubs and café bars. If we want to get cask beer into these outlets this is one way of doing it.'

The issue of the cask breather's acceptability was voted against at the 1982 AGM. But by January 2000 resentment and disagreement was still simmering away. That month's *What's Brewing* featured a full page on the arguments for and against the breather, which only served to fan the flames once again, forcing Colin Valentine to write a special guest column in the March issue to clarify CAMRA's policy on the subject. At that time Colin was Scotland and Northern Ireland Regional Director, but made it abundantly clear that he was writing in a personal capacity. He stated that he felt none of the previous contributors, nor indeed the editor, Ted Bruning, appeared to have any idea what the policy actually was. He clarified that 'what few policies we have regarding the cask breather and its ilk is that if beers are served on cask breather they (the beers) will not be mentioned in our publications, including our flagship publication the *Good Beer Guide*.' Colin went on to clarify that if a publican had a low turnover then using a breather for the sake of having real ale on sale was allowable, but with such a low turnover how could such a pub be considered for the *Good Beer Guide* anyway? He finished with a rousing chorus: 'When we abandon our basic tenets we may as well all pack up and go home to our cans of widgetised Boddingtons.'

In 2018 CAMRA declared itself officially 'neutral' on the subject. This didn't really resolve the root problem though, as the next barrage of letters and articles in *What's Brewing* editions demonstrated. A letter in from April 1980, written by Dave Wilman in Kent, illustrated nicely how these sorts of schisms and controversies were viewed by the bulk of the membership, and outside commentators, as the clear campaigning message of the early days became muddied and confused by dogma. Dave asked for clarity on who their enemies were:

> When I joined CAMRA in 1974 I was delighted to find so many people who shared my concern about what was happening to our beer. Our Campaign was clearly directed against brewers, mainly the 'Big Six,' who promoted and sold principally keg beers and insisted on serving the real stuff by CO_2 pressure. Our friends were the small brewers who produced the real thing and landlords who sold it – simple stuff.

The position now however is far more complex. Our enemies appear to have expanded to include the following:

- Brewers who produce real ale but not mild.
- Landlords who sell strong (Kamikaze) ale.
- People who drink strong ale.
- Pubs which sell a range of different real ales.
- Pubs where the price is a few pence higher than others.
- The LVA and the *Morning Advertiser*.
- Pubs that have been renovated.
- Pubs without Public Bars.
- Other branches.
- The NE and "St Albans".
- People who drink from a glass with a handle.
- Jukeboxes, fruit machines and electronic games.
- Brewers who produce real ale in one area to sell in another.

Are our only friends mild ale drinkers in Public Bars where the ale is cheapest, and is it from these people that our membership comes?

DAVE WILMAN

Lobbying Parliament

One of the great things about the early activity was that we were quite irresponsible about the things we said and the things we did, and we would have thought ourselves radical. I don't really think you could apply that adjective to CAMRA now. It's got a bit serious.

CHRIS HOLMES

Since 1993 the All-Party Parliamentary Beer Group has existed to help MPs better understand the social and economic role played by beer and pubs in British society. There are around 700 all-party groups covering all imaginable topics, from pigeon fancying to stem cell research. These industry facing groups are run by public affairs consultants for MPs and Peers who share a common interest. The beer group is the largest of them. About

350 MPs and Peers right across the political spectrum are members. On average they each have two breweries and eighty pubs in their constituency, so it is in their interests to stay in touch with related issues.

The group came about after the formation of the single market, when a steady flow of white vans filled with booze were making their way over the Channel, causing no end of headaches for the industry. Parliamentary officers, industry voices and CAMRA were brought together by Robert Humphreys, who had worked for Bass for twenty years. There wasn't the will or resource to set up a parliamentary committee so they decided to stage their own enquiry into so-called booze cruisers and their impact on the industry.

It is thought to have been the first time that an all-party group put together a report. It was a detailed piece of PR that emphasised the key issues in the hope of capturing the attention of the government. They employed a clerk and Hansard reporters, and held about eight sessions in Parliament with invited witnesses giving evidence. The costs were huge and the bill was footed by the largest companies. It helped to change mindsets in the Treasury about how the damage to the industry might be mitigated.

The group never did anything quite on that scale again. Since then it has been important for the All-Party Parliamentary Beer Group to remain active as MPs come and go, so there is always work to be done to support the industry in delivering the key messages to Parliament. According to Robert, CAMRA's role in representing the consumer, alongside the commercial organisations that are involved, has been invaluable in giving the Beer Group a real influence and credibility with ministers. There was also a parallel group in the European Parliament, until 2019, in which the Beer Group were equal members with CAMRA thanks to their existing relationships with Europe.

CAMRA played a key role in virtually everything I did.
ROBERT HUMPHREYS, founding Beer Group Honorary Secretary

The current Honorary Secretary, who took over from Robert in 2015, is Paul Hegarty. His role is funded by around sixty-five individual brewing and pub companies, and industry groups like the Society of Independent Brewers (SIBA). This broad base of support, as well as the cross-parliamentary nature of the group's membership, means that it doesn't take a stance on anything politically controversial, like Brexit or minimum unit pricing. Here again, CAMRA's position representing the consumer is important in balancing out the commercial interests, although with the biggest issues, like fighting the beer duty escalator, these interests do tend to coincide.

The work of the Beer Group is 'fun with a purpose' – a brewery visit here, a beer and cheese tasting there – all designed to help the industry build relationships with MPs, as well as a subtle way of demonstrating the good work that beer and pubs do. The other half of its business is more serious, as in February 2020, just before the Budget, when group chair Mike Wood held a Westminster Hall debate to speak about cutting the tax burden on beer and pubs. Normally at these sorts of debates four or five MPs attend, but on this occasion over forty turned out as groups like CAMRA invited all of their friendly MPs.

Each year there is a chairman's dinner, which operates under the Chatham House Rule. The CAMRA National Chairman or Chief Executive is routinely invited along and so this is a great chance to understand government priorities, as well as to put forward the consumer voice and look at future trends. Similarly, before each Budget the group seeks a meeting with the minister responsible for alcohol duty and they always take a representative of CAMRA, SIBA and groups like the Independent Family Brewers of Britain. When Priti Patel was the minister in charge, around five or so years after the duty escalator had been scrapped, she queried whether the cut in duty was being passed on to the consumer. CAMRA were able to show data that demonstrated the pub companies were passing on the savings and the Campaign's independence meant that this data was inherently more believable than if it had come from the pub companies themselves. Similarly, CAMRA also helped the Beer Group make more compelling arguments in Brussels.

The small group that met in the European Parliament included CAMRA and the European Beer Consumers Union (EBCU). CAMRA's positioning meant that they were able to successfully lobby for local exemptions to European legislation – such as overturning the need to label all beer with 'contains fish products' because of the isinglass used to fine it. CAMRA's research showed that the fining agent was part of the process of fining real ale but none was left in the final saleable product. Similarly, when there was a move to prevent use of the word 'light' unless it had 25% fewer calories than the original, CAMRA gained a local exception for 'light ale', which is understood to be a style and not a lower calorie product in the UK. This also, incidentally, protected products like Coors Light and Bud Light from requiring a major rebrand.

CAMRA's GLOBAL INFLUENCE

> I cannot see that any European nation would have formed its own beer consumer group, just out of the blue, had CAMRA not been there ... It started to take off when Europeans would start to go to the GBBF, which was conveniently in London – one of the great international centres of Europe. And then people started to think "Could we do this sort of thing in our own country?"
>
> *TIM WEBB, co-author of* The World Atlas of Beer *and former EBCU Executive, 1974*

Although real ale is a particularly British phenomena, CAMRA exerts a global influence. It is able to command respect as the oldest and arguably most impactful society dedicated to a national beer culture in the world. It is matched in size only by the

American Homebrewers Association, although their purpose is quite different.

The growth in consumer interest in beer around the world was not coordinated. It occurred thanks to synchronous events, in which CAMRA played only a very small part. The Campaign acted as a fire lighter, a source of inspiration, according to author Tim Webb. Much greater impact can be attributed to, for example, the writing of the peerless Michael Jackson, who was given a column in *What's Brewing* from 1979 and wrote massively influential publications like the *World Guide to Beer*.

That said, we know the National Executive were keeping a weather eye on European politics in their early years. They had correctly divined that this was going to be an important political sphere for the UK. Andrew Cunningham remembers that they expended resources on building relationships and visiting the early European Commission. They even had 'middle order moles' he says, who reported back to CAMRA on the comings and goings of the Competitions Directorate. So productive was the relationship that at one time there was a delegation to Europe from Bass Charrington who complained that CAMRA enjoyed too much influence in Europe.

Meanwhile, across Europe, groups were forming that were broadly analogous in purpose or motivation to CAMRA. The Dutch group PINT (Vereniging Promotie INformatie Traditioneel Bier) began in October 1980. It was founded by a CAMRA member who had started up a beer import/export business in Amsterdam, along with the few Dutch-national CAMRA members who had joined because there were a few pubs in the city with British cask on hand pull. When they asked the national CAMRA organisation for more support, they were given a small amount of money and told to start their own organisation because CAMRA was dedicated to British issues.

Some beer lovers see the demise of Dutch beer culture with sad eyes. They become members of the English beer consumer association CAMRA (which stands for Campaign for Real Ale), which was founded in 1971 with the aim of reviving English beer culture. And with success: CAMRA quickly grew into an association with more than 50,000 members.

One of the Dutch CAMRA members thinks that what is possible in England should also be possible in the Netherlands. In the early 1980s he placed a call in 'What's Brewing' CAMRA magazine. This call led to a group of people coming together, who then submitted a request to CAMRA to set up a Dutch department. However, CAMRA rejects this request because the Netherlands does not belong to its field of activity.

The initiators are reluctant and decide to set up their own association. On October 14, 1980 the statutes are signed at the notary and with a starting capital of 50 British pounds, donated by CAMRA, the association PINT is a fact. The first board of PINT is formed by Nico van Dijk, Casper van Gijn, Rob Gras, Ben Kegge and Paul van Oosterom.[9]

The history of PINT

Meanwhile, unrelated to CAMRA, the Belgian group OBP – the Objectieve Bierproevers – was started in 1984 and succeeded by Zythos in 2003.

CAMRA's Research and Information Manager, Iain Loe, was key in bringing these disparate national groups together for the first time. When he joined CAMRA he was aware that a lot of British legislation was coming via directives and regulations from the then European Commission, so he felt the Campaign would benefit from talking to similar minded campaigners on the Continent. As the unofficial representatives of just one country in Europe, Iain felt CAMRA's voice would not be strong enough to effect any changes.

At a beer exhibition in Belgium in 1989 Iain was introduced to the heads of the OBP and PINT, so he suggested a collaborative approach. Iain was tasked with organising a meeting in Bruges for the three groups the next year, and in May 1990 the European Beer Consumers Union (EBCU) was born. A CAMRA

9. https://www.pint.nl/over-pint

member since 1978, Terry Lock was elected as founding chairman and thereby gained the nickname 'El Presidente'.

After the foundation meeting in Oslo, the group agreed to meet every six months in a different host country. They had no funding so representatives were paid for by their respective organisations. CAMRA members John Cryne and Mark Taylor, along with Terry, helped to start the EBCU by formalising the structure and drafting a constitution. This constitution was signed off by all members at the Brewers of Europe building in Brussels.

Terry believes that CAMRA's lasting influence on the other groups in Europe was to provide ambition. People in other countries saw them preserving and protecting a unique beer tradition and they wanted to do the same. He feels that these groups would probably have come about of their own volition eventually, but CAMRA's example inspired quite a number at roughly the same time, each with their own individual focus. The Danish group, Danske, actually began as an association of beer and food lovers, for example, and moved later to solely representing beer. Within five years of its inception there were over 100 microbreweries in Denmark. Knowing the potential customers were out there gave the businesses a reason to start. Similarly, there were fewer than twenty breweries in the Netherlands when PINT started in 1980, and there are now more than 500.

Over time Iain made enquiries and found more regional beer groups who were willing to join the EBCU, including ones in Denmark, Sweden, Norway and Finland. Along came the Amis de la Bière, a slightly eccentric group of French ex-brewers who enjoyed dressing up at their ceremonies. They made Terry a *Chevalier* of their order – a fancy way of saying beer taster! There was also the Swedish Svenska Ölfrämjandet, founded in 1985, Norwegian NORØL, founded in 1993, and more. Because German beer drinkers are very provincial they were one of the toughest nuts to crack when it came to national representation on the EBCU, but even they were brought into the fold eventually. At the time of writing there are eighteen full and associate members of the EBCU.

The purpose of the EBCU is to give all of these diverse groups a chance to lobby together regarding the legislation of health and alcohol duty related issues. Working together gave their voice more power in Europe than they would have as the representatives of consumers from one country alone. As John Cryne observes, there was an increasing concentration of brewery ownership and beer production in an increasingly small number of company's hands. Variety and choice for the consumer were diminishing and so the three founder organisations set out to build a strong campaigning voice, and to protect small breweries from assimilation by multinationals. They look to protect consumer rights regarding quality and value in the marketplace. The EBCU also sets out to preserve beer traditions where local producers use traditional methods, as well as the promotion of local or national beer styles and breweries Europe-wide.

CAMRA, as a part of the EBCU, has influenced a number of legislative changes, including, famously, the threat to 'The Great British Pint' when the European Union looked at standardising measurements across the EU. CAMRA lobbied against this, and the decision was informed by other factors, such as keeping trade in alignment with the US which also uses different systems. Along with the troy ounce and the mile, it was clear that the United Kingdom and Ireland wished to keep the pint as a measurement for both milk and beer. This was allowed as the measurements were in local usage and did not impact cross border trade. No end date was set for the exception when it was set in 2007.

The problem faced by the EBCU is that beer consumers in different countries face different issues – accessing traditional ale on a hand pump simply isn't a consideration in Finland, for example. But despite these differences, there is still an important role for CAMRA in the EBCU going forward, even though the UK has left the EU. CAMRA recognises that brewers can be multinational in their reach and things that happen in Brussels will still have an impact on the UK consumer, so it is important to maintain its role in the organisation.

The Great American Beer Festival

> I was one of the first people that really got infected with
> the passion for what beer could be [...] and also discovering
> what was going on in other parts of the world, such as what
> CAMRA were doing in the UK. *CHARLIE PAPAZIAN*

Christine Cryne says that CAMRA led the way for people around
the world to question beer quality for the first time. Nowhere
did this idea take hold more forcefully than in the United States,
leading to an explosion of new microbreweries.

Charlie Papazian, an affable native of New Jersey, made his
first batch of beer while a student at the University of Virginia.
This was the start of a lifelong obsession that arguably changed
the shape of the modern brewing industry in the US. In 1978 he
founded the American Homebrewers Association when home
brewing was finally legalised for the first time since Prohibition
in 1919. This has since become the Brewers Association, a not-
for-profit trade group.

Charlie is the legendary godfather of homebrewing in the
United States. He was introduced to CAMRA by members of his
association who had travelled to England and experienced the
Campaign first hand, like the *Washington Post* journalist Paul
Friedman. Paul was excited by CAMRA because he knew beer in
the US was in a dismal state, and CAMRA gave him hope things
could be changed. He and his colleagues began to write about beer
in the UK, particularly CAMRA and real ale. Charlie remembers
how 'every story that people wrote in those days was revelatory.
They were revelations that caused revolutions. Because we had
never really understood what was behind beer in other places
and we were enthusiastic. Maybe we could make something work
in the United States.'

Just like CAMRA, the nascent American homebrewing scene
was concerned with quality and flavour. Influenced by the heritage of German brewing, the US market had been flooded with

light lager and very little else. The deregulation of the airlines and more affordable travel saw more Americans leaving the country and discovering new flavours, ingredients and techniques for themselves. Just as in the UK, the American brewing marketplace had become extremely aggressive. Breweries were being forced out of business and by the 1970s there were barely more than 40 left in the entire US. The stage was set for the proliferation of homebrewing, ultimately leading into a new generation of microbreweries being founded. However, there was no information available about how to brew: everything was aimed at brewing on a huge commercial scale. To learn to do something new the homebrewing community had to glean what information they could from bottle and label collectors who had accessed beers from around the world. CAMRA's publications also provided a rich mine of information:

> The reason and the premise for making homebrew was
> to make a better beer. And we could make better beer
> with the simple procedures that were often portrayed in
> the English books. *CHARLIE PAPAZIAN*

The growth of the homebrewing community and the new beer scene was a slow one, because it was limited to direct transfer of knowledge through local communities and newsletters at first. Charlie and his partner, Charlie Matzen, started their own magazine, *Zymurgy*, to share information more efficiently. Their main difficulty was convincing people that any amateur had the ability to make beer at all, so alien was the concept in America that beer could be anything but light lager. It remained a struggle for at least the first decade or two of the association's existence.

While Charlie was establishing a new scene in the States, he also visited the UK for the first time. In 1981 his destination was the Great British Beer Festival in Leeds. His primary contact was the celebrated writer Michael Jackson, who had visited Charlie's homebrewer's conference earlier that year. First he stayed with

Michael in Hammersmith and explored the local pub scene, then they both went up to Leeds.

> I will never forget the first impression I had when I walked in the hall. I saw all these people and all these different kinds of beers, all real ales for the most part. I'd been invited ahead of time to judge the best of the show at the Great British Beer Festival that year, and I'll never forget the photographs of myself and two other people on the little stage [...] between the three of us we decided the grand champions.
>
> The idea that struck me when I walked into the hall and saw all these people enjoying beers and the beer culture everywhere, you know, this awareness of beer and how it was made, and how it was to be served. We didn't have any of that in the United States. But it struck me that I wonder, I wonder if we could ever have something called the Great American Beer Festival in the United States. And I proposed that idea to Mike and he said, "that'd be a great idea, Charlie, but where are you gonna get the beer?" And he was right, you couldn't really have a beer festival just serving light lager. Everyone thought we were crazy, but that's when you know you have a good idea.
>
> *CHARLIE PAPAZIAN*

As well as visiting the GBBF, Charlie also spent some time hopping around the UK, visiting rural pubs, malt companies, hop farms. He remembers the trip fondly as the time when a lot of his thinking really evolved as he experienced where beer came from for the first time. He also felt a kinship with CAMRA as they were branded as revolutionaries in the same way that he and his peers were in the US. He admired them going against the mainstream direction and trying to do something about the monopoly of big business.

Upon returning to the USA, Charlie and his growing community of homebrewers were realising that there were tiny pockets of speciality beers being made regionally in America, but only people who lived in the vicinity knew about them.

Without a reliable consumer base, they were going out of business left and right. In 1982 Charlie gathered the support of 22 breweries who donated beers for an event, in the same way as the original CAMRA beer exhibitions, and they sold admission tickets to interested people.

This was the first time a beer festival had been held in the United States. Bringing a totally new concept to the American market was not without its pitfalls. When they first began, festival organisers gave tastings in half pint servings. After the first two years it became abundantly clear that this wasn't sustainable. They were nearly shut down because of punters getting very drunk rather than celebrating beer culture and education about the diversity of beer. They began limiting serving sizes. There were protests at first but in time the consumers appreciated it in the same way that the GBBF audience does with third of a pint legal measures. Many visitors enjoy the opportunity to experience a wide range of beers through smaller tasting glasses.

> It was one of the very first beer festivals. There was a gentleman named Fred Huber. His family had a brewery in Wisconsin for over 100 years. He was the current president and CEO. He had come to our event to see what he was donating his beer to [...] He saw all these young people, mostly younger people, trying all these different beers from all these different breweries under one roof. And he was stunned. He said, I never thought I'd ever live to see a day like this. Now what he was observing was the very first time different breweries were serving their beer at one event. That was unheard of in the United States. *CHARLIE PAPAZIAN*

The Great American Beer Festival (GABF) was an anchor for the development of microbreweries in the States. People drinking a beer at a festival in Colorado weren't necessarily able to buy it at home, mainly because of the distances involved and because it is illegal to transport alcohol across some states. However, people did take away ideas and inspiration.

Just as Charlie had been influenced by the GBBF, now a generation of homebrewers turned their hobby into a commercial enterprise and the GABF went from strength to strength. Nearly 40 years on, some 700 brewers exhibit to 46,000 people, while the microbrewery scene numbered over 8,000 breweries and brewpubs at its peak. There are many more beer festivals around the country, but they all derive from Charlie's original.

Of course, CAMRA were not Charlie's only source of inspiration and Charlie was not the only driving force behind the US craft beer movement. Influence from the UK also came from David Bruce founding the Firkin chain in London in 1979, for example. The concept of brew pubs created a lot of interest in the US as brewing beer to sell directly to the customer was unheard of there, and today it is arguably more successful there than it is here in the UK.

Dave Bossie of Santa Cruz, California, was an American homebrewer who was inspired by Charlie Papazian. Dave saw Charlie's writing as technical but also anecdotal and fun, which is what attracted a lot of people to reading his books. Michael Jackson's influence also loomed large when Dave began brewing in the early 90s: it was required reading for understanding beer styles. CAMRA didn't feature as much in Dave's beer education because he did not need to know a lot about cask. Like most American brewers, he was not set up for more than the occasional dalliance with brewing cask. However, he does have a strong affinity with beer festivals, both on the local level and the Great American Beer Festival. He describes it as 'packed and loud, with crazy long lines to get to the hottest beer of the year.'

Beer Campaigning

When it's on form, cask ale is one of the most sublime
alcoholic drinks you can get.

ADRIAN TIERNEY-JONES, beer writer

ISSUES of quality are never far from the mind of the discerning
CAMRA member, and, unsurprisingly, the bulk of their campaigning focuses on how customers can enjoy the very best real
ale, kept and served properly. One legendary early member with
an eye for excellence was an estate agent by the name of VDS
Fowler – Valentine Danes Seaward Fowler. Val didn't like any of his
given names and after an accident on a boat on the Isle of Wight
he simply became known as Boathook Fowler. He is fondly remembered as one of the founding members of the Isle of Wight
branch, from where he wrote to a range of breweries in the line
of campaigning.

The most famous story from all of Boathook's exploits was
when he wrote to one particular brewery telling them that he
thought their beers would have been very good, if it weren't for
the forced carbonation they used so abundantly. The chairman
of the brewery wrote back, exhorting Mr Fowler to remember
that carbon dioxide is a by-product of brewing and, therefore,
an essential part of the process. Boathook took some exception
to this response, writing back simply. 'Sir. Manure is a natural
by-product of a pig, but you wouldn't want it served up with
your roast pork, would you?' People often misquote this now
legendary statement, suggesting that Boathook had written 'shit'
rather than 'manure', but CAMRA founder Michael Hardman
saw the letter and can confirm he definitely used the more
demure language.

CAMRA PUBLICATIONS

What's Brewing

> *What's Brewing* in those days was required reading because that's how you got all the news about pubs, breweries, beer, everything.   DAVE GOODWIN

Unsurprisingly for an organisation founded by journalists, they crafted a fairly sensationalist newsletter aimed at catching the eye of news desks around the country. It was a very effective early campaigning tool, as well as being good for keeping the membership informed. The name of the monthly newsletter was *What's Brewing*, coined by founder Bill Mellor. It was first released in June 1972 as a simple two-page sheet compiled by Michael Hardman. He went on to edit *What's Brewing* professionally as a member of CAMRA's paid staff from 1974.

> CAMRA has won its first battle against the flashy gimmicks that disguise bad ale.
>
> *The headline story of the first issue of* What's Brewing, *June 1972*

The first edition featured a front page scoop on the aptly named Dirty Dicks on Liverpool Street in London. The pub was being forced to stop its 'fraud', according to the headline. The problem was that they were advertising beer served from the wood, but in reality there was a pipe going through the wooden cask and feeding out from a standard keg behind. The matter was raised with the Competitions Authority and the pub was forced to apologise and change their advertising so as not to mislead. Dirty Dick's already had a long and venerable history (including dead cats behind the bar) and managed to overcome the reputational damage to survive to this day, although some grumble about overpriced pints there.[10]

---

10. https://spitalfieldslife.com/2012/01/09/at-dirty-dicks

Misleading dispense was a big problem that CAMRA came up against a lot in the early days. Unscrupulous publicans wanting to bypass the complexities of keeping and serving cask ale properly would put hand pumps on the bar which would trigger a switch and dispense keg. Dave Goodwin eventually became a CAMRA National Chairman, but he had already come across a few examples of misleading dispense before that. He found that, as a customer, his complaints to pubs and breweries had made no difference. Then a local trading standards officer pointed him to LACOTS – the Local Authorities Co-ordinating body on Food and Trading Standards. In around 1990, Dave wrote a paper for them on CAMRA's behalf. LACOTS agreed that the actions of the publicans were indeed misleading. Although not part of a concerted campaign, real change took place following Dave's evidence being submitted to the committee. This landmark decision gave some official recognition that the hand pump was a sign of real ale.

It is an example of CAMRA having a direct influence on the industry, even though there were still some brewers who refused to take them seriously and saw them as interfering amateurs. Unfortunately, CAMRA has had to practice eternal vigilance against misleading dispense. As late as 2001 the Stockport & South Manchester branch named and shamed four pubs in their branch newsletter, *Opening Times*, for carrying signs advertising cask beers despite having had their hand pumps removed.

*   *   *

What's Brewing featured a cartoon called 'Cheerless Charlie', illustrated by John Simpson. This was joined by the popular 'Kegbuster' by legendary illustrator, Bill Tidy. Bill continued the comic strip until ill health forced him to officially step down from the role in April 2020. However, Bill's store of Kegbuster appears not to have bottomed out quite yet, as the November 2020 *What's Brewing* still carried the strip.

Beer writer Adrian Tierney-Jones started receiving *What's Brewing* when it was edited by Roger Protz, who had also edited the *Socialist Worker*. This gave a real campaigning feel to the newsletter in Adrian's eyes, the antagonistic and rousing language making it look like a trades union newspaper. Eventually, Adrian began writing for them himself, as well as writing for his local branch newsletter from September 1996.

What's Brewing was a noticeably balanced newssheet, with early editors striving to include a range of opinions. In the December 1973 edition Malcolm Charles was invited to write a point of view column. He was a self-styled consumer expert in the brewing field and wrote 'In Defence of Keg'. He evinced the opinion that the commercial success of keg was undeniable and relatively unstoppable due to its consistency in comparison to draught ale. This was, of course, anathema to the CAMRA faithful, but it is heartening to see accepted truths being challenged in the Campaign's own publication.

Former Regional Director Mark Enderby joined CAMRA in 1981 mainly for the *What's Brewing* subscription as it was the only reliable source of information about beer at the time. He remembers it being avidly consumed by members. Due to its large number of eminent contributors, *What's Brewing* was really the only early source of regular beer news, with the exception of 'Boston on Beer' in the *Guardian*. The godfather of British beer writing, Michael Jackson, generously allowed his travel column to be reproduced free of charge in *What's Brewing*, although his column was later axed by editor Ted Bruning as Jackson was 'not doing as he was told'. Ted felt that Michael was just submitting whatever he fancied, and often featuring foreign beers, rather than pitching stories that were relevant to the membership.

As well as professional beer writers, *What's Brewing* has provided a democratic platform for members to submit letters and pitch articles for over twenty years. CAMRA member Ed 'Quoth The Raven' Taylor has found a home there because of his self-confessed hobby of 'expressing his opinion'. Ted Bruning was the first editor to encourage this sort of contribution and nurtured a good number of members through the editorial process to allow them to contribute to their own magazine. The mantle has since been taken up by Alex Metcalfe, who encourages members to submit content to the Learning & Discovery section of the CAMRA website.

The contemporary incarnation of *What's Brewing*, with Tim Hampson at the helm, is steered by an editorial board, which is made up of National Executive members and individuals working on a specific issue. They act as a sounding board and critical friend for the editor. Tim is also the editor of *BEER*, CAMRA's quarterly magazine.

Writer Matthew Curtis enjoys the challenge of writing articles for *BEER* because of the focus on cask ale. This forces him to push his boundaries and think more deeply about his approach to beer, and it has encouraged him to make a return to cask-conditioned beers that he had previously overlooked. For example, when returning from a trip to the United States, and excited by American craft beers, he might have turned his nose up at classics like Hopback Summer Lightning. But taking the time to write about, consider and appreciate cask for *BEER* meant that he was able to appreciate its quality alongside other styles.

The Good Beer Guide

> We used to go away every weekend before we had children, just put the tent in the back of the car, and off we'd go with our beer guide. We'd tick pubs off all round the country.
>
> CAROL KELLY, *Kinver Brewery*

What's Brewing is made specifically for CAMRA members, but the *Good Beer Guide* (GBG) has, arguably, been a more successful campaigning tool as it appeals to the general public as well. The first edition, compiled by Michael Hardman, was a looseleaf affair of eighteen pages released in 1972. It contained around 300 entries and was stapled together and posted out to members. The guide was mostly based on information provided by Andrew Cunningham. Andrew had been keeping a diary of how many pints he had drunk of what and where since 1968, and this provided some 200 suggestions of pubs with hand pumps that might be considered for inclusion in the guide.

Lists like Andrew's were combined with other sources, like Frank Bailie's *The Beer Drinker's Companion* of 1974. Michael Hardman designed a page of information about each brewery – the beers they made, where they were based, which pubs they owned – and then submitted the page to them for approval or amendment. The only place he didn't get an answer from at first was Watneys. When he called to follow up they said that he had made an error in not describing their Special Bitter as a *premium beer* because 'it had been through more processes' than other beers. Needless to say he took that particular suggestion with a pinch of salt.

Andrew Cunningham's list-making had begun with a light-hearted challenge against a friend in 1964. They decided on a race to consume a pint of beer from a hundred different breweries. Andrew insists that he 'wasn't very competitive,' but he carried on with the challenge even once he had beaten his friend to supping beer from those hundred breweries. Then it got to the stage where there were only two breweries in the United Kingdom remaining that Andrew had not visited, both on the Isle of Man.

Andrew was developing the Brewery Liaison Officer system at the time and took the opportunity to visit the Isle of Man with Michael Hardman to survey the two brewers for the database, and tick off those final beers at the same time. Details of the trip and the visit to the Castletown brewery are hard to come by from the tight-lipped pair. Apparently 'what happens on the Isle of Man stays on the Isle of Man.' The men could not have imagined that from around 180 breweries in the British Isles in the early 1970s there would be more than ten times that amount 50 years later. As microbreweries began to pop up here, there and everywhere Andrew gradually gave up on his quest, although some 'completists' still exist who try to work their way through the huge number of British breweries that are now in operation.

*   *   *

Since 1972 the guide has grown into a weighty tome of over 1,000 pages. The first properly printed guide, published in 1974, was compiled solely by a team of roving volunteer 'inspectors', but the responsibility for collating entries was mainly devolved to the branches from 1975 onwards, with a team selected by the editor being sent out to cover areas where no branch existed.

From humble, yet still ambitious beginnings, the annual creation of the GBG has become a phenomenal logistical challenge. The National Beer Scoring System (NBSS) was developed by Brett Laniosh to inform the long list of pubs for possible inclusion. Brett sat on the National Executive from 2006 to 2017 and he unified the numeric systems that branches were previously using to collate entries. This made the whole system a little more scientific than when 'a group of CAMRA members would meet in a darkened room and put up their hands to vote for their favourite pub'. Having a uniform system of scoring meant members could submit a score on individual beers wherever they were in the country – at first on paper and now online.

A professional editorial team compiles the listings of pubs, breweries and beers submitted by the branches and BLOs, as well as commissioning articles that give the reader added insight into the world of beer that year: trends, techniques and social impact. One of the key priorities for branches is surveying pubs and providing entries to fulfil their allocation to the *Good Beer Guide* editorial team, as well as selecting local award winners for branch Pub of the Year. It is hardly surprising that a survey of the best pubs and beers in the whole country is a mammoth undertaking that takes almost a full year to complete: the GBG 2020 and 2021 both contained over 4,500 handpicked pub entries as well as some 1,850 breweries and 7,500 beers.

*   *   *

Before CAMRA had actually started, I was aware that
something was a bit wrong with the drinking scene and
everywhere I used to go I used to make notes of my own of
what was happening in pubs. CAMRA came on the scene
and of course we produced the first [printed] GBG in 1974,
which sold for 75p. It had 1,500 pubs in it.

JOHN HANSCOMB, Editor of the GBG 1974

The first printed edition of the *Good Beer Guide* is affectionately known by many as the 'Plague Edition'. The end of the book
was devoted to listing 'all the breweries in England, Wales and
the Isle of Man, plus three in Scotland whose products are available south of the border.' Each listing is accompanied by a brief
comment, 'intended as a guide to the traveller who comes across
a pub not listed in the *Good Beer Guide*.' The entry for perennial
CAMRA target Watneys was written by editor John Hanscomb
and reads simply 'Avoid like the plague'.

John stands by this judgement today: 'it was awful beer.
Very, very low gravity, no taste in it whatsoever and everywhere
you went there was this damn thing on the counter: a red barrel,
you couldn't avoid it.' So he did the logical thing for a man in his
position and recommended that right-thinking consumers
steered well clear.

The guide was being published by the printing arm of Waddington's, the makers of Monopoly. Their Chief Executive, Beric
Watson, was not happy about the unflattering description of
such a powerful brewery. He came to the CAMRA AGM at York
to discuss the problem. Deadlines were already pushed as the
printing had been delayed by about six weeks while Waddington's had negotiated the distribution of the Guide to bookshops
nationally with a large publishing company. But after a meeting
with the National Executive that evening, it was nonetheless
agreed that the offending statement should be taken out and the
book be reprinted. CAMRA's level of solvency was so low that

they couldn't afford to be sued, says Andrew Cunningham, and Waddingtons weren't willing to take the risk either. 'Any brewer could have ruined us at that stage,' Andrew remarks.

Luckily the list of breweries was on the final two pages of the publication, so the offending Watneys entry was printed on the inside of the back cover. This meant that only the cover needed to be replaced. It was a good job as there wasn't enough money in the CAMRA kitty to pulp the first run and reprint the whole thing. The text was amended to 'avoid at all costs', which was accepted by Waddington's. Meanwhile, a carload of guides had already been delivered to the De Grey Rooms in York for all the members attending the AGM who had pre-ordered their copies. A very small number of copies managed to liberate themselves and find their way into the wild before the rest were recalled and given new covers. Proper 'Plague Edition' *Good Beer Guide*'s are now quite valuable collector's items.

Most people who were party to the incident agree now that there probably wasn't anything particularly libellous in the statement at all. To the casual reader it seems no more or less cutting than some of the other brewery descriptions John had penned. Of the Barnsley brewery he wrote, 'a shadow of its former self; due to close.' Barnsley had been taken over by Imperial Tobacco in 1972 and was indeed closed not long after, in 1976. For Phipps of Northampton, Hanscomb simply wrote 'Don't bother', and Gibbs Mew of Salisbury are described as 'a disaster'. Phipps had already been acquired by Watneys in 1960. Cask ale brewing was wound up and the brewery was mostly demolished in 1974 to make way for a Carlsberg lager plant. Gibbs Mew made it all the way to 1997 before the brewery was closed and their tied houses were bought up by Enterprise Inns.

*　　*　　*

This should really set people thinking about real ale. There's never been a guide before which selects pubs purely on the merit of their beer and I hope the *Good Beer Guide* will have a lot of impact. Whenever people are in a strange town, they will now know where they can get a pint of good ale.

JOHN HANSCOMB, writing in What's Brewing *February 1974*

What is the value of the *Good Beer Guide*? For brewery manager Stephen Boyle 'it is the first thing I would look at if I'm planning to go to a new city.' It has a venerable history of taking beer tourists around the highways and byways of the British Isles, searching out the perfect pint. For later GBG editor John Hanscomb, Michael Hardman's looseleaf Guide of 1972 had been a true revelation. He was living in a village outside of St Albans from where 'we had to literally travel about ten miles to find a pub that sold real ale [...] You'd need the Ordnance Survey map to find where the pubs were that sold decent beer, they just didn't exist at all.' The GBG made a huge difference to the ease of finding good quality pubs, although there were still huge parts of the country where there weren't any real ale pubs at all back in the early seventies.

Freelance beer writer and former editor of the *Good Beer Guide* Jeff Evans grew up in Wales with only tied pubs and keg beers available. He didn't think anything of it until he went to university where he was introduced to cask beer. This spoiled him, and upon returning home after university he had to grumble his way through many nights out because the beer was so bad. It led him to buying a copy of the 1984 *Good Beer Guide* and seeking out the beers and pubs it listed. He says the publication brought 'colour and life' to his travels around the country, at a time where many beers were only available in the immediate vicinity of their brewery. For Jeff, the GBG let people know they don't have to accept second best – to know there are better beers out there and how to find them. In turn this simple consumerist message also encourages pubs to keep a weather eye on quality and choice.

I was a twenty-year-old and "on tour" hitching around with my pal when I bought my first GBG on Good Friday 1975 from Blackwells in Oxford. It was a life changer. That summer I planned a trip around all the places in Britain I'd never been to, to sample all the beers in the GBG I had never heard of. This took two weeks with a change of accompanying partners at the halfway point. I hired a brand new Mini from Kennings and they could not believe it when it was returned 3,476 miles later.

We started zigzagging down through Wales all around the South West to Penzance, all along the South of England to London and Kent, through East England. Then Leg 2 took us through the North, and Scotland as far as Inverness.

COLIN KEEGAN, CAMRA member

Some question how much longer the physical *Good Beer Guide* will survive as younger people tend to look up information on the go. For just this purpose there is WhatPub, the CAMRA online pub guide. It contains over 55,000 pubs and clubs at the time of writing, which can be filtered by pubs that serve real ale, cider and perry but not by which pubs have made the GBG grade – so rather cleverly it hasn't rendered the paper copy completely obsolete just yet. You can also purchase a GBG app, and that takes up much less shelf space than the paper copy. All of these resources rely entirely on the input and expertise of the CAMRA membership volunteering their time to create and collate the details and descriptions. Each branch has a 'gatekeeper' who approves updates to the listings. Uniquely, publicans can, and are encouraged to, update their own data on the WhatPub website.

Not everyone is a fan of this phenomenal group effort. Writing in the *Guardian* in 2010, author and restaurateur Tim Hayward took the time to comment on Tony Naylor's analysis of the *Good Beer Guide*, saying, 'I'm not sure whose recommendation I'd respect in recommending a boozer but frankly the joint opinion of 100,000 CAMRA members doesn't fill me with confidence …

in fact it just makes me feel a little bit ill.'[11] More importantly perhaps, sometimes the members themselves aren't happy with the GBG recommendations. There was controversy at the 1987 AGM in Manchester when a motion of no confidence was raised in the *Good Beer Guide* editor and staff team. The branches who put the motion forward said that their pub descriptions had suffered a 'wholesale butchering'.

The man who has unquestionably given more than any other to the *Good Beer Guide* is Roger Protz. The journalist and editor joined CAMRA in 1976 as the Assistant Editor of Publications after a very short interview with Michael Hardman: 'you're ex-*Evening Standard*, I'm ex-*Evening Standard*, you'll do.' After about eighteen months, when Michael left to go travelling, Roger took over editing the guide and *What's Brewing*. He edited the Guide between 1978 and 1983, then returned to the role from 2000 until 2017. He remembers National Chairman Joe Goodwin instructing him to make it the best campaigning guide possible, and if they could make a bit of money out of it too then that was a bonus, but it was a campaigning tool first. This guided Roger in his editorial and he feels that the publications helped the public to become more aware of what the big brewers were doing to phase out cask. Under Roger the GBG was always sharply critical of what the big brewers were doing.

The main difficulty with the job, according to Roger, was simply managing the entries as retrieving thousands of submissions on time from volunteers was next to impossible. However, with no rival publications, and despite the complexities, the GBG 'took off like the proverbial rocket', with around 80,000 copies a year flying off the shelves at its peak.

When the 2018 edition was released, a special mention was made of the 'Famous Five', the five pubs that had made it into all forty-five versions of the book. Michael Hardman's 1972 'home-made' edition is not counted as there was a break in 1973 before the 1974 print version. The superstar pubs are:

---

11. https://www.theguardian.com/lifeandstyle/wordofmouth/2010/apr/14/beer-pub-guides#comment-4221496

Buckingham Arms, 62 Petty France, London SW1
Queen's Head, Fowlmere Road, Newton, Cambridgeshire
Roscoe Head, 24 Roscoe Street, Liverpool
Star Tavern, 6 Belgrave Mews West, London SW1
Square & Compass, Weston Road, Worth Matravers, near
Corfe Castle, Dorset

In the 2021 edition all five were still featured, so it is not long before they can have a fifty-year celebration of their own. Carol Ross, the landlady of the Roscoe Head, had cause for an early celebration in November 2020 after winning a decade-long battle to buy the pub's freehold from the PubCo New River Retail, thus securing the pub's future.

Other CAMRA publications

Where the *Good Beer Guide* went, other CAMRA publications were soon to follow. To date, CAMRA Books and its predecessor Alma Books, have published more than 200 titles on a wide range of subjects. Some of the best known include the *Good Cider Guide* and *Good Bottled Beer Guide*.

On 29 October 1987, just before CAMRA officially started campaigning for cider and perry, the first CAMRA *Good Cider Guide* was released. It was written by David Kitton, the maker of Gibbon Stranger Cider. He had coined the title *Good Cider Guide* with a traditional cider directory of his own in 1984. He compiled it by walking through the countryside and visiting every cider and perry maker he found.

Dave Matthews, now proprietor of Bartestree Cider, started writing about cider for *What's Brewing* in 1997 and pitched for a new *Good Cider Guide* in 1999. It was published in 2000 and followed on from David Kitton and a further *Guide to Real Cider* by Ted Bruning. Dave was also a valued contributor to Emma Lloyd's 2005 guide, along with Stephen Fisher, Tom Oliver, and Simon Stevenson.

Susan Nowak released the *Good Pub Food Guide* as a companion book to the *Good Beer Guide*, first in 1989, with five further editions released until 2006 when it was combined into a joint publication with Jill Adam's *Beer, Bed and Breakfast*.

For CAMRA not only champions real ale but was first to champion real pub food – and I found myself an unlikely pioneer when Roger Protz, and Tim Webb of then Alma Books, asked me to edit a new CAMRA guide: *Good Pub Food*. What a project! To spit out all the microwaved lasagne, chicken in a basket and stale Scotch eggs languishing under plastic domes and find the pubs serving honest, tasty fare prepared in their own kitchens from fresh ingredients with real ale and cider to accompany. Unlike the *Good Beer Guide*, branches did not write the entries; I did that myself. But they did send me shortlists of the pubs that met this brief – plus lots of useful detail. I then sent the pubs tough questionnaires about their cooking, ingredients, menus, real ale, and more.

Susan Nowak

CAMRA has always supported bottle-conditioned beers that continue to ferment, condition and mature in the bottle. By 1990 more small brewers were bottling their beers as it presented a way of using up beer that was left over from racking to cask, when carbonation, sterilisation and filtration processing equipment was too expensive. In 1991 a motion was passed at the AGM that CAMRA would do more to promote bottle-conditioned beer and as such a new category was introduced for it at the Champion Beer of Britain contest. From 1992 onwards the GBG also systematically included bottled beers that each brewery produced alongside their cask offering. More and more, bottle-conditioned beers appeared each year until finally, in 1996, Jeff Evans suggested a separate publication to the CAMRA Books Committee. Jeff estimated there were around 100 bottle-conditioned beers around at the time – enough to warrant a book, but not an unmanageable number.

The first edition came out in 1997. It was called the *CAMRA Guide to Real Ale in a Bottle* with a total of 134 entries that Jeff had drawn up by contacting the breweries individually. However, he felt the book's design didn't do justice to promoting bottle-conditioned beer so he petitioned the Books Committee to start again. At quite some expense, they recalled and pulped the unsold copies while Jeff revamped and updated the information he had compiled, now reaching around 170 entries. The new *Good Bottled Beer Guide* was published as a sister publication to the GBG in 1998.

By 2006 the fourth edition contained 778 different beers, and by 2009 it had gone up to 1,346. The most recent edition was in 2013 and that contained 1,847 bottle-conditioned beers, all produced in the UK. Jeff became more selective about which beers he included in additional detail, although the book still aimed to list all bottle-conditioned beers. To accompany the *Good Bottled Beer Guide* CAMRA developed a badge that brewers could use on their labels to show that a beer was bottled conditioned. As they were available in relatively low numbers in the nineties, this logo was helpful for the consumer to know which beers had not been filtered or pasteurised.

In 2016 the Moor Beer Company of Bristol, rejuvenated by Californian brewer Justin Hawke, became the first brewery to receive formal accreditation from CAMRA for producing real ale in a can. According to Justin, it took a long time for the Technical Advisory Group to be satisfied that the CAMRA definition of real ale was being met, but once it had been, Moor were issued with a special certificate by their local branch. They remain the only brewer to have ever received such a commendation. This was especially important for them as naturally carbonated live beer is all that Moor Beer produces – it is a vital point of difference for their brand.

* * *

Unsurprisingly, the history of modern beer writing and the foundation of the British Guild of Beer Writers run very much in parallel to CAMRA's history. Tim Webb and Roger Protz look back fondly on a group of fifteen British beer writers visiting Belgium in October 1988, the first trip of the British Guild of Beer Writers. An iconic photograph of the group visiting the Poperinge Hopmuseum has immortalised the trip – although *Good Beer Guide* editor Neil Hanson is missing from the line up. Tim and Roger claim that during a late-night session at the Brugs Beertje in Bruges they invented the concept of a Good Beer Guide to Belgium and decided that CAMRA should have a publishing arm, although CAMRA had already been publishing books for at least a year by then, so perhaps that was just the beer talking.

The reasoning behind a Belgian guide was much more sound. It was logical for CAMRA to cover Belgium as the only other beer culture that was in much the same state as Britain – i.e., a smallish number of breweries that didn't appear to have much of a future. Tim and Roger hoped that a book would encourage people to hop across and visit the breweries and understand the different types of beer. Tim remembers Belgian beers feeling very different in style at the time, but they were producing beers that were actually very similar to what British beer had been like in the early twentieth century. As Tim had given up his place on the NE to focus on his day job as a consultant psychiatrist, he decided he would have the spare time available to write the *Good Beer Guide Belgium*. Matters soon got out of hand and 'twenty five years later I'm still seen as the Great Guru of the Belgian beer scene', he says.

His beer descriptions made the book entertaining but also gave the Belgian brewers a bit of a kick up the proverbial. Especially the unfortunate product he described as a 'Spice Girls whistling Mozart kind of beer', meaning the brewer was imitating a classic style badly and making it all feel a bit kitsch. He may have ruffled a few feathers but is happy to confirm he is still friends with the brewers he met on his Belgian journeys.

*   *   *

Between them, Michael Jackson, Richard Boston and CAMRA's publications were the pioneers of beer writing. National newspaper columns and CAMRA's campaigning had made beer, cider and perry more newsworthy than ever before. However, this meant that CAMRA's orthodoxy had become the 'Establishment' for fresh new beer writers. In 1998 Pete Brown was at the start of his writing career. He was frustrated that the only narrative he could find was that in 1971 CAMRA came along and saved the world. He felt this was hugely limiting to writers and consumers. For example, the *Encyclopedia of British Beers* had featured no lagers, even though lager made up a huge percentage of the volume of the British market. Pete blamed the 'inherent orthodoxy that was being observed because of CAMRA's definitions'. Adrian Tierney-Jones agrees that 'a lot of beer writing was in a template that CAMRA had laid down,' particularly citing the influence of Roger Protz's elegant writing as a campaigning journalist. Adrian, Pete and others like Melissa Cole looked to change the orthodoxy of CAMRA's consumer-focused writers and developed their own styles, bringing new depth and diversity to the discipline of beer writing.

> When I wrote my first book I deliberately wanted to make an impression. I wanted to be provocative and confrontational. So I really slagged CAMRA off. I think about 70% of what I said was fair at the time and 30% was me just being a bit mean.
>
> *PETE BROWN, Chair of the British Guild of Beer Writers*

When Pete took his first book, *Man Walks into a Pub*, on tour he was quite nervous about meeting people in the flesh whom he'd eviscerated in print. He spoke to the local branch in Salisbury and discovered afterwards that the members thought he was sticking it to St Albans. Indeed, every CAMRA member who read the book and enjoyed it assumed he was slagging off a different part of CAMRA than the bit they belonged to.

BEER FESTIVALS

We all come together, we give up our annual leave and work twenty hours days to put on the biggest beer festival in the world. Then at the end of the week we all go back to work!

NIK ANTONA, Current National Chairman

According to former National Chairman John Cryne, CAMRA's beer festivals are a great way of showing the public what good beer is, as well as recruiting new members. The very first 'beer exhibitions' were members-only events attached to the CAMRA AGM. It did not take long for them to grow and develop into public facing events, although volunteer Mick Lewis jests that 'the customers are an inconvenience, they stop you drinking and having a chat!'

What is a CAMRA beer festival?

All those beers suddenly arrived, many in an unfined form. So we had a local licensee coming in and opening the shive, pouring in a pint or two of finings, tapping it back in and rolling it around. And then humping it up onto scaffolding. There were no electric lifts or anything at the time. Spiling them and seeing the spouts of beer shooting out because a lot of those beers that we had were lively.

Probably the most lively of all were the beers from the Penrhos brewery, which the late Terry Jones [of Monty Python] had set up. They came in wooden casks, they tended to be 18s [18 gallon capacity] so they were difficult to handle. When you spiled them they bubbled for a long time but when they settled down they were actually excellent in taste. It's that hands-on experience in the early days of campaigning that I really found enjoyable.

IAIN LOE on helping to run the Great Western Beer Festival in Bristol at the old Watershed buildings in the late 1970s

CAMRA were not the first to come up with the idea of showcasing beer via an exhibition or festival. 'Britain's Beer Festival' was held at the Alexandra Palace in September 1972 while CAMRA was still in its infancy. CAMRA and the SPBW had both chosen not to attend that affair in protest at the lack of unpressurised beer on offer. Similarly, the NE voted not to attend the World Beer Show in London in 1974 as they did not feel it was appropriate to have a stand at an event where they had no control over the quality or service of the beer.

It sounds like this was the right decision as *What's Brewing* reported it to be 'a cross between an orgy and a trade display,' and 'a sorry shambles' that was only concerned with turning a profit for the organisers. Apparently, you could end up paying some £2.50 for a pint of real beer. This article was presented on the same page as the write-up of the first Cambridge Beer Festival, where 'a dedicated band of CAMRA members have proven that a highly successful beer festival can do without pressurised beer, high admission prices or hordes of PR men,' and all the beers cost 7–9p per half.

> What we were selling them was the Great British Pub
> and the Great British Way of Life.
>
> *STEVE BURY on the first St Albans beer festival*

The CAMRA AGM in York in spring 1974 was probably CAMRA's first beer exhibition, while the oldest public CAMRA beer festival was held by the Hertfordshire branch on 30 March 1974 in the St Albans Market Hall. Tickets were 50p each and it was finally arranged after a year of searching for a suitable venue. They showcased beers from fourteen breweries in the South and Midlands. Then the Cardiff branch held a beer exhibition on 18 May at the Windsor Hotel, Barry Dock.

It's hard to imagine that anyone reading this might not have attended a CAMRA beer festival, but even regular attendees might not realise the huge amount of work that goes into staging them – all done through the goodwill of volunteers. Brewery manager Stephen Boyle eloquently describes their contribution: 'The level of professionalism and the variety of skills blows me away. You'll forget what was done and what was said but you'll never forget how they made you feel – and the CAMRA guys make you feel like you matter, they really do.'

People volunteer at festivals all over the country, visiting friends at other branches to help out with their festivals and staying at each other's houses. Former NE member Ken Davie says 'the friendships go well beyond CAMRA itself.'

The closing celebration parties held at beer festivals are, perhaps unsurprisingly, the stuff of legend, and though most participants are guarded about revealing their anecdotes, it's clear there is plenty of fun and mischief. At one such occasion organiser Mark Parkes was rewarded with a new mallet because he'd had trouble tapping a particularly stubborn cask at the start of the festival. His magnificent new piece of kit came from the Early Learning Centre and squeaked when you hit something with it.

Mick Lewis set up a special surprise one year at GBBF for the cider bar manager who was retiring. He arranged an apple bobbing challenge for him. Once the unsuspecting individual was blindfolded, the bucket was switched out for one full of chilled custard with only one apple placed in it. Of course, he put his head straight in. Thankfully there were plenty of towels on hand! Mick's pranks don't stop there: another year he made a 'special' chocolate cake for the festival working party which contained sixty squares of laxative chocolate. Apparently they were tipped off so nobody was unfortunate enough to eat it.

After the Cambridge festival, committee member Tony Millns would roast 20lb of beef for the hard-working volunteers to enjoy while they finished off the last of the beer. Late-night roller skating around the Corn Exchange was not unheard of in those first years of the festival.

*   *   *

The beer is the star of any festival, and the rows of casks lined up on the stillage are a welcome and familiar sight for most real ale lovers. Dispensing so much beer by gravity makes the signature metal racking a necessity to keep the casks still and properly positioned for the sediment to collect below the tap.

As a rule, responsibility for ordering the beer will sit with one nominated individual on a festival committee, but it is also open to recommendations from other members. Where there are multiple bars at a festival, even at a smaller festival that features a keg or cider bar, each bar has to be a mini beer festival in its own right with a balanced range of styles and ABVs available.

Sarah Durham ordered the beer for the GBBF for nearly twenty years and was always amused when her requests could not be fulfilled by a brewery one day but became possible the very next when it was clear that if they couldn't supply the beer requested she would move on to another brewery. Sarah worked on the basis that if a brewery is decent then it doesn't matter what you pick off their list, it will always be good. It might be their newest line, their best seller or something else entirely, but for the GBBF beer order it needed to work within the mini festival line-up on the particular bar where it would be exhibited. Of course, there are times when even the GBBF can't get a beer that they want – a seasonal beer brewed once a year might already all be accounted for, for example.

As with any event that serves alcohol, beer festivals must have a licence. Thanks to her involvement with the Aberdeen festival, Frances Lock accidentally became the holder of the longest known licence in the UK in around 1990. She applied for the festival's licence to run until 2am 'just in case' as it gave flexibility and matched up with the local pubs. When the licence came it had been granted from 11am on Saturday until 2pm on the Sunday – a full twenty-seven hours! In the event, the festival had run out of beer by 10pm on Saturday, so they didn't need the contingency, or the rest!

Back in the 1980s I was serving behind the bar at Catford SE London Beer Festival. The hall was packed with eager beer hunters and one young man was keen to catch my eye and order. This 'young guy' was perhaps 15 or 16 years old and I politely told him he was too young to be served. He went off in a huff towards the back of the beer hall. Then I noticed the atmosphere in the place hummed with excitement, and the crowd parted to allow the young man to return to the bar with his father.

His dad was clearly a famous face, not usually seen at beer festivals; it was pop star and actor David Essex at the bar. He asked me why I hadn't served his son. I replied I couldn't. David Essex just shrugged his shoulders and said well just get me four pints instead. This I did, and the pair went off beers in hand.

A little while later some other festival goers, seeing Essex & Son in the hall, started an improvised chorus of 'Hold Me Close', a big chart hit at the time. Forever the showman, David Essex joined in briefly before leaving.

DAVID ROBINSON, CAMRA member

Not everyone is a fan of beer festivals. The potential pitfalls have been outlined by the beer marketeer blogger Marc Bishop:

Beer quality at these events can at best be described as variable. Most regional CAMRA groups – the most common of beer festival organisers – don't have the finance or equipment to provide cooling on their beers. Thus, although different methods are used to try and keep the beer cool, much is often served at room temperature, particularly as the festival progresses in time.

The more popular the event, the more people and the hotter the room gets and the more beer in each barrel is drunk, increasing the serving beer temperature a lot quicker.

Not great when most brewers and many pubs are stringent in ensuring their beers are served at perfect cellar temperature. So, more often than not, the beer festival that is designed to promote the sales of cask ale, ends up serving beer that is too warm, indifferent quality, not that palatable and certainly not what consumers are used to experiencing in pubs.[12]

Beer writer Adrian Tierney-Jones has also experienced issues with beer quality at festivals. During a particularly hot spell in the early 2000s he remembers the beer actually began to curdle. He also recalls a separate occasion where he tried a beer that tasted a bit smokey – a phenolic best bitter. The keen volunteer on the bar suggested that veteran cerevisaphile Adrian perhaps hadn't heard of the smoked beers of Bamberg. Adrian pointed out that he was fully cognisant of them, but what he had not previously encountered were the smoked beers of Rutland! He is quick to point out that, in his opinion, CAMRA have really cleaned up their act since then and are much more professional in both how the beers are presented and how volunteers talk about them to customers.

While issues with beer condition have certainly been recorded at some smaller festivals, it is not the case with the GBBF. Christine Cryne and Paul Moorhouse brought in cooling equipment when Christine first became festival organiser in 1992 – and she took the role specifically under the condition that the beer would be served at the right temperature on her watch.

CAMRA beer festivals are now carefully monitored centrally to ensure that they deliver the high standard of quality that members expect. This stops anyone from rocking up and starting their own event using the CAMRA name. Tony Millns recalls a small group of renegade members tried just that in the early eighties. Against national advice, they decided to run a huge beer festival which became apocryphally known as the Battle of Croydon. Bizarrely, they committed the Campaign to bankrolling a massive affair which involved a group of historical re-enactors!

12. http://beermarketeer.blogspot.com/2013/05/the-role-of-beer-festivals.html

Tony was livid that they had gone ahead without permission from the NE, and overhauled the Articles of Association at the Reading AGM in 1983. This brought a new clause into effect meaning that anyone who brought the organisation into disrepute or did anything that was fundamentally detrimental to its interests could be thrown out. After the most tedious meeting that Tony had ever experienced – some ten hours of discussion – the two ringleaders were given enough rope to hang themselves with and duly had their memberships cancelled.

In recent times, along with the Great British Beer Festival, one of the most popular CAMRA festivals is the Manchester Beer & Cider Festival. As beer writer Matthew Curtis puts it: 'the branch is tenacious, stubborn and does things their own way.' They were one of the first to introduce a KeyKeg bar, a bar serving beer in wooden casks, and they have an innovative approach to cider and perry that is likely to set a new standard for best practice. They are also renowned for making good use of unusual venues. One commentator remarked on the festivals held at the Manchester Velodrome in 2013 and 2014 as 'stunning'. Peter Alexander, the current branch chair of Rochdale, Oldham and Bury CAMRA, is one of the organisers and says he has always aimed to innovate. On top of introducing keg side by side with real ale to attract new audiences, he and his committee also look at making their festival inexpensive to attend while still turning a surplus by having themed bars and bringing in new side attractions to keep it interesting.

The Nottingham Beer Festival is also extremely well respected. Andrew Ludlow has been actively involved in the festival every year since 1976 and he has the branded glasses to prove it. It was originally held at the Victoria Leisure Centre in one hall and later expanded to take over the swimming pool hall which had to be emptied and have scaffolding erected over it – probably the best drainage a beer festival has ever had! When it was held at Nottingham Castle it was described as 'the jewel in the Crown of CAMRA festivals'. It now takes place annually at the Motorpoint Arena.

Cambridge Beer Festival

One of the best beer festivals that I've been to in the UK is the Cambridge Beer Festival. I can't believe that it is organised by volunteers. It's an incredible festival that takes place over five days and draws in huge numbers of people ... CAMRA has this power to mobilise and this power to raise beer's profile.

EMMA INCH, Beer Writer of the Year 2018

Cambridge's festival was the first to be run in line with pub licensing hours over several days and was celebrated as CAMRA's biggest beer festival to date. Originally, the festival was held at the Corn Exchange, coinciding with the Cambridge Festival on 24–27 July. The date and the venue were later both moved: the date to the end of May, and the venue first to the Cambridge City Football Ground and then more recently to Jesus Green.

Legend has it that the idea for the event was first suggested by Peter Pearce at the first meeting of the Cambridge & District branch in November 1973. He had been appalled by the attempt of a local catering firm to run a beer tent as part of the Cambridge Festival that year and thought they could do a much better job. Turns out he was on to something and the first Cambridge Beer Festival took place in August 1974.

John Bishopp led the event organisation, along with Peter and their other colleagues, Chris Bruton, Alan and Sue Hill, Nick Haslett and Mark Johnson. John and Chris had both worked in pubs a bit, which was the sum total of relevant experience any of the organising committee had. It's fair to say that they were making it up as they went along. Branch member and local landlord David Short agreed to hold the licence. He is still the beer festival licensee and the success of all the festivals since has been dependent upon him. A club in Norwich that had run a private beer festival for several years was contacted and were able to give lots of helpful advice.

There were fifteen different brews showcased in total, thirteen from East Anglia plus Ruddles County Ale from Rutland and one special guest beer from Germany. The beer list was deliberately designed to mainly showcase beers that came from within easy striking distance of Cambridge so punters could find them again. The foreign guest was a cask of beer from Schumacher Brauerei, the famous Altbier producer in Düsseldorf, which had been brought over specially thanks to the branch chair Alan Hill's German work connections. Alan had driven all the way from Düsseldorf back to the Corn Exchange with the 25-gallon cask of beer strapped into the passenger seat of his car, making his wife sit in the back. They turned the tap on the first night and it wasn't turned off until the cask was empty.

The organising committee had to personally guarantee payment for the beer as the branch had no credit history. The event was more popular than they could have ever dreamed. They ran out of beer at the end of the first day and had to scramble to get more in overnight. Charles Wells had already sent two drays for the festival, but still dropped everything to send a third with a further 25 firkins ready for the second day. Greene King were also local and dropped off more beer at short notice. Already the local CAMRA committee were building a good relationship with these brewers, at least good enough to assure them that the beer would be looked after and their bills would be paid. To begin with they had intended to run the festival with just six people, but it was soon apparent that this was not enough and any unsuspecting CAMRA member who walked through the door was quickly strong-armed into working behind a bar.

For the first couple of festivals most breweries wouldn't deliver the beer in one-off drops a few days before the festival began. Also, the local council wouldn't let them store beer in the Corn Exchange in advance of their booking. This huge storage issue was solved by the friend of a friend who worked at the Barclays Bank on Market Square. He arranged for some of the beer to be stored in the bank vaults to keep it cool. The story goes that the branch was so generous in their gratitude to the bank staff that distressed bank managers had to send word asking for their team to be returned safely from extended lunch breaks.

As a venue, the Corn Exchange itself was a perfect choice as the high cathedral-like nave was built to allow air to circulate, thus preventing the concentrated corn dust from igniting. Even in July, the combination of the draught through the space and thick walls proved ideal for keeping beer cool.

A friend of organiser John Bishopp, George Abbott, ran a travel agency around the corner but kept sneaking in to help out with the festival. At one point he arrived simmering in anger because the press had run an article about the 'Abbott and the Bishopp' running a beer festival. George's cover had been blown and his wife had found out where he'd been sneaking off to that week.

Tony Millns was the beer manager at the early Cambridge festivals, and instituted a customer-friendly policy that if anyone didn't like a beer they could exchange it for something of similar value. One evening a bar volunteer let him know that he had exchanged a pint because the customer complained it smelled funny. Tony took a sniff and confirmed he'd done the right thing. However, when he poured a measure of the same beer, there was no smell. He checked it with a few colleagues, then wondered if something was contaminating the glasses, but couldn't find anything. Meanwhile, the customer had cause for complaint again with his next pint, and once more with his third. Tony decided it was time to get involved personally to solve the mystery. The young man passed Tony his glass: same as before, a few mouthfuls taken out of it and a strange smell. Then it twigged. Tony asked the chap to lean in towards him and sniffed his cheek. He had put on about a gallon of aftershave, so each time he got a third of a way down a glass of beer, all he could smell was his own aftershave. When this was explained his friends roared with laughter.

Chris Bruton and John Bishopp wrote up the formula they used to run the festival and gave it to CAMRA headquarters.

By luck more than design they had effectively hit upon the template that has been used for beer festivals ever since. The relationships they had built with head brewers and brewery directors were to pay dividends when the Cambridge committee were drafted in to organise CAMRA's first national festival at Covent Garden the next year.

> We generally reckoned that running a good festival and providing a wide range of interesting beer was the best and subtlest form of campaigning, so we tried not to beat people over the head with heavy messaging.
>
> We got a very wide range of drinkers, and one evening leaving the hall were two blokes, both dressed in black leather with assorted piercings and safety-pins etc (Cambridge was a bit ahead of the curve on that sort of thing), and I overheard the one with a purple Mohican say to the one with a green Mohican, "I've had three pints of that Robinson's Old Tom – tastes like Coca-Cola but takes your fucking head off." Well, I thought, if we can achieve that sort of broad appeal, we're going to change the country's drinking habits.
>
> *Tony Millns*

The first national CAMRA beer festival

> I think that creating a mass movement of 200,000 people who are enthusiastic about a product is a great thing. They did that mostly by creating the phenomenon of the beer festival. They are two a penny now, but only because of CAMRA.
>
> *Steve Thatcher, CAMRA member*

In 1975 John Bishopp organised a trip for CAMRA members to the Oktoberfest in Munich. This initiative was enough to raise his profile and eventually be elected to the National Executive. He then invited his fellow NE members to bring their branches along to the Cambridge Beer Festival, and that was enough to convince them he should organise the first ever national festival in September that year. Everything had been arranged to take place at one of the old warehouses in St Katharine's Dock in East London, but at the last minute the fire officer stepped in and they realised it would be too expensive to install the fire curtains that were required, so a new venue had to be found.

It was only because Covent Garden was being partly demolished and therefore in the news at the time that they thought of using it. The wider refurbishment project had left the old floral market empty. It was not in a great state, but was sufficient to hold a festival and the Greater London Council let them use the space rent free. The cast iron flower stalls were still intact and worked excellently as beer stillage. Member Peter G. Scott remembers attending the festival and seeing a lone water tap at the end of one of the stalls with a handwritten chalkboard above: 'WATNEYS ON DRAUGHT'.

Alongside John Bishopp, the organising team included Chris Bruton on administration, Mike Nutt as cellarman, Christian Muteau organising the stalls and Dennis Palmer on staffing. Gill Keay remembers being put on duty looking after the food offering – bread, cheese and pork pies. Shark Enterprises under Herrick Spraggot did everything else. Herrick organised the refurbishment of the disused space, including building toilets and organising new wiring.

Because of the last minute change of venue, they hadn't procured a license for the event. Fortunately, Chris Bruton had a good relationship with the Fuller's directors, who stepped in and offered to take the licence. They were in court at 10.30am when the event opened at midday. Fuller's also generously provided thousands of plastic glasses when all the branded glasses ran out. The brewery was quick to see the benefits of supporting CAMRA, despite receiving a lot of criticism from them at the time because many of their pubs weren't selling real ale.

The event was a runaway success. The longest queue was recorded at a quarter of a mile long. The sergeant of the Metropolitan Police stopped by to see whether he needed to pull the plug on the event because of the vast crowds. There were just over 100 UK breweries in existence at that point and thirty of them were present at Covent Garden, supplying around two beers each. This was quite possibly the largest number of British beers that had ever been together in one place before. The festival was also the reason that the first dray from Brains brewery ever crossed the Severn Bridge and entered England. Other breweries travelling from geographical extremes included a large van from Belhaven brewery and the Laird of Traquair House bringing his bottled beer down from the Scottish borders.

Chris Holmes, who was to become National Chairman the next year, remembers signing up Sir Kingsley Amis, the English novelist, as a CAMRA member at the festival. The novel new event attracted a number of celebrity visitors to its central London location.

One of the most infamous incidents at the event happened on the day before the festival opened. John Bishopp had been working in the south of London that day and came back to help with the festival set up. There was an office allocated on Henrietta Street so he left his briefcase there and joined the crew. After finishing in the flower market they headed to the Young's pub across the road for a well-deserved pint. Gill Keay went to lock up the office and agreed to bring John's briefcase across for him.

A little while later, someone came into the pub saying everything was closed down because of a bomb scare. John suddenly remembered his briefcase and dashed to Bow Street Police Station. Gill had put the suitcase down while she locked the office door and then completely forgotten about it as she walked away. As this was at the time of a major bombing campaign by the IRA, the unattended briefcase had soon aroused suspicion. The police told John that it was only the 'Covent Garden is alive with Real Ale' sticker on the front that prevented them from destroying the case on the spot. In fact, the unfortunate incident paid back in dividends as not only were Bow Street very good about the whole affair, but they then kept a professional eye on the smooth running of the rest of the event. The organising committee were happy to look the other way when an off-duty police officer flashed a warrant card to jump the queue. Even off duty they were very handy to have around on the one or two occasions that some of the punters got a little rambunctious.

The first Great British Beer Festival

> It was the star of beer festivals in my opinion. It was such a great event for the public and for CAMRA and for the people who worked there. It was such good fun. We sold a lot of beer and introduced a lot of people to real ale.
>
> *DAVE MCKERCHAR, former NE member*

After the success of the first national festival at Covent Garden, the very first Great British Beer Festival was organised in 1977. James Lynch chaired the committee that ran the festival. He was hugely grateful to be invited by the Greater London Council to run a Queen's Silver Jubilee beer festival in June 1977 at the Alexandra Palace beforehand. This gave them the opportunity of a dry run at the venue before they held CAMRA's event. The Jubilee event was two days long and 50,000 pints were served, while the GBBF was five days long with three times the amount of beer served. Beer writer Matthew Curtis sees GBBF as CAMRA's greatest success, setting the playbook for the large format beer festival.

The first GBBF was opened by Monty Python member and Penrhos brewery co-founder Terry Jones pouring six pints of beer over his head, saying, 'beer tasting should be different from wine tasting. You can tell real ale by the way it dripped over your shoulders and ran down into your boots.' He then had to repeat the stunt for the assembled press photographers, who had apparently missed it the first time round. A lifelong beer lover, Terry wrote a contribution for the 2003 *Good Beer Guide* entitled 'My Love Affair with Beer'. The 'Monty' of Monty Python also has a beer connection, as the name came from a regular at

Eric Idle's Worcestershire local. Eric had wanted a name that represented the quintessential British drunkard.

John Bishopp owns the only branded glass made for the first GBBF at Alexandra Palace, because the company producing them was hit by a strike and beyond the sample glass they never completed the order. Commemorative glasses for the Silver Jubilee celebration organised by CAMRA earlier that year do exist, however, and feature the CAMRA logo.

GBBF was held at the Ally Pally for four years in total, the last (1980) being held in tents outside as large parts of the venue had been destroyed in a fire. By 1979 the event, opened by TV personality and botanist David Bellamy, attracted well over 80,000 visitors who between them sank a quarter of a million pints.

The Great British Beer Festival tradition

From these ambitious beginnings the tradition of large-scale beer festivals grew. The Great British Beer Festival has run continuously except for two years: in 1984 the venue, Bingley Hall in Birmingham, burned down, and in 2020 the Covid-19 pandemic lockdown caused the cancellation, with the festival being replaced with a virtual event.

Writer Adrian Tierney-Jones thinks that the appeal of the GBBF is that it's The *British Beer* Festival, not The *Real Ale* festival, so the general public find it to be more welcoming, easier to understand and more inclusive. British Beer Writer of the Year 2019 Jonny Garrett first got interested in beer at the 2010 GBBF. He loved trying all of the different styles and breweries and enjoyed the incredible size and variety of the beer scene that was laid out before him. It inspired him to start reading beer blogs and books to find out more after the event. CAMRA continued to play a role in Jonny's ale education, through *BEER* magazine and the GBG as well as reading the seminal works of CAMRA great, Roger Protz.

Even though I no longer drink, I still believe in what CAMRA stands for. Also, it's fun. I've made a lot of friends over the years, and the Festival is like a family outing and reunion rolled into one. Nobody writes over the year but when we walk into the hall it's hugs and handshakes all round.

Pre-festival feature interviewing diabetic member
BOB WATERS, WB March 2002

The planning for each festival starts more than a year in advance with a very committed team of volunteers at the helm. Current festival organiser, Catherine Tonry, is the main point of contact with the venue in the lead up to the event. There were 1,100 volunteers working over thirteen days at the 2019 festival. Volunteers enjoy a range of perks in exchange for their committed graft, like a free staff bar, help with accommodation costs and a subsidised staff canteen, but the main draw for most is the camaraderie. The core group of people who volunteer for the full week of the festival, some four or five hundred people, are a close-knit family.

In *What's Brewing*, Ted Bruning called volunteering at the festival 'the ultimate activity holiday'. Marc Holmes organised the festival for an astonishing eleven years from 2002 while raising a young family. Some people have, quite incredibly, volunteered at every single GBBF: they are Sara Hicks, Arthur Cruttendon, Roger Mayhew, Bob Waters and Richard Larkin.

The great hall of Alexandra Palace burning down in July 1980 allowed festival organisers to put on a bigger and better event than had originally been planned. The blitz spirit of organiser Pat O'Neill and his team shone through to bring an area of 70,000 square feet (one and a half football pitches) under canvas – this included two beer tents and an entertainment tent, all interconnected. Including the outdoor seating, the festival was nearly 50% bigger than had been originally planned. The 300-beer line-up the largest ever assembled on one site in Britain. One tent was air conditioned while the rest of the casks were kept cool with lumps of ice and damp sacking in the other. This festival was opened by the Kegbuster himself, illustrator Bill Tidy.

The fire also gave as good a reason as any to try a new festival location and so the 1981 GBBF was moved to Queens Hall in Leeds. Leeds local Denny Cornell-Howarth is a familiar face at the Great British Beer Festival and her long career as a volunteer started thanks to this move:

> I was a bit of a punk in those days. I was on the Tube train in London going up to King's Road just to see what was going on and I spotted a fly poster in the Tube that said "Beer festival at Alexandra Palace". I thought, that looks like more fun than shopping, so I got on the relevant Tube and got to Alexandra Palace. I wandered into this big tent, because that was the year that Alexandra Palace burned down and found lots and lots of people and all these barrels, wooden things and I thought, this looks good! I'll enjoy this. *DENNY CORNELL-HOWARTH*

The following year, when Denny found out the festival was coming to her home city, she decided to get involved – and stayed involved. Denny volunteered at thirty-seven GBBFs in total, giving up two weeks of annual leave for the cause every year until 2017. When she worked as a publican her fellow branch members thought she was mad for going on holiday for two weeks – to work behind a bar!

Denny remembers the Leeds CAMRA branch planning the 1981 festival in the front room of the Pack Horse and deciding they needed to put posters out around town. She volunteered to do this job as she had a 650cc Suzuki with waterproof panniers, like toilet cisterns with a lift off lid. So out she duly went with her boyfriend of the time, one pannier filled with posters and the other filled with wallpaper paste. Denny remembers:

> [we] drove around Leeds in the dead of night, fly posting everywhere for CAMRA. Probably in the region of 800 posters, so it was quite a bit of work. I think my proudest one was in the centre of Leeds. There was a very nice statue, because Leeds

was twinned with Dortmund which was a brewing town in Germany, and they have a lovely picture of a man with a great big beer barrel [The Dortmund Drayman]. I posted a poster right on the front of his beer barrel. And I was quite pleased with that.

DENNY CORNELL-HOWARTH

CAMRA member Colin Keegan also got involved with that first GBBF outside of London because he was a Leeds local. He remembers the new location causing a big problem:

The brewers south of Nottingham all refused to deliver over that distance, and you can't have a GBBF without the classic ales from the likes of Fuller's, Youngs, Sheps, Adnams, Brains, Hook Norton, and Wadworths. Barrie Pepper [by that point a former National Executive member] knew I was working as a transport manager and could drive a lorry, so I was asked nicely if I would go around the country to collect casks from twenty-four breweries. This was an offer not to be refused, and the late night planning commenced! It took six days to collect, and the same to take the empties back again, a different crew for each leg.

COLIN KEEGAN

The first year in Leeds was a qualified success as it was the first time an event of this nature and scale had been held in the north of the country, and after that it became a complete sell out. Colin was enlisted to drive again:

This time the return trip was crewed by my then-fiancée Teresa. After four nights sleeping in the cab, we arrived at Alma Road one evening, with hopes of finding more comfortable accom-modation. Apart from a bathroom there were no facilities there, so poor Iain Dobson received a piece of Mrs K's mind. We were quickly found a room in a nearby B&B, treated to lasagne at a local restaurant, and Iain lived to tell the tale.

COLIN KEEGAN

The national festival returned to London in 1991, where it has remained ever since. The Great British Beer Festival Winter, however, has been held in a number of locations since its inception in 1997. First held as the National Winter Ales Festival it was rebadged in 2018 and is typically held in the North or Midlands to allow members from around the country to access a national festival.

> You look round and think "I hope someone's got some photos because we're going to be proud of this." I enjoy the actual physical effort. And I enjoy it even more when it's finished and I can put me feet up.
>
> *MARK PARKES, GBBF Winter Festival Organiser*

The GBBF temporary community has built up its own traditions over the years. Denny was honoured to be the recipient of the Christian Muteau Award, an annual prize given to a volunteer who has made an amazing difference. Denny's was given in recognition of her work as bar manager, taster, beer orderer, technical manager, trainer, logistics team and more over four decades. You name it, Denny has done it – providing the role was directly involved with being hands on with the beer that she loved.

Her award was named in memory of Christian Muteau who was a larger-than-life GBBF volunteer. He is fondly remembered as the voice of the tannoy for many years. As well as volunteering on the door at beer festivals across the country, he was also a tireless worker for charities like Macmillan Cancer Relief.

Referred to in more than one *What's Brewing* as Christian 'Whoops, I've split my jeans' Muteau, he sadly passed away, aged 62, in 2001.

Another much-loved tradition for the GBBF team is Mick Slaughter's Monday night walking tour (or historical pub crawl, depending on who you ask). Each year he produces a handout of the local pubs so that volunteers can join him on the tour or go on their own at a more convenient time. This is a great opportunity for volunteers to get to know each other (or catch up) before the festival begins.

*　　*　　*

A particular strength of the GBBF is the Bière Sans Frontières international beer bar which provides easy access to beers from around the world. This has been a feature of the GBBF for over thirty years and has now expanded so much that it physically takes up four bars and includes both casks and bottles. The explosion of microbreweries around the world can very much be thanked for this growth, and no doubt this huge range of hard-to-find styles and types of beers being brought together under one roof gives an extra draw for brewers and specialists to visit the festival alongside the public. Rumour has it that a secret party arranges an exchange of a shipping container of beer with the Great American Beer Festival each year, ensuring that an unmatched selection of hard-to-find American beers grace each GBBF.

Jonathan Kemp is a current member of the National Executive who has spent a huge amount of time looking after the international beers at both GBBF and his local festival in Glasgow. He thinks these bars are fantastic for letting people try beers of different styles from brewers and countries that they wouldn't necessarily see in their local pub. For Jonathan the most important factor for serving these beers in the best possible condition is time. The beers need to settle, but you only have four days of preparation time at the biggest festivals, and much less at the smaller ones.

On the whole, these issues are dealt with finesse. Jaw Brew, now considered one of the best craft breweries in Scotland, chose to launch their business at the Glasgow Festival in 2014. This was the first time they showed their beers in public and a clear vote of confidence of the quality and condition of the beers shown there.

Husband and wife team Bagsy and Sarah Durham looked after the beer order at the GBBF for nearly twenty years until 2018. Recommended beers were ordered and then split geographically over the festival bars. They would get in touch with each brewery to get the details of where the beers could be sourced. Their responsibility would also include ordering the beers for the judging of the Champion Beer of Britain competition which takes place at the festival. Before email became common currency, the Durhams had a fax machine and 'would come home from work to find the whole of the floor of the living room completely covered in paper on the day that the post had arrived with the orders.' Once the planning was done, they also looked after stock control on site, controlling deliveries, marking up beers, moving them to the stillage and counting the empty casks out again.

As the festival, and therefore the beer order, got bigger and bigger, it stopped being a one-person job. Now the beer ordering, writing the beer descriptions and onsite stock control are all managed by separate people. Oversight of the casks, bottles, ciders and perries and international beers are also managed by separate volunteers.

Sarah remembers plenty of times when the ordering process could try the patience of a saint. Casks could blow their keystones and spray beer all over the inside of the van they came in. Or they would arrive safely, only to then fall out of the lorry and explode. On one occasion the access to the delivery bay was blocked by an illicitly parked car. It was so disruptive that Sarah had to seek Olympia's permission to remove the offending vehicle to a more suitable parking place. Forklift trucks are integral to the logistics of the GBBF, but this was the only time one was used for parking enforcement.

Visitors to the GBBF tend to be only about 20% CAMRA members, which provides a great campaigning opportunity and differentiates GBBF from the local festivals, which tend to be much more heavily visited by members. It is a national event with size and budget to match, which gives the organisers the chance to innovate. From 2006, 'nips' – one-third of a pint serves – were offered at the GBBF in addition to the standard half-pint and pint measures. So not only is CAMRA thought to be responsible for the introduction of the oversized lined glass, but it can also claim to have resurrected an almost forgotten serving size.

CAMRA fundraising

Fundraising has been an important part of CAMRA's work since the beginning, to allow it to keep moving forward. Even the very first edition of *What's Brewing* mentioned a raffle. There have been campaigns under many guises and names, like the exciting sounding 'Fighting Fund', but one of the most interesting and longest running fundraising endeavours is the Games and Collectibles Committee, which started life as CAMRA Fundraising (or FUN-raising – geddit?). Formed in 1985, they aimed to raise money through entertainments at festivals. Beer festivals were seen as quite limited, being solely vertical drinking experiences, so more diverse activities helped to keep the clientele entertained for longer, for a modest sum.

John Cryne has been involved on and off with the committee ever since its formation in 1985. He remembers the founding meeting at the Fleur des Lys in Bedford with Andy Shaw, Mick Slaughter, Christine Cryne and Mike Bennion. The committee looks after tombolas and auctions as well as pub games and collectibles stalls at beer festivals around the country, including the wide selection on offer at the Great British Beer Festival. They also organise the National Breweriana Auction annually. Branches are supported by the committee purchasing copies of their locally produced pub guides to use as prizes on tombolas. This can help with the branch's overall publication costs by increasing the size of the print run.

The infamous 'Every 1's a Winner' tombola was the brainchild of Mick Slaughter. It debuted at the Bedford beer festival in 1981. Mick had cut his tombola teeth at church events and had worked out the odds for picking a ticket with a 1 in the number as 5.64 to 1. As the tickets are five for £1 it means everybody who enters stands a very good chance of winning. The sound of the bell ringing when there's a winner, or shouts of 'and another winner on the tombola', are now familiar to beer festival goers across the country. So famous is this catchphrase, people regularly shout it at Mick when he walks into a pub.

The committee scaled up the tombola so that it could be used at other festivals without relying on Mick running it, and then the same principle was applied to other pub games that could be adapted for festivals. All of this work was formalised around the turn of millennium when Mick worked with Pete Giles from the East London and City branch to write up proper rules for each game. They ensured that each was an attractive game to participate in and, most importantly, to make sure people won regularly. This last criteria made happy staff as well as happy customers, and so raising money from the activity took care of itself.

Each time a new games idea was developed it would be trialled at a festival to test the rules and functionality. Then the team created blackboards with the rules on and built a stock of the resources needed to play the games. These are kept in a St Albans warehouse along with all of the other resources that branches are able to borrow to help run their beer festival.

Some games are extremely rare outside of CAMRA festivals: only in Lewes, East Sussex, will you find 'toad in the hole' where brass 'toads' are thrown at a hole in the table for example. There is just one league in existence with twenty-one teams at the time of writing. Similarly, 'Caves' in Suffolk has only ever been recorded in one pub. It is a type of indoor quoits that was invented and patented by the landlord of the Black Boy in Bury St Edmunds in 1930. The Games and Collectibles committee have given new life to dying pub games, and thereby have, incidentally, helped to preserve an important aspect of pub heritage.

Those running the games need to obtain a certain number of items to use as prizes. These are usually donated brewery and pub memorabilia. Once this practice was established it became clear that some people actually just wanted to buy specific items from specific breweries, rather than just winning them ad hoc. This led to breweriana stalls being set up at festivals alongside the games. Eventually, the most valuable items were taken off sale and put up for people to bid on instead, and this has turned into the National Breweriana Auction, which is held each year in October, usually in Burton upon Trent.

The Games and Collectables Committee's recorded profits, plus the donations made by branches for the supply of the pub games, has amounted to more than £1.2 million since 1985.

Beer tickers

> It's no coincidence that there is a big overlap between CAMRA members and trainspotters.
> *PETE BROWN, Chair of the British Guild of Beer Writers*

Although not necessarily a strictly CAMRA phenomenon, no beer festival is complete without its own beer tickers. These are hardy souls who 'collect' beers. Originally they would record the beers they had tried with a tick in their copy of the *Good Beer Guide*, with the ambition of ticking them all off.

Nowadays the *Good Beer Guide* isn't necessarily involved and many tickers just want to try any new beer they can find. Ticking, also known as beer scooping, demands that at least a half pint of each beer is imbibed to gain the sought-after tick, although newer tickers, including those adopting the hobby in the United States, see even a mouthful as sufficient to deem a beer as ticked.

Some enthusiasts, known as 'Bottlers', collect small quantities of beer to sample later or share with fellow collectors – getting their nickname from the bottles that they carry to decant the beers into. In urban folklore Bottlers are said to specifically use 'Panda Pops' bottles, the miniature tuck shop favourite. However, that particular soft drinks brand folded in 2011 so contemporary Bottlers must be using an alternative.

Arguably the first ticker – or at least the spiritual father of the tickers – is Andrew Cunningham. The record keeping of his quest to drink a pint from every brewery in the country became the foundation of the original *Good Beer Guide* in 1972.

One of the great legends of the ticking game was Mick 'The Tick' Baker, who had begun ticking when his wife, Betty, bought him a copy of the 1975 *Good Beer Guide*. As there were fewer than 100 breweries in the country at the time, he could only notch up around forty ticks (different beers) in a year, but as the number of breweries increased and Mick reached his ticking peak he was able to reach over 2,000 annually. Mick was the first person to reach 10,000 recorded ticks – the gold standard amongst hobbyists. He certainly amassed more than 35,000 all told as Church End brewery created a Mick The Tick beer to celebrate the achievement in 2009. Sadly, Mick passed away, aged 79, in 2017.

Mick wasn't the only ticker to enjoy the notoriety of ticking off his own eponymous beer. Super-ticker Tara Johnson's 5,000th real ale was her own 4.6% ABV special ale, TJ's 5K, which she brewed with John Eastwood of the Barge & Barrel in Elland.

It is notable in the press and on social media that people can be derisive or indeed downright rude about tickers, which seems odd for such a benign hobby. However, when they were made the subject of a short film by Sheffield-based independent filmmaker Phil Parkin in 2009 they were much more sympathetically treated. *Beer Tickers: Beyond the Ale* showed the public some truly endearing characters in the ticker community.

Michael Hardman admits he wasn't a natural empath to the first tickers he met: 'I was amazed to meet, in the early days, people who had no other interests than beer. Delighted to find people with such enthusiasm but I just wondered what they did with the rest of their lives.'

*   *   *

> It's gone beyond a hobby now. It's kind of a way of life.
>
> *Si EVERITT, Completist*

Another set of dedicated collectors are the Completists. Rather than collecting beers, they aim to tick off the pubs in the *Good Beer Guide* by having a pint in each one, or at least to visit every new pub that appears in a particular edition. Si Everitt is an example of the latter. He started his quest on 5 April 2014 and had steadfastly worked towards his goal until his unbroken pub visiting streak was ended in April 2020 due to the Covid-19 outbreak. He returned to his endeavours as quickly as the lockdowns have allowed.

Si enjoyed going to see Hull City play and experiencing different towns and people at away games, particularly visiting pubs before a match. He wondered how to recreate this experience more regularly, which led him to the *Good Beer Guide*. As well as finding great pubs, he thought it would be a brilliant way to explore new parts of the UK. He joined CAMRA in 2014 when he started his mission. He thought it was only right to become a member since it was their book he was using.

There are around 4,500 pubs in the current guide and at the time of writing Si is working his way up to 1,800 of them. However, over the years he has notched up a gross total of over 3,000 pub visits – that means over 1,000 that are no longer in the guide, predominantly due to closure rather than issues of quality. He prefers to take his trips alone so that he is 'master of his own destiny'. When he takes friends, they inevitably want to mess about with second drinks or meals in the pubs, but Si needs to maintain strict discipline to stay on schedule and fit in all the pubs he has planned. He sometimes takes his dad, or meets up with fellow Completists, who are more sympathetic to what he is trying to achieve.

Some older Completists are up to about 90% completion, with three or four hundred pubs left to do. Of course, with each new guide the goal posts change, but Si is at around 38% and feels that one day he will hit 100%. His lifetime aim is to get it finished. He keeps a database with every pub listed and his date of visit, as well as a list of pre-emptive pubs that are new or have been recommended so that he can tick them off if they crop up in the Guide. Friends and family think it's a bit of a crazy hobby, but as it is what he enjoys doing he feels like it's a worthwhile use of his time. There are definitely worse hobbies.

REAL CIDER AND PERRY CAMPAIGNING

Had it not been for CAMRA having perry at beer festivals on the cider bar, I would claim that perry might have disappeared by now. *MICK LEWIS, founder member of the APPLE committee*

Before CAMRA took real cider formally under its wing it could only be found in thirty or so pubs in the whole country, and the majority of perry was sold at the producer's own premises. However, support for the cause of real cider and perry started early in the Campaign's history. Jon Hallam, current chair of Gwent branch, says the first CAMRA event with cider he attended was in 1975. Iain Loe recalls the motion being put to conference that CAMRA should campaign for cider came from the Hertfordshire branch and was also passed in 1975.

Dick Budgen convinced the Great British Beer Festival Working Party to establish a separate cider and perry bar at the Bingley Hall, Birmingham festival in 1983 with himself at the helm as cider bar manager. Despite all of this activity, it wasn't until 1988 that the Apple and Pear Produce Liaison Executive (the APPLE committee) was formed, to clean up how cider and perry was offered for sale at festivals and promote it as an alternative drink to be sold in pints in pubs.

Most festivals didn't have a separate cider and perry bar, they just had the odd polycask shoved on the beer bar. Sometimes names for the ciders and perries were made up for comic effect by the bar staff. Neither practice gave cider and perry a positive image. Mick Lewis proposed the motion of starting a national cider committee at the 1987 AGM. He says he saw APPLE as the Militant Tendency of CAMRA – reflecting the eighties political group 'because they said what they thought and did what they wanted to do to campaign and didn't wait for permission from above,' and the APPLE committee formed with Mick as secretary. One of its first actions was creating a definition of real cider.

For Andrea Briers, the current Regional Director for East Anglia, one of APPLE's main successes was the introduction and acceptance of bag-in-box for serving real cider. Bag-in-box cider comes in a range of sizes and prevents the cider from being adversely affected through contact with oxygen. Having to sell the product quickly had been a real barrier to publicans taking it on previously. Polycasks would begin to oxidise as soon as they were vented and the empty vessels had to be returned to the producer, no matter where they were located. These are the same issues as experienced with real ale, so it's interesting that bag-in-box has gained acceptance more readily in some quarters for cider and perry, although only for cold-filled bag-in-box, not hot-filled, pasteurised ones.

CAMRA has focused on getting the public to understand the products. 'CAMRA have introduced good beer, good cider and good perry to a population that wouldn't have otherwise known it existed,' says Dave Matthews, who founded the Welsh Perry and Cider Society. Dave thinks that CAMRA's influence has been particularly important in parts of the country where there isn't an established tradition of real cider making or fruit growing as these are the areas where the public benefit most from education about cider and perry. Campaigning methods have included holding dedicated cider bars at beer festivals, the launch of Cider and Perry Month in 2003 and the introduction of Cider Pub of the Year in 2005. A 'Real Cider sold here' sticker for pubs and venues was developed and introduced in 2009. Information collected by members about pubs that sell cider and perry has also been integrated into the WhatPub website.

Raising awareness and supporting cider producers is important because making orchards financially sustainable is difficult. Around the country, orchards are being grubbed up to make way for more profitable land use. Perry in particular was under threat because it is not especially easy to make and had been lost from the public awareness. However, both drinks are very interesting, says festival cider bar manager Chris Rouse, because they are a natural product. Every year the apples and pears in each harvest are different, thanks to the vagaries of nature, so there is always something new to look forward to.

Technical debates rage about the definition of real cider and perry, just as the definition of craft beer continues to occupy ale lovers: the need for full juice, or at least a high juice content being a perennial point for discussion, along with quarrels over the acceptability of the use of pasteurisation and the addition of fruit, spices and herbs. But at least now CAMRA members are talking about cider, and more importantly, customers are choosing to buy it.

*   *   *

At festivals, cider bars are fabled to have been the first to offer free tastes to a public who did not know what they were buying. In the last year or two, the introduction of learn and discover zones at festivals, and increased freely-accessible content online, detailing how cider is made and the differences in apple and pear varieties has been pivotal according to Chris Rouse: 'The public are interested in the provenance of what they are drinking and it's a question of being able to attract them to a situation where you can educate them. That's the beauty of the learning zones. They are staffed by people who have the time to explain.'

For Chris, this is what a cider festival can offer that a pub can't – passionate experts are on hand. Often cider makers will volunteer on the bars at festivals to share their knowledge, while pubs necessarily function as a business so education isn't their primary purpose.

Since CAMRA first began officially campaigning for cider and perry, there have been three national cider and perry exhibitions held in London. Making these a success was a real achievement. Because the public was so poorly informed about what real cider was, getting people enthusiastic about attending was difficult and venue hire costs eventually proved prohibitive for these relatively niche events. At the first festival in 1988 there were roughly sixty producers from the east and west of the country, which were the traditional cider and perry making areas, as well as the single producer that had survived the twentieth century contraction of the industry in Wales.

Sara Hicks recalls volunteering at the Great Welsh Beer and Cider Festival and a customer asked for the driest cider. As products had been graded 1–12 (with 1 being dry), she was able to recommend one easily. Sometime later the customer returned to the bar and thanked Sara for getting it spot on: he was a diabetic and the cider had made no difference to his blood sugar whatsoever!

*   *   *

The National Cider and Perry Championships have been held at the Reading Beer & Cider Festival for about fifteen years, having previously been hosted in Stockport and London. Chris Rouse has been running the Reading competition for around twelve years, coordinating the regional competitions via Regional Cider Coordinators who submit the winners for the national championships at Reading. Samples are anonymised for the regional panels so they don't know what they are judging and the panels are composed of members of the public, very often CAMRA members. The finals are conducted by invited specialist judges.

For Chris the best part of being involved with the championships is when a cider maker you know and think is good gets through to the finals or even into the top three. When East Anglia's Pickled Pig was awarded the bronze placing in the 2010 competition for their Porker's Snout it was the first time since

Chris had been running the competition that an East Anglian cider had achieved a national placing. He describes it as a 'joyous moment', not least because many people see cider as a West Country product and that region has often dominated the awards. Cider is made all over the country, and the Pickled Pig win was special as it opened people's eyes to Eastern style cider.

As well as this annual competition, the Pomona Award was established in 1998. It is not awarded annually, only when a deserving recipient is identified that has made an exceptional contribution to furthering the cause of real cider and perry. Back in 2004 it was won by cider and perry producer Seidr Dai, run by Fiona and Dave Matthews, who said that winning gave their business a real competitive advantage and motivation for them as cider makers. For a fledgling organisation it was a huge benefit to them.

One of the highlights of the calendar for campaigners is the annual National Cider Trip. It is a social event, in October, which helps to educate people on how cider is made and gives them the chance to try new things. Andrea Briers remembers that one year they had lunch in a gazebo while a hailstorm took place, and a quick-thinking guest held their glass out for 'cider on ice'. The first trip was organised by the first chair of APPLE, Rick Zaple, supported by Sara Hicks.

There has been a huge resurgence in cider making across the UK thanks to the so-called 'Magners effect'. This was the explosive success of the Magners brand. Relaunched during the hot summer of 2006 with a multi-million pound marketing campaign, their suggestion to serve their bottled ciders over ice put cider firmly front of mind for a whole new generation of young consumers. Real cider producers of all sizes got a kickback in brand awareness and popularity. Although cider sales have since fallen back, some products like low alcohol and fruit flavoured ciders, as well as premium products, continue to see growth.

APPLE was dissolved in the 2019 governance review because cider and perry had finally been specifically included in the

Articles of Association, putting them on an equal footing with all other aspects of the Campaign. The management of cider- and perry-specific issues moved to their respective umbrella committees with an overarching Real Ale, Cider and Perry Campaigns committee overseeing strategic direction. This came into place in January 2020, but wasn't unanimously welcomed as the way cider and perry campaigning should be managed. Time will tell on how effective it is in continuing to give cider and perry drinkers a voice.

CHAMPION BEER OF BRITAIN

A passion for quality has been at the heart of all of CAMRA's activities for half a century. Creating an award to celebrate the very best in beer was a logical embodiment of this interest. The Beer of the Year competition was introduced at the second Great British Beer Festival, held at Alexandra Palace in 1978, and is now known as the Champion Beer of Britain (CBOB). It is one of the longest-running beer competitions in the world, according to Christine Cryne.

Judging for CBOB begins with members voting for their favourite beers. CBOB coordinators work with Regional Directors and the branches to organise these beers into regional judgings. The four winter styles of beers are judged at the GBBF Winter and all of the winners go on to a final judging at the Trade Day of the Great British Beer Festival in August. A panel of carefully selected judges gather to judge the beers blind. They pick winners in each style category and from these they choose one supreme champion – the Champion Beer of Britain – which is announced to the GBBF crowds.

The demand caused by winning CBOB can be truly transformational for a brewery. Elland brewery won with their 1872 Porter in 2013. Director Dickie Bird is rumoured to have slept in the brewery so that production could continue twenty-four hours a day for a couple of months to keep up with demand.

During 1996 a meeting was arranged at the now-closed
Stones brewery in Sheffield. One of the brewing team at
Tetley's, a true gentleman and mentor to me, called Roy Lindsay,
offered to give me a lift. The speaker giving the paper on this
occasion was Dr John Harrison talking about historic beer
styles. He brought a pint of a 9% Victorian stout with him. As I
wasn't driving I had a few of them. At the end of the meeting,
I asked if he had any Christmas beer recipes that I could brew
at the Feast & Firkin. He said he would look into it and send
me his findings. A letter was eventually received with three
historic recipes, including a porter originally brewed a few
weeks before Christmas 1872 at Flowers brewery in
Cheltenham. I showed the letter to my bosses at Allied
suggesting we brew one of the beers at the Feast & Firkin
but they immediately rejected the idea. 'Not commercial.
We couldn't sell it.' Look what they lost!

After being made redundant from the Firkin breweries,
I got the job as brewer at West Yorkshire brewery at Ludden-
denfoot near Halifax. I was by this time living in Keighley.
Eventually I became the owner of the brewery and decided
to translate the porter recipe into a commercial batch. So it
was first brewed at WYB in November 2001, and when I first
tasted [the porter] it gave me goosebumps, which only happens
rarely when beer tasting. The beer proved very popular.

Early in 2002 my brewery merged to form Elland brewery,
originally called Eastwood & Sanders, and the porter, which
was only supposed to be a one-off winter beer, was brewed
again and became a permanent fixture. It has since gone on
to win many awards through local beer festivals with CAMRA:
Champion Beer of Britain 2013; Champion Winter Beer of
Britain 2010 and 2013; Champion Porter of Britain 2009, 2010,
2013 and 2019. Several SIBA awards also followed and my
personal icing on the cake was a gold medal at the International
Brewing awards at Burton upon Trent in 2004. I think I am

the only GBBF staff member to have created a Champion Beer of Britain. When it won in 2013 I had left Elland brewery, but the owners still insisted I had my photo taken with them. A nice touch, which shows the camaraderie of the industry.

I since moved to Kirkstall brewery in Leeds, and as I did at WYB and Elland, had the pleasure of hosting many CAMRA visits, often to be presented with an award. Some of these visits became legendary. The record at Elland was held by Bradford CAMRA who had the longest visit, with the most members falling asleep! This happened frequently when the porter was served and some of my friends had trouble getting home. One gentleman fell asleep on the train and woke up at Darlington, and was always subsequently referred to as 'Intercity Ken'. Another couple of friends woke up at 5am one Sunday morning, still on the train in the depot!

DAVID SANDERS, brewer

When Nottingham's Castle Rock brewery won CBOB in 2010 with Harvest Pale the brewery owner, Chris Holmes, recalls that they couldn't brew it fast enough. It had been introduced by Castle Rock under the name Trammy Dodger, originally to celebrate the launch of Nottingham's new tram network in 2003. The golden, hoppy beer was intended as a one-off brew, but it proved so popular that they changed the name and kept on brewing it. The brewery had already had to ration it, even in their own pubs, when it won Champion Beer of Britain.

This meant they were also already in the process of expanding the brewery. When Bob Jones and Nik Antona waited with Chris in the GBBF press office to present him as the winner to the assembled press, he took a moment to phone the main contractors working on the brewery expansion. He had to give them the bad news in person; that they were opening the brewery on Monday, no matter what it took. Chris estimates that winning CBOB generated an uplift of some 30,000 barrels at the time. A recent survey by Nottingham CAMRA showed that Harvest Pale is still the most widely sold beer in Nottingham, and it remains available around the country.

Winning CBOB can also create a missed opportunity when breweries cannot scale up quickly enough to benefit from the increase in demand. A motion passed at the 2000 AGM prevented breweries from using the award to promote contract-brewed versions of their award-winning beers, in response to smaller winners like Mordue and Coniston having previously done just that. In 2004 Kelham Island's Pale Rider was the winner. They had to have the beer brewed under license to keep up with demand, and to keep within the CAMRA rules they chose to give this beer the hybrid name of Pale Island to prevent any confusion – making it clear that it was their recipe but not brewed at their brewery. This integrity is important as Chris Holmes remarks: 'We [Castle Rock] were extremely lucky. We were actually in the process of building a new brewery and had spent hundreds of thousands ... we were able to take advantage of the massive demand that comes from winning Champion Beer of Britain. Some microbreweries aren't able to service that demand, they haven't got the production facilities. Some have made mistakes and had contract brews of CBOB that haven't worked out for them.'

Tiny Rebel brewery were CBOB winners in 2015 and the uplift in sales was clearly not at the forefront of their mind – not when there was celebrating to be done. They took the trophy around London to drink out of it and celebrate. When it found its way back to be engraved there was a dent or two from its adventures!

The Champion Beer of Britain had perhaps the most impact on its 1986 winner – Batemans brewery. They picked up the prestigious gong for XXXB, their premium bitter, or as they describe it, an English tawny. Batemans was a traditional family brewer which had been so affected by the rise of keg and the decline of the cask market that some of the family were looking to sell their shares and leave the industry. Only George Bateman remained, fighting with his wife, Pat, and children, Jaclyn and Stuart, to raise the funds to buy out their relatives.

Just a few months before the 1986 GBBF, where CBOB was judged, George Bateman had received a standing ovation at the CAMRA AGM in Southampton for his impassioned speech about his quest to find the funds to preserve his family business. He thanked CAMRA members for their 'overwhelming' support and pledged to do whatever he could to support his loyal workforce. Eventually winning CBOB in the August of that year gave the financial boost needed to allow George to buy the shares and keep the brewery in his family. Batemans still refer to CAMRA as their knight in shining armour, saying, 'if it hadn't been for CAMRA we might easily have not been here today.'

This wasn't the first time that CAMRA had given Batemans their support via a seal of approval. The first time Batemans beer was served outside of its home county of Lincolnshire was in the CAMRA-owned Salisbury Arms in Cambridge.

BEER STYLES

> The really singular success of CAMRA is that the choice
> for the consumer today is really quite astonishing.
> *ROGER PROTZ, former editor of* Good Beer Guide

The Champion Beer of Britain and other CAMRA awards are dependent on a structured approach to beer styles. Having clear definitions allows a beer's quality to be objectively judged. The Technical Advisory Group has informed the groupings and definitions of beer styles in their various iterations over the years.

The most important figure in terms of judging and understanding beer styles in modern CAMRA is Christine Cryne, who did a lot of sensory work during her career in the food industry. She helped to bring a more structured approach to the judging of CAMRA's awards. In the mid-eighties, judges would be tasting 30 or 40 samples each and thus saturating their palates.

Christine instigated tasting panels broken up by beer type so that a judge would not have to consider more than nine samples in one session.

Christine led a review of styles that brought together members, brewers and beer writers to scrutinise the beer market and its future trajectory in order to fairly represent the very best beers in Britain. The results of that review were launched in 2020 and now there are 31 beer styles in 12 categories in the CAMRA system.

This was the latest in a line of reviews that take place every decade or so to take account of changes in trends and the marketplace. Brown, red, old ales and strong milds were contracted into one category, for example, as these styles are only made in limited numbers, making individual categories at a competition impractical. Other areas are expanding: the specialist beer category has undergone notable growth and so differently produced beers like lagers, sours, wheat beers, and flavoured beers like fruit or herb/spiced ones, have been separated out into their own categories. A lot of decisions that were made by the review group's assessment of styles were informed by the National Brewery Information System, which collects the information gathered by the Brewery Liaison Officers.

As well as celebrating new developments in beer styles, CAMRA also attempts to resurrect endangered ones. The annual Mild Month campaign is one of CAMRA's longest-running campaigns. Not everyone agrees that mild could, or should, be saved though. Beer blogger Paul Bailey complains that the annual drive for mild is simply 'flogging a dead horse of a beer style that the public don't want, hence why the campaign makes no lasting inroads into broader mild consumption.'

In order to allow the widest possible participation in scoring beers, tasting panels are held across the country. Training members to be a part of branch tasting panels and festival awards judges has been a part of general practice for a number of years now. Christine has helped to expand upon these training opportunities for active members over the past five years.

As a master trainer, she and Beverley Gobbett have created pro-grammes which cover bar and cellar management as well as un-derstanding beer and beer tasting or judging.

LocAle

One of the most successful pieces of beer campaigning initiated by a branch has been the LocAle scheme. It was started in Notting-ham, which had historically had an enviable brewing record in the Midlands.

> Loughborough's pubs were described in an early edition of *What's Brewing* as "Drinking in a Beer Drinker's Paradise". This was because all the Nottingham brewers were represented (Home Ales, Shipstones and Hardy Hansons), all the Burton upon Trent brewers (Marstons, Bass, part of Bass Charrington, and Ind Coope, part of Allied Brewers) and some of the Birmingham breweries (Mitchell & Butlers, part of Bass Charrington, and Ansells, part of Allied Breweries). In no other town or city in the East Midlands was it possible to drink these brewers' beers, especially as real ale.
>
> *Veteran member, RICHARD SANDERS*

But the three breweries within the Nottingham conurbation, Shipstones, Home brewery and Hardy & Hansons, all stopped production in the eighties and nineties. Although Castle Rock started brewing in 1999 and was to become the biggest brewery in Nottinghamshire, all the old family breweries were taken over and then closed.

Hardy & Hansons was bought out by Greene King and the brewery closed. Their beer recipes were brewed in Bury St Edmunds and brought back to Nottingham for sale, leaving the city with no historic breweries at all. When new breweries did begin to appear, they could not get bar space as all the pubs were tied. The situation inspired the Nottingham branch to fight for beers brewed in the area. They introduced the LocAle scheme in

2007, where participating pubs would serve at least one real ale that had been brewed less than twenty miles away. They even coined the term 'beer miles' to tap into the public consciousness for celebrating local produce.

To formalise their action, the branch put a motion to conference that CAMRA would support local ale in principle. This allowed members to reward pubs that served LocAles and supported their local economy by making them stronger candidates for inclusion in the GBG. Over 120 pubs are signed up in Nottingham and the scheme has now been rolled out nationally. The tangible impact on brewing in Nottingham is clear – from no breweries at all, it is now considered one of the top three beer producing areas in the East Midlands. In just two short years, the Nottingham brewery reported a 17% increase in production, despite their beers travelling fewer miles.

Brown glop for old men

Few beers are as iconic as Draught Bass, although it attracts as many derisive detractors as die-hard devotees. It is perhaps surprising to those who do not know the beer world well that some cask ales attain such a huge cult following. Some are former CBOB winners, like Timothy Taylor's Landlord, which has won the accolade four times in total because of its quality (and is, apparently, Madonna's favourite according to a 2003 interview). Bass is arguably so well known mainly because it is so long lived. It certainly cannot taste the same as it would have originally.

The pale ale was the biggest seller from the Bass brewery, which was founded in 1777. Its iconic red triangle logo was the UK's first registered trademark, registered in 1876, and the beer even featured in the late nineteenth-century painting *A Bar at the Folies-Bergère* by French modernist painter Édouard Manet.

Speculation over the ale's future has rarely been far from the pages of *What's Brewing* over the last few decades, thanks to the complex machinations of the macro brewers. Bass Charrington was, of course, one of the Big Six breweries, but they chose to throw their weight behind the marketing of new brands like Caffreys rather than their eponymous ale in the seventies and eighties. This got Draught Bass fans feeling nervous.

Then Bass Charrington's brewing operations were bought out by Interbrew (now Anheuser-Busch InBev) in the year 2000. It was unclear what was going to happen to the much loved brand. In 2002 the government's Competition Commission insisted that certain Interbrew brands were disposed of, but they were able to retain the rights to the historic pale ale.

At one time Draught Bass had been available in most of the 9,000 Bass tied estate pubs. Now there are fewer than 750 places where it is on sale. Naturally, it is most common in its home region of Staffordshire, and can also be found in Derbyshire and Leicestershire.

Draught Bass was celebrated as being 'brought back' in 2018, but it had actually been brewed in Burton under licence by Marstons since 2005. The bottle, keg and export versions are produced in Blackburn at AB InBev's own brewery. It was originally brewed using the age-old Burton Union system of fermentation, but this came to an end in 1981. *What's Brewing* had warned in spring 1980 that the equipment was coming to the end of its working life and would not be economical to replace. Bass assured customers that they could match the Union flavour using conventional open fermenters. The campaign launched a petition for the preservation of the system, but this was unsuccessful, leaving Marston's Pedigree as the last bastion of the system.

Draught Bass may have moved to conventional fermentation, but this did not diminish its popularity, particularly in the Midlands. In 1989 Alan Merryweather of the Black Horse in Aylestone, Leicester, was cutting his teeth as a landlord at the Navigation in Wilmorton in Derby. It was a small pub but a big Bass house. There were two Bass pumps: 'one as flat as your cap' and the other fitted with a tight sparkler. He would sell through at least

36 gallons every week or two. Unfortunately for him, his first day coincided with the *Derby Evening Telegraph* announcing that Bass was putting its prices up by 2p per pint and it took all of his powers of persuasion to convince the disgruntled locals that the price rise wasn't his fault as the new incumbent at the pub.

For natives of Burton upon Trent, like Ash Corbett-Collins, Bass is a symbol of pride in his hometown, and useful as a barometer when visiting a new pub – if they pull a good pint of Bass it bodes well for how they keep the rest of their beers. Current National Chairman Nik Antona is also a Burton local, and describes draught Bass as 'part of the DNA of Burton upon Trent.'

Former *Good Beer Guide* editor Roger Protz is perhaps the most famous and most vocal proponent of this particular ale. He remembers doing early radio interviews and being asked what his favourite beer was. He would always answer Draught Bass without hesitation: 'I loved that sulphury aroma from the Burton water. I loved the way in which it was so beautifully balanced between malt and hops.'

Roger cites the modern American-style beers as being too aggressively hopped and this style becoming more popular so the balance of Bass stands out for him as a measure of its quality. Beer is made from grain and so you should be tasting the malt in there, according to Roger. He's not alone in his opinion. When he wrote a piece about the beer in *What's Brewing* in 2019 he got a huge response from readers and the conversations led to the foundation of National Bass Day on 11 April, although the inaugural 2020 celebration ended up being cancelled because of the Covid-19 lockdown.

As well as the flavour, Roger also gives a nod to the importance of the nostalgia factor: as it is rarer now, many younger people may not even have tried it, and they certainly won't feel the same attachment to it. John Clarke empathises with Roger's nostalgia. He remembers driving around the Potteries in the early nineties surveying pubs for CAMRA's National Inventory of Historic Pub Interiors and finding all sorts of unusual places that served Draught Bass. 'It was fantastic. It had this beautiful, delicate but pronounced hoppiness which complemented everything else about it beautifully. But it was still brewed at the old Bass brewery. That's gone. You just don't get that any more at all. So perhaps my opinion is coloured by my memory of what I know it used to be like, back in the day.' Indeed, John now describes it unabashedly as 'brown glop for old men.'

Midlands journalist Colston Crawford writes, 'the premise for promoting Draught Bass among those of us who love it stems from the fact that this once national brand is now, in promotional terms, virtually ignored by its owners, the drinks giant AB InBev, the Belgium-based "world's largest brewer."' Author Matthew Curtis feels more strongly about this ownership: 'the fetishisation of Draught Bass is dangerous because it's a fetishisation of an AB InBev brand and I don't believe that companies like InBev or Heineken have the interests of real ale at heart.' Matthew also dislikes the sulphur notes that Roger holds so dear as he thinks that they can be too overwhelming in Draught Bass. It remains to be seen whether the 2020 merger of Marston's with Carlsberg is the final nail in the coffin of Draught Bass.

what's brewing

Journal of CAMRA, the Campaign for the
Revitalisation of Ale   JUNE 1972

Voice of the drinking man...

WELCOME to the first issue of the Campaign for the Revitalisation of Ale's own monthly journal, which will keep members fully informed of progress in the fight to improve Britain's beer. It is hoped you will all help to make What's Brewing a lively newspaper by sending in your own news and views.

TOP PUB IS FORCED TO STOP 'FRAUD'

CAMRA has won its first battle against the flashy gimmicks that disguise bad ale.

The battle began when a number of members reported that Draught Bass being sold at Dirty Dick's - one of London's best-known pubs - was pressurised, even though it was apparently being served straight from huge wooden barrels behind the bar.

Two CAMRA officials ...nt along to the pub and heard more than a dozen customers asking for "Draught Bass from the wood". But on tasting the beer, the CAMRA men found it gassy and sweet.

They tackled a barman about the barrels. At first, he insisted that they were genuine, but later admitted that pipes led from the taps, through the hollow barrels and into the cellar where they were connected to a pressurised cask.

CAMRA's Complaints Committee reported the "fraud" to the City of London Weights and Measures Department, asking for prosecution under the Trade Descriptions Act. Inspectors from the Department visited the pub and complained to Finch's, the wine and spirit merchants who own Dirty Dick's.

The company agreed to avoid prosecution by displaying notices pointing out that the ale was pressurised.

Mr R.J. Hearn, a director of Finch's, told What's Brewing: "We were at fault, and I am very grateful to CAMRA for pointing this out. We don't want our products to be misrepresented."

The CAMRA Complaints Committee is now considering similar action against pubs owned by other firms.

STOP PRESS

A TEAM of area organisers has been appointed to increase CAMRA's membership.

CAMRA: 207 Keats Court
Salford 7

CAMRA officials in brewing study

TEAMS of CAMRA offi....... t bitter, according .... the Sunday Mirror, ...d Guinness's Park ....val brewery.
.......AMRA General Secretary Graham Lees said: ...s type of investigation is vital if we ...... to speak with an ....oritative voice on ....uality of ale. ......by examining brew.......from the inside ....understand what ...o to our pint."

The Editor
What's Brewing

2 High Kingsdown
BRISTOL
BS2 8EN
7th December 1975

Dear Sir,

I should like to congratulate you on introducing a Crossword to your splendid journal.

However, may I make two criticisms. Firstly, I deplore the gratuitous use of vulgar words such as "shits" and secondly there was no fucking clue to 24 Across.

Yours sincerely

Alan Redstone

ALAN REDSTONE

What's Brewing, first printed in 1972, was an effective early campaigning tool, but it also embraced a spirit of fun, as seen in this early letter to the editor.

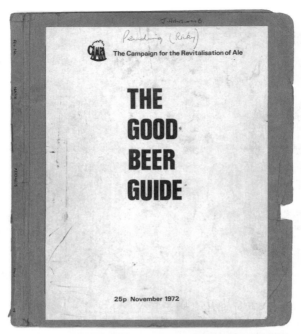

The first *Good Beer Guide* was a loose-leaf affair of eighteen pages released in 1972 and posted out to members.

Photo: John Sturrock

The first Great British Beer Festival in 1977 was opened by Penrhos brewery co-founder Terry Jones pouring six pints of beer over his head. He then had to repeat the stunt for the assembled press photographers, who had apparently missed it the first time round.

TV botanist David Bellamy opening GBBF Alexandra Palace 1979 with National Chairman Joe Goodwin. The next year the festival was held in tents outside as large parts of the venue had been destroyed in a fire.

The Great Hall of the Alexandra Palace, destroyed by fire in 1980 one month before GBBF was due to take place there.

Photo: John Cogill

(L-R) John and Christine Cryne and Mick Hill, returning an empty cask to Timothy Taylor's brewery. Striking up relationships with the breweries was key to getting beer from all parts of the country represented at CAMRA festivals.

Great British Beer Festival veteran Denny Cornell-Howarth has volunteered at 37 GBBFs in total.

The British Guild of Beer Writers visiting the Poperinge Hopmuseum in 1988: Michael Jackson, Ted Bruning, John Simpson, Roger Protz, Ian Golightly, Mike Bennett, Brian Glover, Danny Blyth, Martin Kemp, Tim Webb, Iain Dobson, Martyn Cornell, Tim Clarke and Lynette Arblaster.

CAMRA supported the local community in the campaign to save the
Chesham Arms in Hackney from June 2012 to April 2015.

Photo: Laura Hadland

Beer festivals are a key battleground for cider and perry campaigning. Knowledgeable volunteers are on hand to offer free samples and introduce visitors to products they might not have tried before.

CAMRA's campaigning reach has also stretched into Europe. In 2016 a delegation from CAMRA brought the taxation concerns of small UK cider producers to the EU Commissioner. (L-R) Katie Wiles, Clare Moody MEP, Andrea Briers, EU Commissioner Pierre Moscovici, Anneliese Dodds MEP (with daughter Isabella), Tim Page, and cider-producer Guy Smith.

One of the outcomes of the Revitalisation Project was a focus on the promotion of beer education. Learning and Discovery bars at CAMRA festivals aim to educate drinkers about beer, cider and perry, by offering samples and the opportunity to speak to brewers about how their beer is brewed and the differences in their products.

Brewery Campaigning

TO ensure that members get the very best in beer quality and choice, CAMRA has always gone to source, working to protect and promote local brewers. As well as campaigning against brewery closures they provide advice to brewers on a local level, helping them to reach retailers and wholesalers as well as showcasing their products at beer festivals. Small breweries might bring in local branch members to trial a new beer, while the managing director of a larger brewery could invite the National Executive in to canvas their expert opinion on strategy.

Matthew and Julie Joyce are members of a family that is relatively new to brewing. They took over the Harrogate Brewing Company in 2019 and attach great value to CAMRA's position of influence in the industry and the solid fan base for real ale that they represent. Julie is keen for her brewery to be involved with CAMRA events, festivals and awards because she believes that people recognise the brand and trust their recommendations, in the same way as they would with the Which? consumer organisation.

A short history of modern brewing

Alongside the growth of CAMRA there is a parallel history of microbreweries popping into existence or being re-established on old premises. Traquair House brewery, a part of Scotland's oldest inhabited house, could be seen as the first. The brewery originally dates back to the 1700s, but was rediscovered and brought back into service in 1965. In December 1972, Martin Sykes took over what came to be called the Selby brewery from his uncle. He recommenced sporadic brewing on the nineteenth-century brewery site which had survived being subsumed into the Big Six by acting as a bottling plant for Guinness.

In terms of brand new breweries in new locations, the Miner's Arms in Priddy was probably the first, brewing from 1972. This was closely followed by the self-professed founder of the microbrewery movement, Bill Urquhart, at Litchborough Artisan brewery in Northamptonshire, which started in 1974.

In 1978 James Lynch became the first CAMRA member who had held a National Executive position to start his own brewery, at a time when new breweries could still be counted on the fingers of two hands. While new small breweries like Bourne Valley were starting to blossom, James recalls that the biggest breweries were looking more and more alien to CAMRA members. James visited Courage at Worton Grange with his branch and thought it looked more like a nuclear power station than a brewery. The head brewer was smartly dressed in his chalk-stripe suit with gold watch and chain. In the lounge the barman gave the brewer his 'usual' – a large gin and tonic. That said it all for James. The bigger breweries had been infiltrated by 'non-production people' who were naturally disposed against CAMRA.

While living in Leeds I gained a reputation as a not-bad home brewer, which played a small part in the start of my professional brewing career. Word got out that Allied Domecq was setting up a Firkin Brewpub in Leeds. The reporter was asked if she knew anyone who could brew and my name was mentioned. An interview was arranged for a date during the middle of GBBF 1994 so I had to return to Leeds for it. Fortunately, this was successful and I joined the Firkin brewery covering the Leeds site in August 1994. Hard work and great fun, but dealing with Allied's marketing department, who only thought beer was either lager or bitter, was banging head against the wall time.

The local CAMRA branch was very supportive and helpful, and set up a contest for the best beer on permanently at a Leeds pub. Feast Bitter was the winner in both 1996 and 1997. Allied went to town with the presentation, arranging for the deputy mayor and Allied bigwigs to attend. Special t-shirts were printed but I never told my Allied bosses that only one person had voted (not me) and so I won by the only vote cast. Oops!

Nationally, I thought the Firkin concept was not always liked, with the bad puns and suggestive names, but the beers had a good reputation. Many of the pub convertions worked fine but Allied had a map in their Leeds head office with potential conversions and being the local lad I was called in regularly. They were confused one day when I nearly screamed pointing at the map. They had earmarked the Philharmonic in Liverpool for Firkinisation!!! Can you imagine the outcry if this had gone ahead?

DAVID SANDERS, brewer

With more new breweries and brewpubs being set up, there was a wave of people entering the industry who put the quality of the ingredients above the cost of the beer. The established regional brewers were pleased to help these new businesses. People like James Lynch received help, support and kit from the family brewers when they set up. These family controlled regional breweries are some of the oldest surviving brewery businesses in the UK. Alongside CAMRA they played a vital role in protecting real ale by continuing to brew it. As Geoff Strawbridge puts it, CAMRA 'helped to sustain a market for the beer they liked to brew'. John Clarke describes the family brewers as 'the backbone for the preservation of beer in the UK,' and it's true that if they had all sold up in the 1960s there would be considerably less cask ale in the UK today.

In 1993 the 29 businesses that described themselves as 'the original brewers, intrinsic to the British cultural landscape' set up the Independent Family Brewers of Britain as an association separate from the UK Brewer's Society to highlight their different strengths and different needs. They celebrated with a parade of drays through the City of London before what was by all accounts 'a good lunch' at the Brewer's Hall.

Marc Bishop of St Austell brewery suggests that these days CAMRA members locally are more likely to support smaller, supposedly more interesting, brewers than the family brewers which are often ubiquitous in their home territory and may dominate the choice of beer locally even though they are not widely drunk outside of it.

The new small brewers wanted to have their interests represented, so James Lynch contacted the Brewers Association to enquire about membership for them as commercial brewers. A meeting was arranged in a pub in Wootton Bassett in February 1980. The 25 budding new brewers were grudgingly offered associate membership of the Brewers Association for £50 a year. This would not give them voting rights and they were told that full membership was not available to them. During a heated question and answer session the Brewers Association representative, Mr R.L.Matthews, explained that under society rules no brewer could be allowed full membership if they produced fewer than 10,000 barrels a year.

James was disappointed with this response, since once upon a time even Mr Whitbread and Mr Courage must have been tiny breweries and they were allowed to join then. James was quoted in *What's Brewing*, saying, 'they are supposed to represent the brewing industry as a whole, but for many years the Society has been dominated by the interests of the big national companies while providing an occasional social club for the local brewers.'

What option did they have but to form their own society? They created the Small Independent Brewers Association (SIBA), changing their name to the Society of Independent Brewers in 1995 as many of the family breweries felt more at home there than in the Brewers Association.

SIBA has historically had a good relationship with CAMRA, even though it took the latter a while to realise that small brewers were here to stay. CAMRA massively underestimated the impact this sector would have. Brian Glover, editor of *What's Brewing*, wrote that the small brewery revolution was over in the late 1980s, but he couldn't have been more wrong. There are around 2,000 UK breweries now, but over 3,000 more have come and gone in that time. A relatively hostile environment for independent brewers has been a constant because the tied pub system meant there were relatively few outlets willing and able to stock new beers. In turn this has encouraged the proliferation of brewpubs, freehold or small brewer-owned micropubs and brewery taps.

The support of the Campaign has been invaluable in providing new breweries with eager customers. Without CAMRA, Kinver brewery would not exist, says head brewer Dave Kelly. Dave would not have had the confidence to transition his home brew hobby into a commercial venture without the support of his local real ale scene. He and his wife, Carol, were already CAMRA members when they began the business in the early 2000s. The friends they had made at branch events became customers who were keen to support them and see them succeed.

Because Dave acknowledges the important role CAMRA has played in the life of his business, he is always looking for ways to give something back. He brewed a special beer in 2010 for CAMRA legend Bob Jones. Bob was awarded the CBE for his services to policing as West Midlands Police Authority Chairman, so Kinver brewery produced a beer called 'Commander of the Beer Empire'. Kinver brewery also created a beer called 'Life Begins' for CAMRA's fortieth anniversary, so watch this space to see what they produce for the fiftieth anniversary celebration.

Original Gravity and Alcohol by Volume

People came on board that knew more at a technical level. People who were able to analyse beer and tell us for the first time what the ABV of beer was. Nobody knew, it was all a trade secret. Nobody knew how strong or weak a beer was or what the ingredients were. And being reporters we started making enquiries.

GRAHAM LEES

According to Michael Hardman, campaigning was 'a bit primitive' in the early days, but CAMRA was still able to get some great results in a very short time. The labelling of beer was an early battleground. The strength of beer was not revealed to the customer. Indeed, a newspaper exposé on the increasing weakness of English brews from the Big Six spurred CAMRA's founders into action in the first place.

In the spirit of true investigative journalism, the founders and early members would steal away small vials of beer from the pub and pass them on for analysis to two colleagues who worked in a lab. Janet Pigeon and her husband, Chris, worked at Guinness and agreed to help test the strength of beer samples for publication in the *Good Beer Guide* in 1976.

They tested hundreds of beers for the GBG over the next three years, putting their jobs at risk to do so. Chris Pigeon said, 'the best thing we ever did was to reveal the duplicity of the brewers over beer strength. Some of them even used to cut the strength in summer and put it back up in winter.' Sadly, Janet, a multiple sclerosis sufferer, passed away at the age of just 54 in the year 2000, but her contribution to CAMRA was much celebrated.

Although breweries were outraged at first, gradually the practice of announcing a beer's strength on the label or pump clip crept into vogue even before finally becoming a legal requirement. Breweries that were more inclined towards transparency tended to help push up quality for the consumer. The newer microbreweries were producing better beers with better ingredients and this highlighted how the bigger brewers had been cutting corners. James Lynch remembers his brewery, Bourne Valley in Andover, being one of the first to voluntarily add original gravity information to pump clips when he was there.

It did not take long for the evidence CAMRA gathered to be put to good use by the government. From 1975 The Food Standards Committee considered evidence, including submissions from CAMRA, on the definition, composition and labelling of beer and released a report on the subject in 1977.

> The Food Standards Committee heeded our call via sympathetic MPs to examine the labelling of beer and we were asked for our views. Being a Whitehall civil servant I did have experience of how this kind of business was processed. I oversaw the drafting of our submission and led our delegation to a formal hearing. The core of our submission was that consumers should have an understanding of the strength of the beer they were drinking. To this end we asked that the Original Gravity should be declared. We were perhaps being a little too technical. OG is indeed the most accurate means of measuring strength and is what is used by Customs to determine how much excise duty is to be paid. But it is a somewhat obscure concept and may not have resonated with the public. So the Food Standards Committee was right when it opted for ABV to be declared instead. Still, we essentially got what we wanted. Today, drinkers might be astonished to learn that the strength of a beer was considered to be a trade secret and no business of the consumer. We had cracked a tough nut, and to this day I consider this may have been CAMRA's finest achievement.
>
> *GORDON MASSEY, former CAMRA National Chairman*

The requirement was finally enshrined in law with the EEC Directive of 15 April 1987 – ABV had to be included on the label of beverages over 1.2% alcohol. The ingredients do not need to be printed on the label under European law, but now that Britain has left the EU it is possible that this could be the next thing for CAMRA to push for, according to long-standing member Andrew Cunningham. This would help to inform people about allergens and vegan beers, for example, as well as the nature of any adjuncts.

Duty and excise

> Beer duty is the tax on the production and sale of beer and is calculated on alcoholic percentages. The "beer duty escalator" period between 2008 and 2013 started with the Labour Party's decision to increase the duty on alcoholic beverages by 6 per cent in real terms.
>
> *Taxpayers Alliance*

Campaigning for changes to duty and excise has been a way of life for CAMRA throughout their history. Their first duty-related campaigning success came along in 1993 in the form of the Beer Regulations. They had helped to persuade the government to move from calculating duty on the wort system – based on original gravity before the yeast is pitched into the fermenter – to the factory gate method where excise duty is based on the beer that actually leaves the brewery and its alcoholic strength. With the original gravity system there was a 5% wastage allowance between pitching the yeast and actually getting the beer into casks, bottles or cans. While the well-equipped and efficient big modern breweries could get away with just 0.5% wastage (and get 4.5% of their duty free), small breweries with cobbled together kit could easily have as much as 10% wastage, so they were paying lots of duty on beer that never left the brewery.

Small Brewers' Relief (SBR)

The next major victory came in March 2002, shared with campaigning partners SIBA, when a reduction in beer duty for small breweries was introduced. At its heart was the idea of creating parity between the smallest and largest brewers. The duty relief allowed small brewers to compete on a more or less level playing field with the larger brands who benefited from economies of scale.

The relief is a 50% discount on beer duty for brewers that produce under 5,000 hectolitres, and then it scales down quickly for larger brewers, to the cut-off point of 60,000 hectolitres, after which no relief is provided. While the smallest breweries and people considering starting a brewery celebrated the legislation, some of the family brewers with a regional reach complained that they had been left in the cold, and argued that the upper limit should have been set at 200,000 hectolitres. CAMRA supported these middle-ranking brewers in campaigning to raise the ceiling, but were unsuccessful.

Arguably, this legislation was the catalyst for new breweries to be established and for the craft brewing revolution to take hold in the UK, and as such was key in providing the breadth of choice in beer that we enjoy today. However, the scheme's detractors say that the relief programme holds back growth or even encourages businesses to downsize, which costs jobs and is against the spirit of the discount.

When Derek Moore started Kilburn brewery he waited until the exact week that the duty legislation went through to commence brewing, so influential was the promised relief on his decision to start a brewery. Even now, some eighteen years later, the duty relief helps to keep the business viable as they rely on sales as a guest beer on rotation at various free houses rather than having the security of their own venue to sell their product. However, Derek doesn't agree that the 5,000 hectolitres 'cliff edge' discourages any serious brewer from expansion. He feels that any expansion is by nature a leap of faith, so people will do what is right for their business, taking the relief for small brewers into account but not being held back by it.

The duty relief also helped to save the Three Tuns brewery in Bishop's Castle, Shropshire, which had been mothballed in

2001 after quality issues saw it lose £30,000 a year. The tax break encouraged the owning consortium to take another look at brewing on site, even though plans had already been drawn up to convert the brewery building into letting accommodation. The promised relief tipped the balance back in favour of the miniature Victorian tower brewery and it was returned to life as a going concern. It is still operating today 18 years later.

Critics have been looking at how the programme might be reformed since 2017 and so the scheme's supporters have also been involved in a review as key stakeholders. These discussions include CAMRA, the BBPA (British Beer & Pub Association), SIBA and the newly formed Small Brewery Duty Relief Coalition (SBDRC). The SBDRC is made up of a range of medium-sized breweries who feel that they are struggling to compete with smaller breweries who receive rate relief at a higher level than they do – they talk about the 'market distortions' caused by this.

At the 2018 CAMRA AGM a motion was put forward by the SBDRC that CAMRA should 'campaign for a reduction in the level of Small Brewery Duty Relief coupled with an increase on the barrelage on which it is granted.' The proposer, Brian Sheridan, said that small breweries undercut the cask ale market and destabilised it for larger independents, creating a squeezed middle which the SBDRC wants to protect. This motion was rejected as the aims of the SBDRC aren't really aligned with those of the CAMRA membership. It is in the consumer's interest to have a wide range of breweries of all sizes to drive innovation and quality forward: the SBDRC's proposed changes are likely to put some smaller breweries out of business.

Not all the larger breweries disapprove of the relief measures. Marc Bishop of St Austell recognises that duty relief can be 'irksome' to some medium-sized businesses, but points to how St Austell work hard on their brand presence to overcome any potential issues in terms of competition. They focus on presenting the customer with something they want to drink, not the cheapest product on the market. Those benefitting from duty relief are irrelevant to their business model.

In July 2020 the government proposed reducing the threshold for Small Brewery Duty Relief from 5,000 hectolitres to just 2,100 which would affect around 150 small businesses. This proposal was very much reflective of the SBDRC's view. In response, a letter was sent to the Treasury signed by well over 300 brewers, as well as a parliamentary petition being started, which led to a passionate adjournment debate in November 2020. CAMRA has been actively campaigning against the proposal as for smaller breweries the proposed change would be nothing short of disastrous, particularly when real ale brewers have been so badly affected by UK-wide Covid-19 lockdowns.

Beer duty escalator

Another important episode that really put CAMRA on the map was the introduction of the hated beer duty escalator in 2008, which put up the price of a pint by 2% over the rate of inflation every year. Between 2008 and 2013, when the escalator was scrapped, this equated to a 42% tax hike on beer. The industry was rightly concerned that the excessive taxation was causing pubs to close, and at a particularly high rate in Scotland. Between 2007 and 2012 nearly 20% of Scottish pubs closed down, with a disproportionate impact on community pubs in rural locations.[13]

This clear decrease in the number of pubs and corresponding social impact correlating directly to the escalator gave CAMRA, who were working closely with the Taxpayers' Alliance, a strong footing on which to fight against the escalator. An online petition garnered 104,000 signatures and triggered a debate on the issue, which was held on Thursday, 1 November 2012. In preparation for that debate, the BBPA, the All-Party Parliamentary

---

13. https://www.bighospitality.co.uk/Article/2012/09/24/Molson-Coors-welcomes-beer-tax-milestone-after-report-reveals-scale-of-pub-closures-in-Scotland

Beer Group and CAMRA worked together to fight the escalator. They provided each MP with a breakdown of information on the beer and pub industry's impact in their own constituency, including the numbers of pub closures and job losses that could be attributed to the escalator.

> I beg to move,
> That this House welcomes the essential contribution of brewing and pubs to the UK's economy in providing one million jobs; notes the 42 per cent increase in beer duty since 2008 and HM Treasury forecasts that have shown that there will be no additional revenue generated from beer duty despite planned increases over the next two years; is therefore concerned about the effectiveness of this policy in tackling the Budget deficit, its impact on valued community pubs and the continued affordability of beer in pubs; and therefore urges the Government to support the UK's beer and pub sector by conducting a thorough review of the economic and social impact of the beer duty escalator to report back before the 2013 Budget.
>
> *ANDREW GRIFFITHS, MP for Burton*

A Lobby Day took place on 12 November 2012 and was set up within a few hundred yards of the Palace of Westminster. Over 1,000 people from across the country descended on Parliament to express their anger at the beer escalator. Members were joined by sympathetic MPs from across all parties who spoke to the assembled crowd. A couple of members from the Fife branch even managed to gain an audience with their MP, the former prime minister, Gordon Brown, to discuss the issue.

National Chairman Colin Valentine's MP was Alastair Darling, who had personally introduced the beer duty escalator when he was chancellor. Colin visited him in his top floor offices at Portcullis House. He asked Mr Darling to write to the current chancellor and ask him to scrap the beer duty escalator (although he can't be sure whether he pointedly mentioned 'that you introduced'). Letters were exchanged, and the originals sent to Colin. They were addressed:

Dear George [Osborne], Yours Alistair

and the reply was:

Dear Alistair, Yours George

It was a 'study in equivocation', Colin said. However, it seemed the change was already in the air. There had already been a number of cuts to duty over successive years and then a freeze, then at the next budget after the Lobby Day the escalator was scrapped altogether as CAMRA kept up the pressure on government. The whole campaign had shown CAMRA as a force to be reckoned with and a top trustworthy source for MPs to consult for an impartial and voter-led view.

*   *   *

The fight is far from over for either the paid staff or the volunteers of CAMRA. Issues surrounding duty for brewers and cider makers have been some of the most enduring areas that require CAMRA's campaigning attention. For example, a 2014 petition with over 20,000 signatures was presented to 10 Downing Street asking the government to reject EU calls for increased duty on small UK real cider producers. Since cider duty was introduced there has been an exemption for small producers, who make up some 80% of the British cider market. The government upheld their commitment in 2016 and it was enshrined in EU law in May 2018, saving each small business around £2,700 annually. Now CAMRA has turned its sights to ensuring this continues to be upheld now that Britain has left the European Union.

Petitions to request a cut to beer duty do the rounds pretty much every year. The latest was seen in February 2020, when eighty-five Conservative MPs, along with the All Parliamentary Beer Group, BBPA, and industry-backed campaign initiative

Long Live the Local, put in a petition to the chancellor to cut beer duty in the March budget. This resulted in the chancellor announcing a freeze in duty across alcoholic drinks, along with business rate support for pubs, which was made before the various provisions to support businesses during the Covid-19 lockdown.

Pub Campaigning

Good beer IS available, irrespective of how it is served.
Now the main fight is where it is served – saving pubs.
I am seeing community pubs and family locals being taken
over by developers looking for a quick buck and there is
nowhere left for that community to meet and enjoy.

NIK ANTONA, current National Chairman,
speaking in February 2020

PUB culture permeates British life. Need proof? Just turn on the TV and watch a soap opera. Most of the action will centre around the local boozer. Recent research has shown the pub to be at the forefront of the fight against social isolation and loneliness. The pub is vitally important as drinking real ale is nearly wholly dependent on having a publican who can keep and serve cask ale correctly. At the 2000 AGM in Derby, a motion put forward by the Pubs Group was passed to give campaigning for pubs equal status with campaigning for real ale.

This Conference recognises that the long-term health of real ale, cider and perry is dependent on the long-term health of pubs and pub going. Accordingly this Conference agrees that in future the campaigning for and promotion of pubs shall have equal priority within the Campaign as the campaigning for and promotion of real ale, cider and perry.

Pub campaigning wasn't on the agenda when CAMRA began, even though there had been a slow, steady decline in pub numbers since the 1950s. In 1971 there were some 75,000 pubs in the

UK. The BBPA estimated this had declined to 66,000 in 1986, and there were fewer than 41,000 at the start of 2020 according to research by the Altus Group; a massive decline of over 45% during CAMRA's lifetime.

In the early twentieth century pubs had been the victims of a concerted campaign that attempted to control drunkenness by reducing pub numbers. However, magistrates were forced to compensate the publicans who were losing their valuable licenses. Now it is the economics that are the problem, not the change in drinking culture. Opportunistic developers, the tied pub system and changes in how people use their disposable income have all fed into the decline in pub numbers in recent decades.

These factors have created a slow increase of irresistible pressure against keeping pubs profitable. Social change is certainly partially to blame. Previously, successful pubs would have been part of the communities where people lived and worked, but then people began to live and work in different places, thus breaking those bonds. Similarly, drinking habits have changed over the years and competition for how we spend our leisure time has increased. The impact of the anti-alcohol lobby on our habits cannot be underestimated. Economic challenges have been compounded by changes in duty, business rates and wages, not to mention the physical disappearance of pubs where their buildings are sold off for conversion into mini-markets and flats.

The first CAMRA Pubs Group was set up in the 1980s. The brainchild of Kathy Hadfield-Moorhouse, she brought the issue of pub closures to the fore for the first time. In 2000 a Public House Viability Test developed by CAMRA was given the approval of a government planning inspector. It had been developed in consultation with planners and surveyors to give local councillors a guide to the business potential of pubs that were subject to change of use applications.

Of course, not every pub is viable, but Chris Holmes emphasises that the quality of pubs has improved massively over the decades and their appeal has broadened as they improve their offer to customers. They are now truly diverse spaces that welcome everyone but troublemakers: 'if you don't fight, you're alright,' as Chris says.

The long-standing issues affecting pubs have been compounded recently by the impact of the lockdowns and social distancing measures implemented because of the Covid-19 pandemic crisis in 2020/21. Landlords are struggling to maintain their businesses on a scale never previously seen. CAMRA has repeatedly called for a full package of support for the sector from government, and the legacy of the pandemic on the hospitality industry remains to be seen.

Pub conservation and heritage

> When you have lost your Inns, drown your empty selves,
> for you will have lost the last of England.
>
> *HILAIRE BELLOC*, This and That and the Other *1912*

CAMRA's most significant contribution to broader public life is arguably in the field of pub conservation and heritage. This work has a venerable history which started with a pub conservation group that was formed in York.

Dave Gamston was a particular driving force for pub conservation. He had a personal and professional interest in the built heritage of pubs. In 1979 Dave was a research fellow on a contract studying conservation area designation in Yorkshire, looking at how the Civic Amenities Act (1967) was being implemented in a pilot area, namely Yorkshire. He travelled around the built environment to do this job and had to visit lots of pubs. He saw historic buildings, including traditional pubs with multiple rooms, interesting furniture, panelling, stained glass and other exciting features. They were the 'Cinderella' of building conservation: overlooked, unrecorded and not recognised for their significance in their own right.

Dave was inspired to create a Pub Architecture Committee to help protect these buildings in York. It was soon renamed the York Pub Conservation Group. Colleagues at the Institute of Advanced Architectural Studies at the University of York, and York Archaeological Trust, shared Dave's interests and joined CAMRA to bolster the group. They produced a manifesto for pub preservation, writing about the importance of the ecology of pubs and their relationship to local heritage. It was eventually adopted nationally.

The group worked intensively, publishing a comprehensive local list of historic pub interiors in the York Civic Trust annual newsletter. Dave then extended the inventory he had spearheaded, first to the regional and then the national level: the beginnings of the National Inventory of Historic Pub Interiors that is still maintained today. It was 'a true ground-breaking initiative for CAMRA,' Dave says. In 1982 the first national pub preservation conference was held at York University.

All of this work paved the way for a 1985 CAMRA Manifesto for Pub Preservation, with a specialist focus on the heritage and preservation of pub interiors. Similar groups had popped up in branches around the country, so they were able to consolidate into a national group. Serious work on a national list of heritage pub interiors was begun in 1991 with the foundation of the national Pub Heritage Group and the National and Regional Inventories. Now there is a website used to record entries: the full inventory went online in September 2000. The aim of the group is to identify, record and help protect historic or architecturally important unspoilt pub interiors.

Once they had a list of historic pub interiors to work with, both the local and national groups were able to start getting involved with objecting to potential changes to those pubs through the planning system. The group catalogued which features were important and built the case as to why they needed to be preserved. They objected to proposals to demolish or revamp pubs and brought together police, magistrates, breweries and publicans to have conversations about how best to preserve the buildings. Other local campaigning actions included making representations to local planning authorities, petitioning owners, publicising news and potential sales/changes to buildings and working more with Historic England to make formal requests to get pubs listed.

Andrew Davison worked on a campaign to save the John Bull in York. This had been built by John Smiths in 1937. After being closed for a number of years, it reopened as a real ale free house in the early 1980s and soon gained a cult following. However, the pub's owner was also in possession of the car dealership next door and decided he wanted to expand his car park rather than keep the successful pub.

> Even today, some people talk of it in the way they would talk about a lost friend. They say it was, for a good decade or so, the best pub York had. *The York Press, 24 May 2014*

While the campaign to save the pub achieved a short stay of execution, the listing application was ultimately turned down. On 28 May 1994 the pub closed and the building was demolished shortly afterwards. Although this campaign was unsuccessful it was high profile enough to catch the attention of Historic England, then known as English Heritage. They brought a specialist field worker on board, Geoffrey Brandwood, who created detailed descriptions and documentation for the purpose of listing pub interiors. The John Bull could not be saved, but many more were saved after it through the formal listing process. The 'list' is the National Heritage List for England which gives all the buildings on it national protection. These buildings are graded according to how significant they are: Grade I buildings are the most important and very little can be done to alter them or to negatively impact on their historic character.

The Pub Heritage Group also keeps a separate list of pubs known to be at risk: the Historic Pub interiors in Peril list. Although Historic England's resources are limited, they honour an agreement with CAMRA to enhance the internal descriptions of the most important pubs. The Heritage Group provides a list of about a dozen pubs each year. In February 2020 one of the pubs identified for an enhanced description, the Philharmonic Dining Rooms in Liverpool – the same pub that had been earmarked for possible conversion into a Firkin pub in the late nineties – was identified as having the finest Victorian pub interior in the country. Its listing status was upgraded, making it the first Grade I-listed pub in the country and a huge success for the Pub Heritage Group.

Dave Gamston stood down as chairman of the group in 2003 and was succeeded by Paul Ainsworth, who still holds the position today. The group works with a rolling fifty-year remit and Paul says that some of the pubs the group seeks to protect may surprise people. For example, 1960s estate pubs may not be beautiful, but they are an important part of the social history of an area. They are usually extremely rare because they were made from cheap materials and no one batted an eyelid if they were torn down at the time. Drawing attention to more modern buildings has encouraged Historic England to conduct a study of post-war pubs, with all largely intact pubs dating up to 1970 now recorded, although still only a handful are listed.

Britain's Best Real Heritage Pubs is the main publication of the Pub Heritage Group, but smaller regional inventory books are periodically released to inform people of their findings locally. The early guides in York were able to get sponsorship from the local tourist board because they contained information that was useful to visitors, an approach that was later taken up by other branches. The national inventory was first put into published form in the 1997 *Good Beer Guide*. This was followed up with a booklet in around 1998, and then a glossy publication in 2003. A regional guide for Scotland was put together by Mick Slaughter and launched in 2007. This caught the attention of Historic Scotland and led to several buildings being listed for the first time.

The national and regional inventories, as well as many of the locally produced regional guidebooks, are beautifully illustrated with photographs taken by Mick Slaughter. Mick took an evening class to learn basic photography skills and got lots of tips on how to photograph pubs from one of his lecturers who had a sideline in taking pictures of building interiors. In 2007 Andy Shaw created a website that collated all of the historic pub interior data that had been collected over the years and Mick's images were used there as well. They record the pubs to help raise awareness of them and to preserve them by encouraging people to use them.

An important recent conservation campaign took place in Kilburn. In April 2015 developer CLTX demolished the Carlton Tavern. They did not have permission or any appropriate health and safety planning in place for demolishing the building, which was under consideration for Grade II-listed status. The pub had been the only one on its street to survive the Blitz. The demolition happened without warning, with the local hockey club's trophy cabinet still on the wall and beer still in the cellar ready for the next day's trading.

After global media attention, as well as local and national campaigning, a government ordered inquiry found that developers 'rode roughshod' over the local community and the thriving business. In a landmark decision for pub preservation, CLTX was ordered to rebuild the property exactly as it had been, 'brick by brick'. Work began in August 2017, but as it had not yet been completed by early 2020, it was reported that Westminster Council were considering taking further action against the developer who had thought they were risking, at most, a £5,000 fine and wanted to make millions by building luxury flats on the site.

Assets of Community Value

After some thirty years of dedicated work, the Pub Heritage Group's greatest campaigning success came in 2017 when planning protection for all pubs in England was secured. Originally, no planning permission was needed to change the use of a pub into a shop, restaurant or office. Having these permitted development rights removed helped to slow down the rate of closures as it became harder for developers to shut a pub and change it into something else.

This success was not achieved overnight. The introduction of Assets of Community Value (ACV) in 2012 was an important step: pubs were first protected under planning permission if their local community nominated them as an ACV. CAMRA brought staff on board to support local branches and volunteers in their applications. CAMRA as a national organisation could not nominate a pub as an ACV, but a local branch satisfied the conditions to make a community nomination. They could also advise any other group that might want to protect their locality. Over 18 months, some 2,000 pubs were made into ACVs across the country.

The benefit of being an ACV was limited; it essentially gave the community more time and the right to bid if the pub went up for sale, but the owner was under no obligation to sell to the group even if they offered more than a developer. So the next stage was for the government to change the law so that pubs that were named as an ACV had their permitted development rights removed entirely. This happened in 2015 and was finally extended to all pubs in 2017 so it diminished the importance of ACV status.

Paul Ainsworth considered ACVs as having been valuable in stimulating the community pub ownership revolution, and there are now some 150 community-owned pubs: 'It's a model that just works, so far not one of those pubs has failed. If the community has taken the trouble to get the money together to buy the pub and then to run it either directly or through a tenant then there's an obvious commitment to it. They're going to use it because it's their pub.'

Some community pubs that were written off as unviable by their previous corporate owners have become the vibrant heart of their local area through community pub ownership. The valuable social function that pubs perform has long been recognised by CAMRA. The Red Lion in Preston, Hertfordshire, became the UK's first community-owned pub back in 1983. Locals raised £90,000 to buy it from the Whitbread brewery. In 2019 the Red Lion was a national finalist in the CAMRA Pub of the Year competition, having been judged as one of the top four pubs in the UK.

Some community pubs are supported by funding from charities like the Plunkett Foundation and were thriving prior to the Covid-19 lockdowns, bucking the wider trend for pub closures. These pubs have valuable social impact and often help other struggling facilities to survive in rural locations, providing additional functions as post offices and shops as well as promoting inclusion and supporting vulnerable communities. In June 2010 the George & Dragon, Hudswell, reopened as a community-owned pub. By 2016 it had been judged to be the Pub of the Year:

> When the George & Dragon pub in Hudswell closed in 2008 it left the small North Yorkshire village with no other facilities for its residents apart from a village hall. Within two years, the community banded together to form the Hudswell Community Pub Ltd group and bought back the pub, reopening in June 2010 after extensive renovations. The community was determined that the George & Dragon would offer far more than a traditional pub. As well as acting as a meeting place and venue, it is also home to the village library, a local shop staffed by volunteers, community allotments and free internet access for its patrons.[14]

14. https://camra.org.uk/pubs/campaigns/community-pub-ownership

The Chesham Arms in Hackney, East London

It was built in 1865 and was closed in October 2012 when the family which had owned it sold it to a property developer. The 'Save The Chesham' campaign ran from June 2012 until April 2015. We were a collection of neighbours and regulars, supported by a wider network of pub lovers and organisations like CAMRA and the Hackney Society. I was the campaign secretary.

The ACV provisions were very new, indeed we had the first ACV in Hackney and only the third in London. Communities had only just started to fight back against pub closures, linked together via social media and organisations like Pub is the Hub and Plunkett Foundation.

The closure was half expected as we knew the pub was for sale, but we were told it was to be sold to a restaurant operator. This turned out to be false. The developer, Mukund Patel, was a small-time speculator who had done a few low-key conversions in North and East London. He bought it with a view to carve it up into four flats. Once it became apparent to him, via local press articles, that there would be opposition to this plan, he held off submitting a planning application and instead wasted several months challenging our ACV status, which Hackney Council had awarded in November 2012. After a failed internal review he took the case to the First Tier Tribunal in the General Regulatory Chamber where Judge Nicholas Warren heard the first ever oral challenge to an ACV registration. It took Warren around two hours to throw it out and dismiss the appeal.

Patel then decided to use a new planning option introduced by Eric Pickles (the then Secretary of State for Communities and Local Government) to exploit a temporary permitted development right to change the use of the pub to offices. The offices were in effect a sham but since the law allowed him to do it for two years, he felt a temporary spell in office use might make us all melt away.

Campaign fatigue is always a challenge as pub campaigns are often long and arduous, but we were going nowhere. This pub is in our street, and we have to live with it forever. He used the fake office to mask the fact that he had moved tenants into the flat upstairs, built for the pub landlord and his family. This flat was in A4 ancillary use lawfully and a residential use not connected to the pub was not allowed. We lobbied very hard for Hackney Council to take enforcement action, which they did in October 2013. Patel immediately appealed and demanded a Public Inquiry.

The Public Inquiry sat in the spring of 2014 and Patel's legal team argued that the flat above the pub had always been separate and independent to the pub itself. This was manifestly untrue as one could only access the flat from behind the bar. He then argued that even if a change of use had actually occurred, this should be allowed as there was no public harm and it was, in his view, allowable development. The inspector took three days to hear the inquiry and decided that Patel's appeal should fail. Heritage grounds played a large part in the inspector's assertion that a change of use from pub to residential use would harm the character of the Clapton Square Conservation Area, in which the Chesham Arms sits and is highlighted in the appraisal document as a key building.

Having lost the appeal and lost his associated cost claim, we were informed by Patel's planning agent that his client would 'just keep it shut forever', as punishment for our campaign. This seemed a silly approach to an asset that he had paid £650,000 for just a few months earlier. He was given six months to cease the unlawful residential use from the date of the inspector's decision notice, in July 2014. He then quietly put the feelers out for a buyer, and turned down several offers, one as high as £950,000. In my experience of hundreds of pub campaigns, I find that these developers share one common trait – motivated by pure greed. After realising that no well-informed operator would pay the £1 million he wanted for the freehold, he engaged agents to find him a lessee. In March 2015 he exchanged paperwork with an outfit known as Fletch Fletcher Ltd, who took a 15-year lease on the building and opened a refurbished (tastefully restored) pub in June 2015 to much local acclaim and celebration.

The revenues at the Chesham Arms increased 400% between closure in October 2012 and relaunch in June 2015, demonstrating how pubs thrive under the right management when the needs and aspirations of the local community are sensitively met. The bizarre epilogue is that nobody really lost out. Patel sold the freehold with a sitting tenant in February 2016 for £1.2 million, doubling his investment, minus futile legal costs. He got what he wanted, and moved on. The new operators got a pub and an ancillary flat on a 15-year lease for reasonable terms, creating local jobs and helping to sustain Hackney's thriving beer and pub scene. The community got their pub back, in better condition and with a better operator than previously, and a vastly expanded range of beer, wine and spirits. The Council retained a commercial premises and local jobs and saved a heritage asset in a conservation area from undoubted substantial harm.   *JAMES WATSON*

Pub of the Year Awards

The National Pub of the Year and the Pub Design Awards are an important part of how CAMRA celebrates the best in pubs old and new. The awards have been bringing much needed media attention to the very best pubs since The Boars Head in Aberdeenshire was judged the inaugural National Pub of the Year in 1988. There are local and regional judging rounds for the National Pub of the Year competition, which start with local competitions to crown each branch's Pub of the Year. The branch winners are then judged against others in their region, from which a list of 16 finalists is produced. These are visited by the Regional Directors who make the final award based on criteria like the quality of the beer, cider and perry on offer, décor, service and overall feel.

The Pub Design Awards are held in conjunction with Historic England and the Victorian Society. They were first conceived in the early eighties to celebrate a range of achievements, including the best new build, conversion project and pub refurbishment, as well as the Conservation Award sponsored by Historic England. A great pub interior is hard to define because they are all so different. The judges have to balance factors like purpose, period and character when dishing out gongs. Finally there is a discretionary award, the Joe Goodwin Award, which has recently been renamed the Community Local Award. Joe was a champion of the street corner local and many excellent community pub projects have been awarded the prize that bore his name. Joe was National Chairman when he passed away suddenly in November 1980, at the age of just 32.

It's not just pubs that CAMRA supports, but any venue that serves real ale, especially clubs. There have been specific campaigns over the years in support of clubs and the CAMRA Club of the Year award is given out in association with the *Club Mirror* magazine. In 2019 it went to the Appleton Thorn Village Hall, just outside of Warrington, for the second time. This club has a constantly changing range of seven beers from local and regional breweries and provides a community hub with facilities like a bowling green and garden area. It has also reached the final of the National Cider and Perry Pub of the Year because of its great selection in this regard.

The Beer Orders

> The general mood was triumphal. The Big Six were the arch enemy, they were the devil incarnate and we ascribed most of the ills of the industry to the influence of the Big Six. We could see this golden age coming along where all of these pubs would become free houses, able to sell whatever beers they liked.
>
> *PAUL AINSWORTH*

The major victory that marked the transition of CAMRA's campaigning from its early to mature phase was the passing of the Beer Orders – The Supply of Beer (Tied Estate) Order and The Supply of Beer (Loan Ties, Licensed Premises and Wholesale Prices) Order 1989. This was the legislation that put the final nail in the coffin for the monopoly of the Big Six breweries, although in hindsight it was something of a double-edged sword for the consumer. Beer historian Jessica Boak points out that a range of external societal factors informed the timing of the Beer Orders being passed, but the detail of the changes it engendered was certainly greatly influenced by CAMRA's involvement.

CAMRA had been pushing for legislation to prevent brewing companies from owning or managing more than 1,000 pubs each since 1974, although at the time the Secretary of State for Trade, Alan Williams, said that the introduction of such legislation was not possible. By 1980 there was a hint that the Monopolies and Mergers Commission (MMC) was waking up to the potential issue. The February 1980 edition of *What's Brewing* stated simply:

> Big Six break-up?
> The government is looking into ways of encouraging the break-up of large conglomerate companies as part of a review of monopolies and mergers regulations. Ministers believe industry would be better served through smaller concerns. Big Six breweries are you listening?

This was not CAMRA's first brush with the MMC. An internal CAMRA monopolies committee had already been set up to lead campaigning against the product tie. It had submitted reports to government since 1976 on the issue of local brewery monopolies. Andrew Cunningham had chaired a committee reporting on Watneys pub ownership in East Anglia, which had swallowed up all the pubs owned by the three local breweries. There were also investigations into the Thames Valley, which was being monopolised by Whitbread, and Ind Coope's dealings within the jurisdiction of the Mid Chilterns branch, for example.

CAMRA volunteers like Andrew also fed into the development of the MMC's report entitled 'The Supply of Beer: A report on the supply of beer for retail sale in the United Kingdom', and it was the recommendations that came out of this report that provided the basis for the beer orders.

The CAMRA team were invited to a pre-meeting with the chair of the MMC, Reece Mills, at the very start of the process. This was aimed at establishing exactly which parties the commission should focus on as part of an investigation into the brewing industry, and shows that CAMRA were really in at the ground floor of the investigation. The whole enquiry took two-and-a-half years, and resulted in a massive report of 501 pages.

CAMRA delivered a lengthy written submission and four volunteers met with the commission to give oral evidence, where they were grilled for some four hours. This was a very high-pressure situation for self-professed amateurs to be put under. There was a stenographer at the enquiry and afterwards the four were given a 100-plus page transcript which they had to sign off as a true record.

By the time the report was due to be published in 1989 the Campaign had taken on more staff to support the National Executive in their campaigning work, in particular preparing their submission to the enquiry: a huge piece of work. Previously, there had only been one member of staff working on campaigns, and their time was split between that and *What's Brewing*. Now there was a campaigns manager, a new editor of *What's Brewing*, a research and information manager, and, slightly later, a campaigns assistant. Andrew Cunningham remembers long days working on the commission's call for evidence – including getting a fine in Birmingham for overstaying a 12-hour parking ticket on one especially long day!

*   *   *

When the report was released, Roger Protz, then editor of *What's Brewing*, went to London for the announcement and rushed two copies of the huge report back to St Albans. He was then roundly criticised by the company secretary, Ian Dobson, for only bringing back two copies of the mammoth document. The team put out a brief initial press release then went to a local pub to celebrate, while the campaigns manager, Steve Cox, took call after call giving comments to the national press. Roger remembers rushing out a four-page *What's Brewing* special to highlight just how devastating the report was in its criticism of the Big Six and their 'complex monopoly': 'We felt that we'd been vindicated. We felt that everything we'd been saying since the early seventies had come home to roost and the government really had to pay attention to this.'

The MMC report looked at the vertical integration of the brewing industry under the Big Six – pubs being tied to breweries so that the producers had control over their distribution centres, leading to monopolies which stifled fair competition for giving other brewers access to the market. It was shown that the Big Six owned 74% of brewery-owned tied houses, 75% of beer production and 86% of loan ties (where publicans were given loans in exchange for stocking the brewer's beer). The figures showed a clear monopoly over the market and they were judged to be anti-competitive.

The Haig Whisky company undertook a survey of pub-goers to find out their opinion of the recommendations in the immediate aftermath of the report being published. The majority were in favour of the government implementing the Monopolies Commission report. Some 84% of adults surveyed thought that landlords should have more freedom to introduce more beers. The majority of consumers thought that the recommendations would be good for the traditional British pub, as did the majority of CAMRA members.

The big brewers predictably poured scorn on the report, saying it was clearly written by CAMRA. This was a fair criticism: all of the points the Campaign had been making against the

Big Six since their inception were reflected in it. In the words of Roger Protz, the Big Six acted like a cartel. They fixed prices, they overcharged for beer and they wouldn't allow other brewers to sell their beers in the Big Six pubs.

The commission's recommendations, more or less, came into force. The most publicised provision was that no brewery company could henceforth own more than 2,000 pubs. There were also clauses concerned with the sale of beer, the terms of tied loans and an expectation that wholesale prices would be published, all aimed at protecting tenants and breaking the monopoly. For some people, this meant that real ale could finally be considered 'saved', but unfortunately the issue was far from cut and dried. The recommendation that loan ties should be banned was quietly forgotten by the government.

Initially, it appeared that through the Beer Orders, CAMRA had struck a great victory. The vast estates of the Big Six were going to be broken up. CAMRA members dreamed of a bright future where most pubs were free houses, choosing which beers to sell on merit alone. Nobody in the Campaign initially spotted the unintended consequences that would arise.

The big brewers were being forced to break up their chains and sell on any pubs over the permitted 2,000, but it was only specifically 'brewing companies' that were covered. Investors and property companies bought up the estates, often paying too much with borrowed money. And so the pub companies, or PubCos, were born – often funded by and beholden to the largest brewers. The largest pub company today, Ei Group, originally known as Enterprise Inns, was started with the purchase of 300 former Bass pubs in 1991. In 1997 more former Bass portfolio pubs were bought by the former head of Pizza Express and founder of Café Rouge, which is how Punch Pubs came into being.

Over the years, through rafts of complicated sales, mergers and acquisitions, the PubCos developed a monopoly over the industry more invidious than that of the big brewers, but with the difference that these property companies don't have the same interest in their own product being kept or presented properly in the pubs in the way the breweries did. Their brewing operations tend to be held at arm's length from the main investment company purely to supply product in-house. The PubCos are motivated purely by profit and became asset strippers in all but name. Pubs were closed and often historic buildings and their land were sold for development because this was the quickest way of maximising revenue from the properties.

Former National Chairman Tim Amsden noticed the difference in philosophy first hand. Aggressive though the Big Six had been, they had often still retained important core values: 'Particularly Whitbread, where there was a marked contrast between those in the firm who seriously valued tradition and good ale and those who saw it as a property and profit exercise. They still had some fine breweries and very competent brewers.'

The unintended consequence of the Beer Orders pushed pub campaigning to the fore for CAMRA. The changes introduced by the legislation forced the sale or free from tie of 10,791 pubs and at least half of them were bought up by new independent PubCos. There was another huge blow for campaigners in 1991 when Grand Metropolitan and Courage pulled off a cynical exchange of breweries for pubs: the former owned no breweries and the latter no pubs, thus freeing them both from the constraints of the Beer Orders. The pub group Inntrepreneur, which was the result of these machinations, bought 4,000 venues. They imposed long leases, responsibility for the property and massively increased rents on licensees, while continuing to restrict their beer choice to Courage brands.

Arguably, a new Big Six had been created: Punch Pubs, Greene King, Enterprise Inns, Star Pubs & Bars, Marston's and Admiral Taverns. A government review in 2000 led to the estate cap being scrapped and the Beer Orders were revoked in their entirety in 2003, but by then the damage had long since been done. By October 2004, Punch's acquisition of the InnSpired chain took them up to 8,300 pubs.

However, some people see the Beer Orders as a positive and defining moment for the industry. Former National Chairman and entrepreneur Chris Hutt says, 'I was delighted by the Beer Orders and I think ultimately they freed up the industry so that more choice could be provided to the customer.' Current CAMRA National Chairman Nik Antona agrees that the Beer Orders opened up the market and made a wider beer choice available to the consumer by increasing the number of breweries. However, he also sees the difficulties that have come from PubCos trying to address their increasing debt, usually by saddling the poor tenants with increased rents, higher product costs and so forth in the attempt to claw back as much money as possible. The massive increase in property prices in the period since the Beer Orders, particularly in London, has also been a particular detriment to pubs as developing the buildings became an increasingly attractive option. This really upped the ante for CAMRA's pub campaigning in terms of protecting the physical buildings through working alongside planning legislation but also creating campaigns that focus on the social benefit of pubs, such as the recent Pub is the Hub campaign.

*   *   *

One particular stipulation of the Beer Orders that was positive for CAMRA's aims and objectives was the guest beer provision. Brewers had to allow tenants and tied loan clients to buy one brand of cask-conditioned beer on the open market – a guest ale. It was CAMRA's intervention that confined the allowance to cask ales only, and it inspired a new explosion of small breweries as more space opened up on bars around the country. The first wave of new breweries in the late 1970s had met with mixed success. Now the guest beer provision gave a new stimulus and created more robust businesses that tended to go the distance because there was consumer demand to support them.

There was also an opportunity for existing breweries. Andy Beaton recalls the growth of the Three Tuns Brewery in Bishop's Castle, Shropshire, as its availability in the free trade grew. It is one of the UK's oldest breweries, having been licensed in 1642, and managed to remain independent through the centuries. The Three Tuns Inn adjacent to the brewery was one of only four home brew pubs in operation when CAMRA had begun – the others being the All Nations Inn, Shropshire, the Blue Anchor in Cornwall and Ma Pardoe's (The Old Swan) in Netherton.

However, the Guest Ale Provision wasn't a bulletproof solution. The canny large breweries were even able to find a way to exploit this arrangement. To maintain the monopoly of their own product, more unscrupulous brewers would introduce a 'guest beer' from breweries they had bought and closed down instead of giving a hand pump to a genuinely independent guest beer. Also the provision only applied to tenanted pubs and not managed ones. As the management model was changed across the industry, the number of hand pumps available to guest ales was reduced.

On 5 August 1996 the EU mounted a legal challenge against the provision. The argument was made that cask-conditioned ale is predominantly a British product and so the arrangement was discriminatory against brewers in other EU member states. This arose from a complaint made by a British importer of German beers. CAMRA argued that this provision served the interests of consumers and small brewers. Ultimately though, the guest beer provision was allowed to continue by extending it to allow one bottle-conditioned guest beer as well as one cask-conditioned. Bottle-conditioned beer can be found in other European countries so this addition was deemed to have sufficient benefit to small brewers across Europe without undue monopoly.

The Pubs Code

> The Big Six were proud of their pubs and their licensees.
> Regardless of their many faults I don't think they would have
> treated their tenants as the PubCos are treating them today.
> *ROGER PROTZ, speaking during the first UK lockdown in 2020*

After significant campaigning, the problems with the PubCos' treatment of their tenants was recognised by the government in 2014. A statutory code of practice was announced, along with an adjudicator to arbitrate disputes. It felt like a victory. The Beer Orders had been endlessly reviewed until they were scrapped in 2003, but little change had been forthcoming. The Pubs Code was introduced in July 2016 to regulate the relationship between tied pub tenants and their landlords – the Beer Orders Mark II in effect.

The code applies to all pub-owning businesses with 500 or more tied pubs in England and Wales. One of its guiding principles is that the tied tenant should be no worse off than the free-of-tie tenant. Unfortunately, the code has, so far, not had the muscle it needs to uphold this principle. The adjudicator's powers have not been wide ranging enough to prevent the pub companies from side-stepping their obligations to tenants. For example, there is scope within the code for pubs to pursue a 'Market Rent Only' (MRO) lease from their PubCo, to end all product and service ties and instead just pay an independently assessed and fair rent to them as landlords. This should have been achieved by a relatively simple lease change, but the PubCos demanded unnecessarily onerous new leases, which has resulted in the tenants seeking arbitration through the Pubs Code Adjudicator. The applications have therefore been taking much longer than necessary, even though CAMRA has been trying to support a number of tenants through their MRO claims.

Where tenants are treated unfairly and beer ties are monopolised there is a knock-on effect on quality and choice for the consumer and so CAMRA has supported a review of the code. This process began in 2019 and CAMRA took an active role in the evidence gathering by administering a tenant survey to understand whether pub companies had been acting within the spirit of the code.

Where the code has been effective, it has really highlighted some significant wrongdoing. In December 2019 the adjudicator concluded that Marston's had been selling casks to its pubs as containing 72 pints, despite knowing that at least 5% of that volume was unsaleable yeast sediment due to the inherent composition of real ale. As campaigner Steve Bury describes, you simply can't sell consistently good ale without throwing some away, but these publicans were not being given any allowance for wastage.

Not only did this mean tenants were overcharged for the saleable beer, but, as Marston's calculated rents based on sales, the tenants were charged twice on these fictitious pints.

The 2019 British Beer Writer of the Year, Jonny Garrett, helped to uncover this issue. He believes CAMRA has an important role in educating consumers about issues like the pub tie so that they can make informed purchases. Customers may choose to change their purchasing decisions if they know more about whether a company was involved in the 72 pints scandal, or cancelled rents for their tenants during the 2020 lockdowns, for example. Jonny suggests that for Marston's to cancel rent amassed by all of their tenants during the first lockdown would cost less than they pay their managing director in just six months: a relatively inexpensive choice they could make to benefit some 400 publicans and their families. In the event, they chose not to do this. Instead, they offered rent reductions of up to 50% to some of their tenants during the first lockdown and reduced headline rent by 90% during the second lockdown in November

2020, according to their press releases, even though their pubs could not open at all during these periods.

The first statutory review into the Pubs Code was completed by the government in November 2020 and the 500-pub cap was kept in place. It is unclear what the next steps will be as the various interested parties have reported on the review's outcome quite differently.

The *Morning Advertiser* reported that the review was applauded by the BBPA who represent the PubCos, because it found that no significant changes to the code needed to be made. This is in direct contrast to Nik Antona's response. He said that he was glad the government agreed with CAMRA's assessment that the code was not working and that change was needed to deliver on the principles of tenants being 'no worse off' and enjoying the 'fair and lawful dealing' enshrined by the code.

CAMRA Today

A craft beer revolution

All this cloudy vegan beer now I cannot stand! My local pub
has 12 hand pumps and they've now switched about seven or
eight to cloudy, unfiltered, unpasteurised beer and I can't
drink it. I don't want it. It's not what beer was meant to be.
Beer is supposed to be clear, bright, sparkling, tasty and
delicious at a reasonable price, not vegan-style unfiltered
beer at £6 a pint. I'm sorry, it's just not my scene. To me it's
unfinished beer. I won't say lazy beer. I'll say unfinished.

DAVE MCKERCHAR, Former NE member

IN the 1970s the beery battle lines were clearly drawn. Cask ale
represented the best of British craftsmanship and cellarmanship. Keg beer was its enemy, stealing its space on the bar. It was
a bland, fizzy approximation that was produced to satisfy the
lowest common denominator and maximise profit. CAMRA was
started to make sure that consumers were able to have a choice:
if real ale disappeared there would be no option but to drink keg.
In 1973 Michael Hardman wrote a response to a claim from the
industry that sales of keg had gone up because it had become
more popular through free choice. 'Frost and the Brewers Society
[now the British Beer and Pub Association (BBPA)] should heed
the words of V.D.S. Fowler, CAMRA's leading light on the Isle of
Wight: saying the public prefers keg beer is like ripping up all the
railway tracks in this country and doing away with all the railway stations and then saying the public prefers to travel by bus.'

However, once CAMRA had helped to create an environment more conducive to new breweries establishing themselves successfully, there was a flurry of activity. New breweries had the benefit of access to new technologies as well as better brewing kit, more efficient processes and easier access to high quality ingredients than in years gone by.

Experimentation in brewing was becoming commonplace. New types of beer appeared; or, perhaps more accurately, formerly lost traditional styles were revived. In the UK, the US and across Europe a boom time for beer was created thanks to the rise of craft beer. Outside of the UK this often didn't involve cask-conditioned ale, either because there was no pre-existing tradition or because it was not pragmatic to focus on cask or cellar-conditioned ales. Maybe the beer had to travel long distances or climate made it impractical. These craft beer revolutions – experimenting with flavour, style and technique – took place in kegs. The distinction between the potential quality of cask and keg was no longer an absolute.

The definition of 'craft beer' is a much debated issue. An early mention of a craft brewer in the *What's Brewing* of March 2002 references the size of the brewery as being relevant, craft brewers being micro in scale. Current National Executive member Ash Corbett-Collins agrees that craft is often something on a small scale, but adds that it should also be produced predominantly as a passion product. Even though they are commercially successful, he sees Tiny Rebel brewery as craft, for example, because they brew interesting beers and brew what and how they want. Pete Brown's recent book on craft is the most useful summary of current thinking around how craft breweries and craft beer might be defined.

However you define it, CAMRA had helped to create the conditions for the rise of craft beer in the UK by nurturing and expanding the beer drinking population and thereby creating a market for new brewers to enter. Despite this, people outside the organisation see them as hesitant to live in the brave new world they helped to create. This is perhaps because a mistrust of kegged beer was, and remains, hard-wired into parts of the longer serving membership.

> CAMRA's biggest failure these past 15 to 20 years has been its failure to deal with the term craft, and as a result it is, unchallenged, used liberally to refer to breweries and beers of all shapes, sizes and sorts, there being no definition of the term. Had it come up back in the early years we would have commandeered it, claimed it for ourselves and put it to good use, but instead it has just served to confuse everyone as no one knows what it means. I certainly don't. CAMRA's biggest missed opportunity and a failure of leadership.
>
> *JAMES LYNCH, former NE member and brewery founder*

CAMRA's relentless digs at the Big Six in their early years certainly did lead to a culture, amongst some areas of the organisation, of looking down on keg beers, but not everyone felt obliged to join in. Christine Cryne instigated CAMRA's first ever market research towards the end of her first stint on the National Executive in 1997. She describes how the results of their focus groups led to a change in CAMRA's strategy, no longer knocking keg beer on any official channels but instead focusing on being an organisation that specifically promoted choice for the consumer. The result was a change in language when talking about keg and dropping any promotional materials that ran keg down. The new marketing materials started to promote CAMRA as 'beer warriors'.

> We don't want to tell you what to drink (though we hope you'll give real ale a try!) but we hope that you believe in choice.
>
> *London Drinker's explanation of CAMRA, September 1986*

CAMRA's been sort of standoffish in terms of craft, which to my mind is OK because our interest is real ale, and craft has its own place in the marketplace. It's a case of acknowledging that it's there. Some people think it's a threat but if we can encourage younger drinkers to taste different things then they can drink real ale alongside craft keg and enjoy them both.

KEN DAVIE

Not everyone got the memo. At the 2000 AGM, National Chairman Dave Goodwin encouraged continuing the 'revolt against the false positioning of nitrokegs as having the qualities of real ale. They do not and we're going to let Britain's 15 million beer drinkers know about it.' However, by that point craft pioneers like Meantime Brewing were already off the starting blocks and brewing kegged craft beers. Within a few short years they would be joined by others who also became household names in British craft brewing, like Thornbridge and BrewDog. CAMRA's mixed messaging meant that they were looking the other way as a new wave of beers appeared that ticked all of their boxes in terms of quality and choice for the consumer because they weren't necessarily cask-conditioned. Arguably, this strategic error caused CAMRA to lose resonance with large numbers of new beer drinkers in the first two decades of the twenty-first century.

What was bad about the keg beers of the past was that they were insipid, overpriced products, low in alcohol, which was a deliberate ploy on the part of the big brewers to maximise profit, whereas you can't accuse small craft brewers of that.

GRAHAM LEES

Developments in the US beer scene and the flowering of craft beer were monitored with interest in *What's Brewing*. An article by Ken Brewster and Dave Hadfield as far back as January 1980 featured the distinctive beer made by a certain tiny San Francisco brewery called Anchor Steam. They had begun to brew in 1896 and recently moved to bigger premises. The article describes how neither Anchor Steam nor their porter 'meet the British definition of real beer,' but reported that 'the preparation loosely follows conventional European methods,' and went on to describe the Krausening process for conditioning the beer.

They applauded the brewery in helping to distance a new generation from the 'average American drinker, who has been brainwashed into believing that beer should be ice-cold, gassy and tasteless.'

However you define craft beer, flavour must be the most important factor. Steve Tabbenor, owner of the Real Ale Classroom in Leicester, sees a very wide range of people coming into his pub to enjoy keg beer and notes that independent breweries choose this style of dispense to help with freshness and consistency. When he first opened his pub in 2015, he put on more cask, but over the years the balance has changed to 50/50 cask and keg as most of his customers will happily drink both, whether or not they are CAMRA members.

> To not be seen as the voice of the beer drinker in the most exciting time for beer in over a century was unquestionably an error. *TIM WEBB, beer writer*

It is held that the Campaign missed the boat on craft beer. A significant contribution to this public perception was delivered courtesy of the marketing machine that is BrewDog brewery, whose early promotion relied heavily on setting themselves up as exciting new upstarts in opposition to the boring old fogies of CAMRA. However, plenty of the longest-serving CAMRA members are self-confessed craft enthusiasts. Gill Keay, for example, organised the Kent Beer Festival for forty years and says, 'my husband and I are great fans of the new beers, we do like key keg beers. There are so many people in CAMRA who say they're no good, they're too expensive, they're cold and fizzy. Well they're not, you get some delicious beers.'

The Revitalisation Project

> Everyone expected it was going to be this defining moment, that we'd wake up the next day and everything would be different.

I think people were expecting to be told what to do afterwards. The National Executive in their wisdom will come down from on high and tell everyone what to do. Which is weird because that is exactly the opposite of what CAMRA is and exactly the opposite of what the CAMRA membership wants. CAMRA is a grassroots organisation.

ASH CORBETT-COLLINS, current National Executive member

The lack of clarity, or perhaps more accurately the absence of a CAMRA position on craft and the new generation of kegged beers, was emblematic of a broader identity crisis within the organisation. There were various reviews and reorganisations in the early years of the twenty-first century as CAMRA struggled to find its place in the new landscape that it had helped to build.

Some members, like Peter Alexander, felt disillusioned with a perceived lack of campaigning, expressing that national lobbying work was out of sync with local campaigning. Others saw inherent contradictions in the way the Campaign operated: overseas beers at CAMRA festivals could be kegged and still 'allowed', while a similar beer brewed in the UK would not be permitted. There was a growing awareness that pubs had an important role in communities and that needed protecting, and this was not reflected in the constitution. Finally, a large number of members were increasingly inactive. The active membership was recognised to be an ageing, unreplenished group, significantly outnumbered by disengaged members who didn't attend events or even participate in online questionnaires. CAMRA faced a bleak future if its active membership literally died off.

In the first ten years of CAMRA there were eight chairmen. In the next eight years there were four and then in the 29 years from 1989 until 2018 there were just another four. The same thing was happening in the branches. People wouldn't step aside and give others a chance. CAMRA's membership was ageing as a result and no spaces were made for enthusiastic new blood, fresh pairs of eyes, etc., which any campaign must have. The bed blocking and dead men's shoes were a real deterrent to keen, new, young members. *JAMES LYNCH*

A Fit-For-Purpose review in 2011,chaired by John Groby MP, was intended to look at CAMRA's structure and purpose as it approached its fortieth birthday, but was widely held to not have sufficient depth to make any real impact. However, it did lay the foundations for a much more comprehensive review that began in 2015. Aimed at ensuring CAMRA was up to date and truly representative of the beer consumer, the three-year-long process was known as the Revitalisation Project. This was an oddly backwards looking choice of name, harking back to the original acronym for CAMRA – the Campaign for the Revitalisation of Ale – which had been retired in 1973.

Tim Page was the Chief Executive during the Revitalisation Project. He had a background in change management and was an unusual choice for CAMRA as he had no previous involvement with the Campaign. Tim invited Michael Hardman to lead the review committee. Michael was seen as nominally independent from the standing National Executive and says that his brief was 'to find out what CAMRA could do better and how it could reinvent itself.' He saw 'a good opportunity to bring CAMRA screaming into the twenty-first century' – in particular to accept that there were some very good non-cask beers on the market, whether in bottle or in keg.

The review set out a number of proposals that were tested at meetings and roadshows with members all around the UK. The overriding memory of this process in the minds of everyone, from the regular member right up to the National Executive, was that it was divisive. Tim Page knew that he was asking the members to make decisions on issues that could potentially split the Campaign completely, and indeed there was a hugely mixed response. On the negative side, Tim has the dubious honour of easily being the most controversial figure in the Campaign's history – being loved and loathed in equal measure for his take on revitalisation. On a more positive note, his process meant that feedback was gathered from some 25,000 members in total, whereas previously it was estimated that only around 5–8,0000 members were actively engaged. So at least the problem of participation was being addressed!

The results of the consultation were made up into a series of resolutions. They were put to the vote at the 2018 AGM as proposed changes to CAMRA's Articles of Association. For Tim this was a 'pretty tortuous process with significant watering down': he felt it was difficult to get the engaged volunteers of the National Executive to fully embrace the suggestions made by the broader membership as they held very strong personal opinions on CAMRA's purpose which didn't always match with the consensus.

Many commentators couldn't understand why the Revitalisation Project ultimately came down to an argument over Articles. Tim Webb thought the approach was confusing and wasn't mincing his words when he described it as 'the absolute epitomy of the CAMRA conversation with itself – with its head up its arse.' The National Chairman during most of the process was Colin Valentine and he stoutly defends the way the project unfolded, saying that it was important to evaluate CAMRA's purpose and 'bake it into the Articles of Association'.

*   *   *

The most controversial and widely reported Special Resolution was that CAMRA should 'act as the voice and represent the interests of all pub goers and beer, cider and perry drinkers.' It would have made CAMRA a much broader church, embracing all pub goers and all beer, cider and perry drinkers within its remit – cask, keg or otherwise. The proposal was rejected, but only by the narrowest of margins. As a Company Limited by Guarantee, 75% of the vote was needed under company law to pass a Special Resolution. This resolution received 72% of the vote – a huge mandate by any measure, but not enough to 'bake it in'.

The other Special Resolutions proposed at the AGM as part of the Revitalisation Project also widened inclusivity and participation. They did receive enough votes to pass:

- To secure the long term future of real ale, real cider and real perry by increasing their quality, availability and popularity;
- To promote and protect pubs and clubs as social centres as part of the UK's cultural heritage;
- To increase recognition of the benefits of responsible, moderate social drinking;
- To play a leading role in the provision of information, education and training to all those with an interest in beer, cider and perry of any type;
- To ensure, where possible, that producers and retailers of beer, cider and perry act in the best interests of the customer.

Colin Valentine saw the passing of so many Special Resolutions as a good indication that the membership was in agreement with CAMRA's direction of travel, but the current National Chairman, Nik Antona, thinks the scale of the process may have set up an expectation that things would change massively overnight: simply not possible in such a large organisation. However, it did finally formally enshrine more than 30 years of campaigning in the pub, perry and cider spheres into the organisation's objectives.

Graham Lees thinks the project was mainly CAMRA getting itself in a twist about non-issues, just like when he resigned over the Scottish air pressure contretemps in the late seventies:

> I found the whole thing rather confusing and distracting because as CAMRA now says, the real issue is the survival of pubs – it's about people going back to pubs and drinking. CAMRA was splitting hairs about what was real ale, what was craft beer and what was acceptable. This proved a distraction from the saving of pubs.
>
> *GRAHAM LEES*

*   *   *

Having reviewed their objectives, CAMRA was in a position to undertake a governance review. This took a further year and resulted in significant changes to the committee and organisational structures. The changes were approved at the AGM and enacted at the beginning of 2020 with the aim of making the organisation more flexible and agile. The new committee structure allows decisions and policymaking to happen more quickly so that CAMRA can be more responsive and let those with the best specialist knowledge and expertise make the decisions. There were also changes to the allowed tenure for National Executive membership to encourage more regular changes in personnel to keep the strategic direction vibrant and energetic.

Learning and Discovery

> We are the Campaign for Real Ale whatever form it comes in. We also know there are other formats and styles of beer out there and we see educating as a vital part of our role. Telling people what's good about various beers. We're not the campaign **against** anything, we are **for** real ale, **for** choice.
>
> *MARK PARKES, GBBF Winter Festival organiser*

After the Revitalisation Project, Alex Metcalfe was brought on to the paid staff team to help realise the new commitment to playing a leading role in providing information, education and training to all those who love beer, cider and perry of any type, which, as Alex says, was pretty revolutionary thinking for CAMRA. His role as Learning and Discovery Manager was intended to manage opportunities for members of CAMRA and members of the public to learn more about beer, cider and perry in the most holistic sense.

Alex has created an informal learning programme at festivals. Thanks to sponsorship and support from key industry stakeholders, along with voluntary support from beer writers, brewers and cider makers, Discovery Zones at festivals have been able to showcase ingredients and explain production methods in an accessible way. Anyone can drop by and take away some new knowledge or taste something new. The buy in from emerging talent in brewing and cider making has made this one of the most vibrant and exciting parts of recent CAMRA beer festivals. Rather than aiming to deliver all of this himself, Alex has been keen to empower festival volunteers to make use of their years of accumulated knowledge and expertise to the benefit of other festival goers. Alex has found CAMRA keen to try new things as an organisation, so instituting the learning programme across the country has been 'pushing at an open door'.

> Too many people think it's a simple drink, brown liquid you pour down your throat, so they don't give much thought to how it's made and the ingredients that go into it.
>
> *ROGER PROTZ*

Looking forward

> The biggest battle will come when Covid-19 is over. There will be a battle cry to revive what CAMRA is really about because without pubs, without beer, without cider we might as well all pack up and go home. And that would be devastating.
>
> *CHRIS ROUSE*

This book was researched and written over the course of the 2020 calendar year. This chapter is being written as we languish in the second national lockdown. It's fair to say that it has been a memorable year, although no doubt many would prefer to forget it.

The year began with Britain leaving the EU on 31 January 2020. The transition period is still in place and is due to end on 1st January 2021. CAMRA's future trajectory will undoubtedly be shaped by the repercussions of this exit. For example, there will be an opportunity to push for more flexibility on how excise duty is levied on alcohol products, applying a lower rate to beer sold in pubs than that in off licences and supermarkets. This sort of targeted benefit to the pub industry was illegal under European Directives on Excise Duty as different rates of tax cannot be applied depending on where a product is sold.

The duty exemption for small cider producers is hoped to continue even without the imperative from Europe, so this may also become a campaigning issue. Some 80% of Britain's 500-plus cider makers are small producers and the exemption is vital for maintaining a strong, diverse and vibrant industry.

Brexit, though, would be overshadowed by a more serious, and global, threat. Nobody could have foreseen how 2020 would be dominated by the Covid-19 pandemic and its attendant national lockdowns, wreaking havoc on the brewing and hospitality industries.

Reflected in the issues the lockdowns have raised for beer drinkers, publicans and breweries we see a microcosm of some of the most important battlegrounds on which CAMRA has, over the past 50 years, taken a stand. For consumers to have access to a wide range of good quality live beer they need pubs and breweries. To be effective in protecting these interests CAMRA has to be flexible enough to adapt with the times.

> This is a make or break moment for the beer and pub industry as we know it.
>
> *NIK ANTONA, writing to Secretary of State for Health Matt Hancock, 25 November, 2020*

The campaign to protect the great British pub couldn't have been brought into starker relief than when our pubs were forced to close for months at a time, and then cope with tougher restrictions than almost any other sector. CAMRA founder Michael Hardman worries that we might experience a massive loss of real ale pubs in the future, seeing the Covid-19 pandemic as the 'only threat of its type to beers of all kinds in my memory and definitely in my lifetime. I don't know what threats there were ever that match the threat now.'

Chris Holmes, the majority shareholder in Castle Rock brewery, talks of having 1,200 casks of beer with an eight-week time limit on them as the country went into the first lockdown in March 2020. They sold what they could at a Covid-safe drive-through at the brewery site, but it wasn't enough to really make a dent – most had to be poured away. Chris knew that Castle Rock was in a fortunate position as a bigger business. They are able to weather the storm to a degree and keep their 200 staff employed, with government help through the furlough scheme. However, many smaller businesses live a much more hand-to-mouth existence and will not be so fortunate. We wait to see what the beer industry looks like on the other side of the pandemic.

The new CAMRA committee structure that was implemented in January 2020 to give more flexibility couldn't have been better timed. It was brought in just as the country went into its first national lockdown. As a national volunteer organisation, CAMRA was already well versed in remote working and now their structure allowed for quick responses to rapidly changing circumstances. Within just a couple of weeks they had launched their #PullingTogether campaign along with SIBA and Crowdfunder to support the pub and brewing industry.

The social arm of the campaign was the Red (on)Lion virtual pub, which was aimed at helping to continue to create a sense of community for members missing their pub, while also supporting their local pubs by encouraging them to share what they are drinking on their profile. Beer writer Melissa Cole saw the virtual pub as a 'wonderful thing', and commented that putting mental health at the forefront of their activities is not something she would have dreamed of hearing from CAMRA ten years ago.

By May 2020 CAMRA had launched its Brew2You app, giving thousands of pubs and breweries a virtual shop window for their takeaway and delivery products. The not-for-profit app saw beer lovers supporting their local beer businesses by ordering over £100,000 worth of beer, cider and perry in less than six months.

Melissa was again pleased to see this change in focus to being more inward looking at the industry and how they can practically support it, which is an 'incredibly valuable thing to do'

As the pandemic progressed, CAMRA ramped up the online learning resources it offered to members. Online resources had already started to be rolled out since May 2019, but the need to provide resources for members who weren't able to access their normal membership benefits meant things happened much more quickly. Work that had taken place in 2019 made it clear that there was a big gap in provision for people who were keen on CAMRA but didn't really know anything about beer yet: they needed to be given the opportunity to get entry level information about what beer is and the tools to understand more about what they were drinking.

Written content, video and audio productions aimed at beginners, experts and connoisseurs were quickly commissioned by Alex Metcalfe and added to the Learning and Discovery section of the CAMRA website. New content has been added weekly since March 2020 and this looks set to continue well into 2021. The popular podcast 'Pubs. Pints. People.' also began, featuring expert commentators speaking on a range of beer-related topics.

The cancelled GBBF also got a new lease of life as a virtual tasting event. Perhaps surprisingly, this was not a first for CAMRA. The St Albans beer festival in the year 2000 had offered a virtual tour of the festival at the Alban Arena on its website, allowing punters to visit the bars and see what was on offer to try and 'encourage cybersurgers to abandon their mousemats (!) and spend time in the real world of ale.' Unfortunately, though, the virtual GBBF's festival glass featured a stylised coronavirus design that was not particularly well received on the whole, given that tens of thousands of people in the UK had already died of the virus by the time it was released, but this was perhaps the only misstep taken by the Campaign in their rapid response to Covid-19 in the UK.

Epilogue

I think we did genuinely save cask-conditioned beer.
We changed the drinking habits of the country.
TONY HEDGER, Battersea Beer Festival organiser

IT started as a bit of a joke and turned into one of the biggest and most successful single-issue consumer organisations on the planet. CAMRA has changed the face of the beer industry in the UK and beyond through their campaigning for beer, breweries and pubs. They took on the relentless march of keg beer and kept the fires burning for traditional cask ale. They have protected hundreds of pubs, saving venues that are valuable lynchpins of their communities as well as historical treasures. CAMRA has supported breweries and the brewing trade, advocating to governments both at home and abroad about the regulation and taxation of the industry.

Now, as GBBF Winter Festival organiser Mark Parkes acknowledges, CAMRA has got to remain relevant. The time has passed for members to stand up at the AGM and wax lyrical about how things were when they joined the Campaign back in the seventies. Things have changed, things continue to change, and CAMRA has to continue to adapt if it is to remain an important feature on the British beer landscape.

Pub campaigning was rightly highlighted by most of the people interviewed for this book as a key future battleground. Well-kept real ale can only survive and thrive if there is someone to serve it properly. As the events of the 2020/21 pandemic have swept over us, the threat to pubs has increased significantly.

As a consequence, the future of real ale is uncertain once more. The commercial market is so large that it is unlikely we will see live beer die out altogether. However, it is not hyperbolic to suggest that real ale faces a bigger existential threat now than it did in 1971, when four young men from the North West took a boozy tour of Ireland.

With new Covid-19 vaccines recently approved for use in the UK we now squint hopefully towards a pinprick of light at the end of a very long tunnel. Many breweries and pubs, however, particularly small independents, will not survive to join us on the sunlit plains of post-Covid Britain. Consumer choice and quality is once more in peril. In 2020 CAMRA has surprised commentators with a rarely seen fleetness of foot, by its adaptability and clear, principled stance. The Campaign is now in a great position to free itself from the image problem that has plagued it for decades. It has grown more inclusive and welcoming. A huge investment into learning resources has made it easier than ever before for CAMRA to guide newcomers on their own journey of real ale discovery. All of these characteristics should see the consumer organisation step boldly forward into its next half century.

> CAMRA is a brilliant example of People Power. Together
> we question, encourage and challenge so that quality,
> value for money and choice is better for all consumers.
> Long may CAMRA roar!
>
> *GILLIAN HOUGH, National Executive member*

Appendix 1

National Chairmen and AGM Locations

Year	AGM Location	Chairman
1972	Nuneaton	Michael Hardman (1)
1973	London	Michael Hardman
1974	York	Chris Hutt (2)
1975	Nottingham	Gordon Massey (3)
1976	Brighton	Chris Holmes (4)
1977	Blackpool	Chris Bruton (5)
1978	Cardiff	James Lynch (6)
1979	Keele	Joe Goodwin (7)
1980	Loughborough	Joe Goodwin
		Ian Mitchell (acting chairman after Joe's death)
1981	Durham	Tim Amsden (8)
1982	Bradford	Tim Amsden
1983	Reading	Tony Millns (9)
1984	Edinburgh	Tony Millns
1985	Southport	Tony Millns
1986	Southampton	Jim Scanlon (10)
1987	Hull	Jim Scanlon
1988	Birmingham	Jim Scanlon
1989	Aberdeen	Rob Walker (11)
1990	Norwich	John Cryne (12)
1991	Sheffield	John Cryne
1992	Bristol	John Cryne
1993	Salford	John Cryne
1994	Scarborough	John Cryne
1995	Wolverhampton	John Cryne
1996	Portsmouth	John Cryne
1997	Llandudno	John Cryne
1998	Edinburgh	John Cryne
1999	Hove	Dave Goodwin (13)
2000	Derby	Dave Goodwin
2001	Newcastle	Dave Goodwin
2002	Scarborough	Dave Goodwin
2003	Exeter	Dave Goodwin
2004	Southport	Paula Waters (14)
2005	Glasgow	Paula Waters
2006	Blackpool	Paula Waters
2007	Wolverhampton	Paula Waters
2008	Cardiff	Paula Waters
2009	Eastbourne	Paula Waters

2010	Douglas	Colin Valentine (15)
2011	Sheffield	Colin Valentine
2012	Torquay	Colin Valentine
2013	Norwich	Colin Valentine
2014	Scarborough	Colin Valentine
2015	Nottingham	Colin Valentine
2016	Liverpool	Colin Valentine
2017	Bournemouth	Colin Valentine
2018	Coventry	Colin Valentine
2019	Dundee	Jackie Parker (16)
2020	York (cancelled – AGM held online)	Nik Antona (17)
2021	Sheffield	Nik Antona

National Chairmen and the location of their respective AGMs, compiled by Nik Antona

Appendix 2
Champion Beer of Britain Winners

Year	Beer	Brewery	GBBF Location
1978	Best Mild and ESB	Thwaites and Fuller's	Alexandra Palace, London
1979	London Pride	Fuller's	Alexandra Palace, London
1980	Best Mild	Thwaites	Alexandra Palace, London
1981	ESB	Fuller's	Queens Hall, Leeds
1982	Landlord	Timothy Taylor's	Queens Hall, Leeds
1983	Landlord	Timothy Taylor's	Bingley Hall, Birmingham
1984	—	—	
1985	ESB	Fuller's	Metropole, Brighton
1986	XXXB	Batemans	Metropole, Brighton
1987	Dark Star	Pitfield	Metropole, Brighton
1988	Old Thumper	Ringwood	Queens Hall, Leeds
1989	Chiswick Bitter	Fuller's	Queens Hall, Leeds
1990	Burton Ale	Ind Coope	Metropole, Brighton
1991	Black Adder	Mauldon	Docklands Arena, London
1992	Norfolk Nog	Woodforde	Olympia, London
1993	Extra	Adnams	Olympia, London
1994	Landlord	Timothy Taylor's	Olympia, London
1995	Norman's Conquest	Cottage	Olympia, London
1996	Wherry Best Bitter	Woodforde	Olympia, London
1997	Workie Ticket	Mordue	Olympia, London
1998	Bluebird Bitter	Coniston	Olympia, London
1999	Landlord	Timothy Taylor's	Olympia, London

(cont.)

Champion Beer of Britain Winners *(cont.)*

Year	Beer	Brewery	GBBF Location
2000	Black Cat	Moorhouse	Olympia, London
2001	JHB	Oakham	Olympia, London
2002	Deuchars IPA	Caledonian	Olympia, London
2003	Bitter & Twisted	Harviestoun	Olympia, London
2004	Pale Rider	Kelham Island	Olympia, London
2005	Brewers Gold	Crouch Vale	Olympia, London
2006	Brewers Gold	Crouch Vale	Earls Court, London
2007	Mild	Hobsons	Earls Court, London
2008	Alton's Pride	Triple fff	Earls Court, London
2009	Ruby Mild	Rudgate	Earls Court, London
2010	Harvest Pale	Castle Rock	Earls Court, London
2011	Oscar Wilde	Mighty Oak	Earls Court, London
2012	No 9 Barley Wine	Coniston	Olympia, London
2013	1872 Porter	Elland	Olympia, London
2014	Boltmaker	Timothy Taylor's	Olympia, London
2015	Cwtch	Tiny Rebel	Olympia, London
2016	Vanilla Stout	Binghams	Olympia, London
2017	Goats Milk	Church End	Olympia, London
2018	Broken Dream	Siren Craft	Olympia, London
2019	Shere Drop	Surrey Hills	Olympia, London
2020	—	—	

Appendix 3
Membership

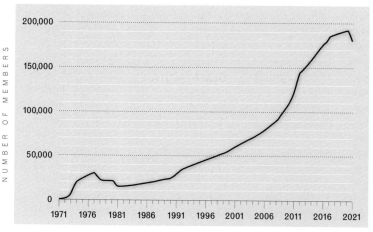

Appendix 4
Editors of *What's Brewing*

June 1972–February 1977: MICHAEL HARDMAN
March 1977–April 1979: ROGER PROTZ
May 1979–August 1988: BRIAN GLOVER
September 1988–January 1989: ROGER PROTZ
February 1989–April 1990: LEWIS ECKETT
May 1990–January 1991: ROGER PROTZ
February 1991–May 1991: IAIN LOE
June 1991–December 1998: ROGER PROTZ
January 1999–December 2006: TED BRUNING
December 2006–February 2019: TOM STAINER
February 2019–Present: TIM HAMPSON

Appendix 5
Acronyms and Abbreviations

ABV	Alcohol by Volume
AGM	Annual General Meeting
BBPA	British Beer & Pub Association
BLAG	Brewery Liaison Advisory Group
CAMRA	Campaign for Real Ale
CBOB	Champion Beer of Britain
CMIC	CAMRA Members Investment Club
GABF	Great American Beer Festival
GBBF	Great British Beer Festival
GBG	Good Beer Guide
LACOTS	Local Authorities Co-ordinating body on Food and Trading Standards
MRO	Market Rent Only
NBSS	National Beer Scoring System
NE	National Executive
NERD Weekends	National Executive & Regional Director weekends
OG	Original Gravity
SBDRC	Small Brewer's Duty Relief Coalition
SIBA	Society of Independent Brewers
SPBW	Society for the Preservation of Beer from the Wood
TAG	Technical Advisory Group
WB	What's Brewing

Index

Page numbers in italics refer to illustrations

Celebrating 50 Years

The Campaign for Real Ale is celebrating its 50th anniversary in 2021. For more information on the events planned to mark this milestone year, and how you can get involved, visit **camra.org.uk/50-years**

CAMRA Books

From the first, loose-leaf *Good Beer Guide*, published in November 1972, CAMRA has always been proud to publish books on pubs, bars, beer and brewing. Discover the full range at **shop.camra.org.uk**

The Good Beer Guide 2021

The UK's best-selling beer and pub guide, featuring detailed entries recommending 4,500 of the best real-ale pubs, in rural and urban areas, selected by 190,000 CAMRA members across the UK. The unique Breweries section lists all operating UK real ale breweries and their regular beers, including CAMRA tasting notes. A full-colour introduction features commentary and industry analysis, including a foreword by chef Tom Kerridge.

RRP **£15.99**   ISBN 978-1-85249-366-0

The Family Brewers of Britain

ROGER PROTZ

Britain's family brewers are stalwarts of beer making. Some date back as far as the 17th and 18th centuries and have survived the turbulence of world wars, bomb damage, recessions, floods, and the hostility of politicians and the temperance movement. This book, by leading beer writer Roger Protz, traces the fascinating and sometimes fractious histories of the families still running these breweries, in this lavishly illustrated limited-edition hardback.

RRP **£25.00**   ISBN 978-1-85249-359-2

Beer by Design

PETE BROWN

Beer is the most popular alcoholic drink on the planet. However, few who enjoy it have seriously thought about how it has managed to cajole, intrigue and persuade us to buy it in the first place. The design of the pump clip, beer label or can will often tip us into a decision about which beer we choose or continue to prefer. This is a lavishly illustrated book, tracing the history of beer label design back to the UK's first-ever trade mark and beyond.

RRP **£15.99**   ISBN 978-1-85249-368-4